China, Cultural Heritage, and International Law

China is a country that is rich in antiquities, but it is also a victim of looting that occurred during the period from the First Opium War to the end of the Japanese Occupation (1840–1945) when innumerable cultural objects were lost overseas. The Chinese Government insists on asserting its interest over its wrongfully removed cultural heritage and has sought for the return of lost cultural heritage by all means in accordance with relevant international conventions and Chinese laws. However, securing the return has been, and continues to be, problematic. Little research has been done regarding the question as to whether China has a legal basis for recovery, which is the first legal hurdle that China needs to get over. In addition, China does not have a legal basis for all cultural heritage taken during the period of 1840–1945. Claims for return without a legal basis are usually silenced or, at best, discussed only but very rarely facilitated.

This book provides an answer for the return of Chinese cultural heritage. It examines the law contemporaneous to the removal of Chinese cultural heritage and its application. For this lack of a legal basis, this book argues that a new customary international law is emerging, according to which the interests of the states of origin in their wrongfully removed heritage should be prioritised. This proposed customary rule supports the return of wrongfully removed heritage. Once this proposed customary rule is accepted, it will provide a stronger argument not only for China, but also for other states of origin with a similar dilemma, including South Korea, Egypt, Greece, Cambodia, Turkey, Peru, and Italy, to recover their wrongfully removed heritage.

While dealing with a large pool of return cases, this book is valuable to museums and art collectors in the event of buying and accepting art objects, and settling recovery disputes with states of origin. It will also be of interest to researchers, academics, policymakers, and students in the fields of cultural heritage law, international law, international trade, and human rights law.

Hui Zhong is a research fellow at South China Sea, Xiamen University, China.

Routledge Research in International Law

For a full list of titles in this series, visit www.routledge.com/Routledge-Research-in-International-Law/book-series/INTNLLAW

Available:

Peacemaking, Religious Belief and the Rule of Law
The Struggle between Dictatorship and Democracy in Syria and Beyond
Paul Zwier

China, Cultural Heritage, and International Law
Hui Zhong

The UN Security Council and Domestic Actors
Distance in International Law
Machiko Kanetake

Human Security Discourse and International Law
A Principled Approach
Shireen Daft

Fighting and Victimhood in International Criminal Law
Joanna Nicholson

Prosecuting Juvenile Piracy Suspects
The International Legal Framework
Milena Sterio

Nationalization, Natural Resources and International Investment Law
Contractual Relationship as a Dynamic Bargaining Process
Junji Nakagawa

Queering International Law
Possibilities, Alliances, Complicities, Risks
Edited by Dianne Otto

Sovereignty Conflicts and International Law and Politics
A Distributive Justice Issue
Jorge E. Núñez

China, Cultural Heritage, and International Law

Hui Zhong

Routledge
Taylor & Francis Group
LONDON AND NEW YORK

First published 2018 by Routledge

2 Park Square, Milton Park, Abingdon, Oxfordshire OX14 4RN
52 Vanderbilt Avenue, New York, NY 10017

Routledge is an imprint of the Taylor & Francis Group, an informa business

First issued in paperback 2019

Library of Congress Cataloging-in-Publication Data
Names: Zhong, Hui (Writer on law) author.
Title: China, cultural heritage, and international law / Hui Zhong.
Description: Abingdon, Oxon [UK] ; New York : Routledge, 2018. | Series: Routledge research in international law | Includes index.
Identifiers: LCCN 2017036625 | ISBN 9781138093249 (hardback) | ISBN 9781351605700 (web pdf) | ISBN 9781351605694 (epub) | ISBN 9781351605687 (mobipocket)
Subjects: LCSH: Cultural property—Protection—Law and legislation—China—History. | Cultural property—Protection (International law) | Customary law, International.
Classification: LCC KNQ3183 .Z465 2018 | DDC 344.51/094—dc23
LC record available at https://lccn.loc.gov/2017036625

ISBN: 978-1-138-09324-9 (hbk)
ISBN: 978-0-367-89045-2 (pbk)

Typeset in Galliard
by Apex CoVantage, LLC

Contents

Table of Cases

Table of Legislation, Conventions and Treaties

Legislation

Conventions

Treaties

Preface and Acknowledgements

I always felt very proud when I saw Chinese art treasures exhibited in foreign museums, until Christie's announced that the two bronzes, a rat head and a rabbit head would be auctioned in Paris in February 2009. These two bronze statues were taken from Beijing's Summer Palace by Anglo-French troops during the First Opium War (1856–1860). After Christie's announcement, the Chinese Government resolutely urged Christie's to stop the sale, stating that the auction would "seriously hurt national sentiment". For many Chinese, the looting of the Summer Palace has become a source of bitterness, as China's highest culture had been ignored and violently destroyed by Anglo-French troops. A group of Chinese lawyers tried to block the auction, but a French court allowed it to proceed. The two bronze statues were still auctioned for sale, but the auction ended in controversy. This auction made me start thinking about the reasons that make recovery difficult, as well as the possibility for recovery.

To answer these questions, I began my research at the University of Queensland, Australia. Until then, I had not realised the difficulties involved in returning these treasures to the place where they were originally created. China is a country that is rich in antiquities, but it is also a victim of looting that occurred during the period from the First Opium War to the end of the Japanese Occupation (1840–1945). Innumerable cultural objects were lost overseas. However, there are relatively few studies relating to the looting and destruction that occurred between 1840 and 1945. While the Nazi's looting of before and during the Second World War has been condemned, Japan's systematic plunder and destruction of China's cultural heritage during the same war is seldom discussed. The damage to Chinese cultural heritage tends to be forgotten. Furthermore, instead of pressing formal demands for repatriation, the approach used to bring scattered Chinese arts home is still limited to donation, buying-back and diplomatic negotiation. One of the reasons for this is that there is no clear answer as to whether China has a legal basis for the recovery. Little research has been done regarding the law in the Qing Dynasty (1644–1911) and law in the Republic of China (1911–1949), and its application to the removal of China's cultural heritage.

As the research progressed, I also realised that China is not the only country that has been active in pursuing the return of its cultural heritage. In the past few decades, other states of origin have been expecting the return of their cultural heritage: Greece has been requesting the return of the Parthenon Marbles for decades; South Korea has been requesting the return of its Ugiew, the historical books about its Joseon Dynasty (1392–1910); Egypt has been seeking the return of the Rosetta Stone and Nefertiti; and Nigeria has been demanding the return of the Benin bronzes. However, securing the return has been, and continues to be, problematic. As removals often occurred a long time prior, many claims are time barred, additionally many records and other evidence may have disappeared, and international conventions are not retroactive. Most importantly, there is no law contemporaneous to the removal determining such taking as illegal. Even though the taking was morally wrong, it was perfectly legal. Claims for the return without a legal basis are usually silenced or, at best, discussed only but very rarely facilitated.

For this lack of a legal basis, this book aims to provide an answer. This book argues that a new customary international law is emerging, according to which the interests of the states of origin in their wrongfully removed heritage should be prioritised. This proposed customary rule supports the return of historically removed heritage, including Chinese cultural heritage that was lost overseas between 1840 and 1945. During the past two decades, more and more cultural heritage objects have been returned to the states of origin by individuals, museums and states. Both international and national laws have evolved in the direction of favouring and respecting the interests of the states of origin in their cultural heritage. One of the consequences is that museums have adopted stricter policies when buying and accepting art objects. These facts support the idea of a new, emerging customary rule. Once this proposed customary rule is accepted as a new customary rule, it will provide a stronger argument not only for China, but also for other states of origin with a similar dilemma, including South Korea, Egypt, Greece, Cambodia, Turkey, Peru, and Italy, to recover their wrongfully removed heritage.

This book is based on my thesis submitted and defended at the University of Queensland for the degree of Doctor in Philosophy. And this brings me to many thanks. The most sincere thanks are due to Professor Craig Forrest, who supervised my doctoral thesis. I really appreciate the way he guided me to undertake academic research and gave me this opportunity to have my questions answered. He provided me with illuminating guidance, precious advice and constant encouragement through the years of my study. I am incredibly fortunate to have had such a good supervisor. I also owe a debt of gratitude to Professor Janet Ulph who offered precious comments and support during my visiting study at the University of Leicester. Thanks also to Dr Justine Bell, who commented on my work and allowed me to improve my thesis.

I also wish to thank Professor Elina Moustaira and Dr Christa Roodt for their valuable advice and comments on all aspects of my thesis. Thanks also to the anonymous reviewers. Their feedback was nothing less than extraordinary.

I am so grateful to my colleagues in the South China Sea Institute, Xiamen University. Special thanks to Professor Kuen-chen FU for offering the opportunity to continue my research in underwater cultural heritage and law of the sea.

I would also like to express my gratitude to China Scholarship Council for funding my study in Australia. I am fortune with the opportunity of doing my PhD in the TC Beirne School of Law.

A special thank you goes to my parents, for their unfailing encouragement, for their continuous belief in me and for their unreserved love.

1 Introduction

1. Introduction

On April 26 2013, the French Pinault family announced that they would donate two $40 million bronze statues to China.[1] The two bronzes, a rat head and a rabbit head, were among 12 animal heads, replicating the Chinese zodiac, in a central fountain clock at Beijing's Summer Palace, also known as Yuanmingyuan and used by rulers of the Qing dynasty, spewing water to tell time. All disappeared after the Palace was destroyed by Anglo-French troops during the Second Opium War (1856–1860). The return of the two bronze statues enjoyed a warm welcome in China, with the State Administration of Cultural Heritage in China stating that Mr. Pinault's offer was "an expression of friendship toward the Chinese people". At the same time, however, it also reminded the Chinese people of the auction of the same two bronze sculptures four years earlier.

In 2009, when the statues were put up for auction in Paris, China attempted to stop the sale. The Chinese State Administration of Cultural Heritage (SACH) resolutely urged Christie's to stop the sale, stating that the auction would "seriously hurt national sentiment".[2] To China, the looting of the palace epitomises the humiliation it suffered at the hands of imperial Western powers during the Second Opium War. However, Christie's refused to pull the bronze statues from the auction, as it continued to believe that "sale by public auction offers the best opportunity for items to be repatriated as a result of worldwide exposure".[3] A group of Chinese lawyers also launched a legal bid in a Paris court to stop the sale. However, the court ruled against stopping the auction, concluding that the plaintiff did not have a direct interest in the two statues and therefore no standing before the court. The auction ended in

1 Edward Wong and Steven Erlanger, 'Frenchman Will Return to China Prized Bronze Artifacts Looted in 19th Century', *The New York Times* April 26 2013 <www.nytimes.com/2013/04/27/world/europe/frenchman-will-return-to-china-prized-bronze-artifacts-looted-in-19th-century.html>.

2 'China Condemns Christie's Auction', *The BBC News* February 26 2009 <http://news.bbc.co.uk/2/hi/asia-pacific/7911691.stm>.

3 Ibid.

controversy. After China failed to block the sale legally, a Chinese businessman successfully bid for them, but refused to pay as a "patriotic" act. Convinced that he had fulfilled his duty as a Chinese citizen, he further stated that "these cultural relics belong to China . . . they were looted by the West in time of war and illegally taken abroad".[4] After the auction sale, the SACH announced new limits against Christie's.[5] Specifically, the Chinese Government tightened the ownership control over all cultural relics that Christie's seeks to import or export.

This auction case clearly reflects the importance that societies attach to their cultural relics, which is why related discussions can easily become emotional.[6] Cultural relics are often the symbols for times of victory, defeat, great suffering, or important occasions in the history of a society.[7] However, a large number of such cultural relics were taken out of China during times of war and peace, and particularly during the period beginning with the First Opium War to the end of Japanese Occupation (1840–1949). China has since been expecting the return of its scattered cultural relics.[8] During David Cameron's 2013 visit in China, he was inundated with demands for the restitution of cultural objects taken from the country.[9] When the British officials set up the official page on the Chinese social network "Sina Weibo", China's version of Twitter, one of the most popular questions concerned the return of Chinese cultural relics. However, securing the return of the relics taken during this period has been and continues to be problematic.

4 Yu Zhang, 'France Returning Treasure to China Sets Precedent for Further Restitutions', *Global Times* September 9 2015 <www.globaltimes.cn/content/941506.shtml>.
5 'China Tightens Control on Christie's After Auction', *The Xinhua News* February 26 2009 <http://news.xinhuanet.com/english/2009-02/26/content_10901300.htm>.
6 Scholarship in this area now clearly differentiates these terms, such as cultural heritage, cultural property, return, repatriation and restitution. For more discussion, see Lyndel Prott and Patrick O'Keefe, '"Cultural Heritage" or "Cultural Property"?' (1992) 1(2) *International Journal of Cultural Property* 307; Wojciech Kowalski, 'Types of Claims for Recovery of Lost Cultural Property' (2005) 57(228) *Museum International* 85.

But in Chinese legal documents, the terms antiquities, ancient objects, and cultural relics, are more commonly used. This book will use cultural heritage and return in most of its context as the primary purpose of this book is arguing for a new customary rule based on the increasing recognition of connection between states of origin and cultural heritage. But when analysing Chinese legislation, this book will use the relevant terms according to the context in which they appear.
7 Stefan Gruber, 'The Fight Against the Illicit Trade in Asian Cultural Artefacts: Connecting International Agreements, Regional Co-operation, and Domestic strategies' (2013) 3(2) *Asian Journal of International Law* 341, 343.
8 China's recovery efforts will be discussed in Chapter 2.
9 '"Give Us Back Our Treasure": Chinese Demand Cameron Returns Priceless Artefacts Looted during 19th Century Boxer Rebellion', *Mail Online* December 4 2013 <www.dailymail.co.uk/news/article-2518111/China-demand-David-Cameron-return-Boxer-Rebellion-artefacts.html>.

2. A Victim of Loss of Cultural Heritage

China has an abundance of cultural relics created through its history of more than 5,000 years. However, due to the decay of the Qing Government and the military superiority of European forces, China was forced to open its gates after the defeat in the First Opium War in 1840, and incurred invasions from foreign countries.[10] During this period, China was dragged into the First Opium War (1840–1842), the Second Opium War (1857–1860), the Sino-French War (1883–1885), the First Sino-Japanese War (1894–1895), the Pillage of Beijing by Eight-Nation Alliance (1900),[11] the British invasion of Tibet (1903–1904), the First World War (1917–1918) and the Second World War (also known as the Japanese Occupation, 1937–1945).[12] China lost almost all of the wars it fought, and was forced to give major concessions to the great powers in the subsequent treaties. At the same time, China was plagued by destruction and a large-scale loss of its cultural heritage on a large scale.[13] Generally speaking, Chinese cultural heritage was lost in two ways: first, plunder and looting in times of armed conflicts; and, second, taking by individual behaviours, such as expedition, theft and exportation, during both times of war and peace.

Large-scale looting during wartimes have resulted in massive losses of Chinese cultural heritage, in particular, during the sacking of the Summer Place by Anglo-French troops during the Second Opium War (1856–1860), the plunder of Beijing by the Eight-Nation Alliance in the Battle of Beijing (1900); and the Japanese looting in the Second Sino-Japanese War (1931–1935). For example, the Old Summer Palace was where the emperors of the Qing Dynasty lived and handled government affairs. Reputed as the "Garden of Gardens", the Summer Palace is well-known for its magnificent architecture and extraordinary history, as it took the Qing people from 1709 to 1772 to complete this grand complex of buildings and gardens. Also, countless priceless Chinese artworks, antiquities, unique copies of literary works and compilations were collected from all over the country and stored in this Palace. However, when Anglo-French forces occupied Beijing, the invaders torched

10 For more historical backgrounds, see John King Fairbank, *The Cambridge History of China Volume 10: Late Ch'ing 1800–1911, Part 1* (Cambridge University Press, 1978); David Scott, *China and the International System, 1840–1949: Power, Presence, and Perceptions in A Century of Humiliation* (State University of New York Press, 2008).

11 The Eight-Nation Alliance was an international coalition set up in response to the Boxer Rebellion by the nations of Japan, Russia, the British Empire, France, the US, Germany, Italy, and Austria-Hungary.

12 Japan started fighting against China intermittently since 1931, but the total war started in 1937.

13 This book will not go to the details of the loss of Chinese cultural heritage. For more details, see Lei Peng, *A Research on Legal History of Return of Relics (in Chinese)* (Nanjing: Yilin Publishing, 2012); Zuozhen Liu, *The Case for Repatriating China's Cultural Objects* (Springer, 2016), Chapter 1.

or levelled as many as 200 buildings, stripping a nearly thousand-acre site of sculptures, silk robes and jewellery.[14]

Japan is another major destination for the looted Chinese cultural heritage. During the Second Sino-Japanese War, public museums, libraries, imperial palaces and private houses were all targets of pillage for Japanese troops due to Japan's notorious "Three Alls Campaign", also known as "Burn all, loot all, and kill all".[15] The damage to China's cultural heritage during the armed conflicts was massive.[16] For example, Chongqing, with a long history dating back at least 3,000 years, enjoys a prestigious historical reputation and is famous for a series of Chinese religious sculptures and carvings, depicting and influenced by Buddhist, Confucian and Taoist beliefs. However, the 1939 carpet bombing of Chongqing in two days of air raids was described by a survivor as "a sea of fire". It was reported that 741 historical sites, more than 15,000 paintings and over 3,000,000 books were damaged or destroyed in this act.[17] It was also reported that only in 1944, 11,022 volumes of ancient books in the Forbidden City and 1,372 pieces of treasures in the Peking History Museum were pillaged by the Japanese.[18]

Apart from war looting, countless Chinese cultural heritage was stolen, excavated, and exported from China by individuals during both times of war and peace. Since the end of the 19th century, foreign explorers, sinologists and missionaries had come to China to collect Chinese cultural heritage. During the period of 1850 and 1940, 151 archaeological explorations were conducted by foreign expedition teams in Northwest China.[19] The most well-known example occurred in 1907 when Auriel Stein convinced the guardian in the Mogao Grottoes to sell a collection of 260 paintings and more than 8,000 manuscripts to the British Museum.[20]

In a recent donation case in 2014, seven marble columns from the Summer Palace were handed over to China from the KODE Art Museums of Bergen, a

14 Karl Meyer, 'The Chinese Want Their Art Back', *New York Times* June 20 2015 <www.nytimes.com/2015/06/21/opinion/the-chinese-want-their-art-back.html?_r=0>.

15 Louis G. Perez, *Japan at War: An Encyclopedia* (ABC-CLIO, 2013), 484.

16 For a general account of the Japanese plunder, see Yan Changhong and Li Xia, 'A Review of Japan's Cultural Aggression against China during Anti-Japanese War' (in Chinese)' (2005) 25(4) *Journal of South-Central University for Nationalities (Humanities and Social Sciences)* 12.

17 'War Damage on Cultural Relics Commission under the Department of Education', *China Cultural Relics* August 22, 2007 <www.xhgxt.com/html/View_9270.html>.

18 Peng, *A Research on Legal History,* above n 13, 26–34.

19 Twenty explorations were conducted by Germans, 53 by Russians, 30 by British, one by Hungarian, 13 by Japanese, eight by French, three by American, 22 by Swedish, and one by an unknown expedition team. Ibid, 34–55; Liu, *Repatriating China's Cultural Objects,* above n 13, 13.

20 James Cuno, *Who Owns Antiquity?: Museums and the Battle over Our Ancient Heritage* (Princeton University Press, 2008), 88–89.

Norwegian museum.[21] The columns were part of an over 4,000-piece collection of Chinese artefacts in the KODE museum that were donated by Johan Munthe between 1907 and 1935. Munthe lived in China from 1886 to 1935 and was first employed in the Chinese customs service. He fought on the Chinese side in the First Sino-Japanese War and was named a lieutenant general by Yuan Shikai, who would later become the first president of the Republic of China. As an avid collector of Chinese art, Munthe had a significant collection of Chinese sculpture, jade, porcelain, paintings and Chinese antiques. However, it was unclear how he obtained and transported them to Norway.

From 1840 to 1949, Chinese cultural heritage was lost in amazing figures, calculated in millions of pieces, including hundreds of thousands of works of superb quality, scattered over 47 countries.[22] Britain has the richest collection of Chinese cultural objects, next comes France. It is estimated that the British Museum has around 23,000 cultural heritage objects, including Chinese paintings and calligraphy, ancient books, jade, porcelain and bronze dating from different historical periods.[23] In Guimet museum, over half of the works collected are of Chinese origin, more than 30,000 pieces in number.[24] The US is another destination for a great deal of the lost Chinese paintings and calligraphy. It is estimated that the Freer Gallery alone has a collection of over 1,200 paintings and the Metropolitan Museum of Art owns more than 500 pieces.[25]

All of this loss and the taking of Chinese cultural heritage have made the return all the more important and meaningful. China has begun insisting on asserting its interests over cultural heritage removed during this period. In the auction case of 2009, China's State Administration of Cultural Heritage stated that:

> China does not acknowledge what it called the illegal possession of the two sculptures and would continue to seek the return of looted and/or stolen cultural objects and other illegally exported relics by all means in accordance with relevant international conventions and Chinese laws.[26]

21 Bree Feng, 'Despite Frigid Relations, Chinese Relics Coming Home From Norway', *New York Times* February 12 2014 <http://sinosphere.blogs.nytimes.com/2014/02/09/despite-frigid-relations-chinese-relics-coming-home-from-norway/?_r=0>.

22 'Chinese Experts Demand Return of Cultural Relics' in Lyndel Prott (ed), *Witnesses to History* (UNESCO, 2008) 119, 119.

23 *'Give Us Back Our Treasure'*, above n 9.

24 Irini A. Stamatoudi, *Cultural Property Law and Restitution: A Commentary to International Conventions and European Union law* (Edward Elgar Publishing, 2011), 25.

25 'Culture Insider: Chinese Cultural Relics Lost Overseas', *China Daily* Ausgust 15 2014 <www.chinadaily.com.cn/culture/art/2014-08/15/content_18311574.htm>.

26 'China Condemns Christie's Sculpture Sale, Warns of "Serious Effects"', *Xinhua News* February 26 2009 <http://news.xinhuanet.com/english/2009-02/26/content_10900960.htm>.

However, when the Chinese Government made this statement, it did not refer to a specific law that entitles China to claim for the return of the disputed art treasures. On the other hand, to obtain the return of removed heritage, repatriation cases have suggested that the first legal question China needs to deal with is to prove that China has a legal basis for the recovery.

Although international legal instruments, such as the 1954 Hague Convention,[27] the 1970 UNESCO Convention[28] and the 1995 UNIDROIT Convention,[29] which provide for the restitution of cultural heritage, have emerged over the last 70 years, they do not apply retroactively. Most historical events, for example the Looting of the Summer Palace, that have given rise to current restitution claims occurred before the promulgation of such measures. Thus, one of the fundamental reasons for disputes being unresolved is that there was no law contemporaneous to the removal regulating such taking as illegal. In other words, current possessors are under no legal obligation to return. The usual result for the recovery claims is that enforceable legal action is not an option, resulting in an unsatisfying outcome both legally and ethically.

3. Increasing Demand for Return, but Lacking a Legal Basis

China is not the only country that has been active in pursuing the return of its cultural heritage. In the past few decades, other states of origin have been expecting the return of their cultural heritage: Greece has been requesting the return of the Parthenon Marbles for decades; South Korea has been requesting the return of its Ugiew, the historical books about its Joseon Dynasty (1392–1910); Egypt has been seeking the return of the Rosetta Stone and Nefertiti; and Nigeria has been demanding the return of the Benin bronzes. In many situations, in order to bring their heritage home, many states of origin have taken legal action against current possessors. Turkey petitioned the European Court of Human Rights for the return of the Helicarnassus; Italy took legal action against Marion True, the former curator of the Getty Museum, which was revealed to have accepted stolen Italian cultural objects; and Cambodia requested the US Government to apply civil forfeiture for the return of Khmer statues. As commented by a Turkish archaeologist, "we know

27 Convention for the Protection of Cultural Property in the Event of Armed Conflict (1954 Hague Convention). The Convention was completed by the Protocol for the Protection of Cultural Property in the Event of Armed Conflict (First Protocol—May 14 1954, 249 UNTS 358) and Second Protocol to the Hague Convention for the Protection of Cultural Property in the Event of Armed Conflict (Second Protocol—March 26 1999, 38 ILM 769 (1999)).

28 Convention on the Means of Prohibiting and Preventing the Illicit Import, Export and Transfer of Ownership of Cultural Property (1970 UNESCO Convention).

29 Convention on Stolen or Illegally Exported Cultural Object (1995 UNIDROIT Convention).

100 percent that these objects at the Met are from Anatolia. And we only want back what is rightfully ours."[30]

However, the lack of law regulating such removals as illegal makes it difficult for the claims to be successful. In May 2015, Greece stated that it had ruled out taking legal action in its battle to reclaim the Parthenon marbles from the UK, which ended the legal battle in one of the world's most debated cultural disputes.[31] Arguments for the return of the marbles have been made on both cultural and ethical grounds, and diplomatic efforts have been attempted since the mid-1980s.[32] The case was brought before the UNESCO Intergovernmental Committee; however, very little progress has been made. The fundamental reason for the dispute being unresolved is that there is no law contemporaneous to the removal regulating such taking as illegal. Neither the British Government nor the British Museum is under any legal obligation to return the Parthenon marbles to Greece.[33] In other words, claims for the return of relics without a legal basis are usually silenced or at best discussed, but very rarely facilitated.

In the absence of mandatory obligation, although return could still be trigged through diplomatic negation or voluntary donation, the fate of disputed cultural heritage is left to the current possessor to decide. The available practices demonstrate that relying on another party's goodwill is unpredictable and unrewarding. In 1978, the Netherlands handed over to Indonesia some colonial art treasures of cultural and historical significance; however, earlier requests from Indonesia related to a list of 10,000 objects.[34] Therefore, an ethics discourse is ineffective and inadequate to prompt large-scale restitution. Both China and other states of origin need a stronger argument to claim for the return of their cultural heritage.

4. Is a New Customary Rule Emerging?

In the past two decades, an increasing number of cultural heritage objects have been returned to states of origin by governments, museums, and individuals throughout the world. In particular, many claims that had been largely

30 Dan Bilefsky, 'Seeking Return of Art, Turkey Jolts Museums', *New York Times* September 30 2012 <www.nytimes.com/2012/10/01/arts/design/turkeys-efforts-to-repatriate-art-alarm-museums.html?pagewanted=all&_r=0>.

31 Helena Smith, 'Greece Drops Option of Legal Action in British Museum Parthenon Marbles Row', *Guardian* May 14 2015 <www.theguardian.com/artanddesign/2015/may/13/greece-drops-option-legal-action-british-museum-parthenon-marbles-row>.

32 Michael Reppas, 'Deflowering of the Parthenon: A Legal and Moral Analysis on Why the Elgin Marbles Must be Returned to Greece' (1999) 9 *Fordham Intellectual Property,Media and Entertainment Law Journal* 911.

33 'UK Government Rejects Parthenon Marbles UNESCO Mediation', *Elginism* March 27 2015 <www.elginism.com/elgin-marbles/uk-government-rejects-parthenon-marbles-unesco-mediation/20150327/7859/>.

34 Jos van Beurden, 'How to Break the Deadlock in the Debate About Colonial Acquisitions?' in Valentina Vadi and Hildegard Schneider (eds), *Art, Cultural Heritage and the Market: Ethical and Legal Issues* (Springer, 2014) 165, 167.

unsuccessful in the late 20th century have now been successfully negotiated and settled. In 2006, the Metropolitan Museum of Art stated that it would relinquish ownership of a 2,500-year-old Greek vase to Italy, reversing a position it had held for more than 30 years.[35] In the case of *Iran v Wolfcarius*, while the Iranian Government initiated legal action in the Belgian court in 1981 for the return of disputed art objects, the litigation was pending until December 2014. The court finally acknowledged the Iranian government's legal right to all the disputed cultural relics and ordered for them to be returned to Iran, more than 30 years after Iran first sued for the return.[36] In 2011, Japan eventually returned to South Korea over 1,200 precious ancient royal manuscripts, known as the Uigwe collection, more than 100 years after they were taken to Japan.[37] The evolving law and retuning cases strongly contribute to the idea that the interests of states of origin in their wrongfully removed cultural heritage have been increasingly respected and recognised. Based on the increasing recognition, this book argues that a new customary rule is emerging and will likely come into existence in the future. The proposed customary rule recognizes that the interests of states of origin in their wrongfully removed heritage should be respected and such heritage should be returned.

To argue for the proposed customary rule, this research critically examines the types of state practices that should be considered as relevant evidence for the formation of the customary rule. Against this background, it is timely to identify the types of return that will be analysed in the following chapters: (1) historically removed heritage; and (2) illegally removed cultural objects, which were removed either, (a) during armed conflicts; or (b) because of individual illegal behavior, such as theft, illicit excavation or illegal export during times of both war and peace. The reason that cultural heritage should be treated differently is that the legality of various types of legal removal is determined by different bodies of law. As for illegal removal due to war or occupation, the question remains as to whether the law of war prohibited such taking and provided for the return of cultural heritage afterwards. The illegal removal of cultural items by individuals during both times of war and peace is an issue due to the contravention of national laws. One further clarification is necessary for illegal removal due to individual behavior and its sub-categories: (1) stolen heritage and (2) illegally exported heritage. The difference is that a foreign court may be inclined to help an original owner recover stolen property, but will be reluctant to help a foreign government enforce its export

35 Randy Kennedy and Hugh Eakin, 'The Met, Ending 30-Year Stance, Is Set to Yield Prized Vase to Italy', *New York Times* February 3 2006 <www.nytimes.com/2006/02/03/arts/03muse.html>.

36 Janet Blake, *International Cultural Heritage Law* (Oxford University Press, 2015), 62–63.

37 Danielle Demetriou, 'Japan Returns Looted South Korean Documents to Homeland', *Telegraph* December 6 2011 <www.telegraph.co.uk/news/worldnews/asia/japan/8937503/Japan-returns-looted-South-Korean-documents-to-homeland.html>.

rules.[38] In other words, even though an object may be classified as illegally exported, the illicit removal does not necessarily constitute an illegal import, as a state is not obliged to recognise and enforce a foreign state's export law in the absence of a treaty or bilateral agreement.[39]

Despite the increasing returns made throughout the world, it should be admitted that the fundamental reason for many successful repatriations is that the states of origin generally have a legal basis and strong evidence to convince the courts that the disputed objects were illegally removed. However, for historically removed heritage, the obstacle standing in the way of return is a lack of law regulating such taking as illegal. In order to argue for the proposed customary rule, the crux of this research is to link the return of illegally taken heritage to historically removed heritage. Thus, the central questions lying at the basis of this book are whether an increasing recognition of states of origin's interests can be in found in state practices when illegally removed heritage is returned, and whether such recognition is sufficient to create the proposed customary rule to support the return of historically removed heritage. The increasing recognition of the interests of states of origin in their wrongfully removed cultural heritage is the bridge between illegally removed heritage and historically removed heritage. If state practices suggest that illegally removed heritage should be returned, it may reflect an increasing recognition and respect for states of origin and therefore constitute strong evidence for the formation of the proposed customary rule. Once state practices have shown a uniform and general recognition of states of origin's interests, this proposed rule will be recognised as a new customary rule. In other words, it will create a legal basis for states of origin to claim for the return of their historically removed heritage against current possessors. There will be more than just a moral and ethical connection between removal and return.

However, a question may arise as to whether the proposed customary rule is an overly optimistic view. To create a new customary rule, it is essential that the states whose interests are "specially affected" by the proposed customary rule should be in favour of the creation of this rule. Put simply, the uniform state practice in the specially affected states is required. In this regard, although there is an increasing recognition that foreign states should have sufficient interests to argue for the return of their wrongfully removed heritage, the uniformity among specially affected states is still lacking. For example, unresolved recovery issues during the Second World War suggests the lack of concurrence of those particularly affected states with the proposed customary

38 James Gordley, 'The Enforcement of Foreign Law: Reclaiming One Nation's Cultural Heritage in Another Nation's Courts' in Francesco Francioni and James Gordley (eds), *Enforcing International Cultural Heritage Law* (Oxford University Press, 2013) 110, 110–118; Yunxia Wang, *Cultural Heritage Law* (The Commercial Press, 2012), 376–378.

39 Paul M. Bator, 'An Essay on the International Trade in Art' (1982) 34(2) *Stanford Law Review* 275, 287.

Is a New Customary Rule Emerging?

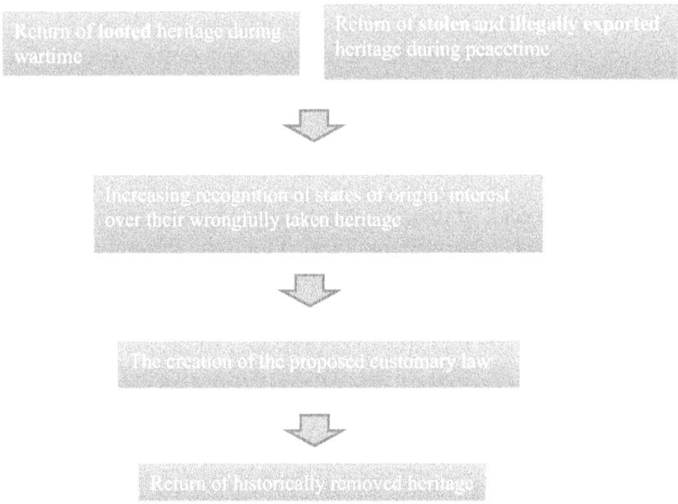

Figure 1.1

rule. Further, despite the return cases during the past two decades, actions by individuals and institutions do not constitute state behaviour and can therefore not create customary international law. More importantly, there is no indication that countries holding foreign cultural heritage removed in early times were willing to give them up at a large scale. All these issues raise uncertainty about the future of the proposed customary rule: whether the proposed customary rule can continue to develop, and eventually be recognised as a new customary rule.

5. Book Scope

Starting with the dispute surrounding the Chinese bronze statues, this book first aims to answer the question as to whether China has a legal basis to recover its cultural heritage taken during the period of 1840–1945. Although China has been expecting the return of its cultural heritage lost overseas, securing the return is problematic. Instead of pressing formal demands for repatriation, the approach used to bring scattered Chinese arts home is still limited to donation, buying-back, and diplomatic negotiation.[40] The main rea-

40 Gao Sheng, 'Recovering Illegally Removed Cultural Property and Improving Cultural Property Protection: A Chinese Perspective' (2009) (1) *Art Antiquity and Law* 1, 9–14.

son for this is that there is no clear answer as to whether China has a legal basis for the recovery. While many contributors have studied the topic of China's cultural heritage, they mostly focus on the cultural heritage law in the People's Republic of China (1949–present) and on other specific issues, including regulating the art market, preventing theft, illegal excavation and illegal export of cultural heritage, and promoting international cooperation. To the extent that these studies have considered the issue of the return of Chinese cultural heritage, they have focused on present day illegal trafficking of cultural objects instead of items that were looted before the founding of the People's Republic of China. Little research has been made on the applicable laws contemporaneous to removals that occurred during the period of 1840–1945, which is law in the Qing Dynasty (1644–1911) and law in the Republic of China (1911–1949). On the other hand, the question as to whether China has a legal basis for recovery is the first legal hurdle that China needs to get over. Thus, this research aims to examine the availability of a legal basis for the recovery of China's cultural heritage.

While the first part of the book is aimed at China specifically, the positioning of China in this book is not merely as a case study. This book is also valuable to all states that are active or involved in the field of restitution of cultural heritage. When ethics discourse is ineffective and inadequate in promoting large-scale restitution, the proposed customary rule will provide a solution. The proposed customary rule will allow not only China, but also other states of origin with a similar dilemma, to obtain the return of both illegally and historically removed heritage. In other words, all states of origin should have a right to the return of their wrongfully removed cultural heritage according to this proposed customary rule. China has been used as a case study in this book because of its experience with the process.

As it will be analysed, China does not have a legal basis for all cultural heritage taken during the period of 1840–1945, in which case the proposed customary rule may provide an answer. The second part of this book will answer questions about whether the proposed customary rule is emerging. Premised on the assumption that the new rule has come into existence, it will provide China and other states of origin a stronger and legal argument to claim against museums and art collectors for the return of cultural items. To argue for the proposed custom, this book provides a systematic and critical examination of the types of state practice that should be considered as relevant evidence for the formation of the customary rule. This book argues that the available state practice has shown a clear tendency towards supporting the return of wrongfully removed heritage.

Several further aspects necessitate clarification. First, this book focuses on the return of Chinese cultural heritage taken from the First Opium War to the end of the Japanese Occupation (1840–1945). The proposed timeframe (1840–1945) falls short of the period during which some of the most important Chinese material was relocated to Taiwan from the mainland by the Kuomintang. The reason that this book does not go beyond the date of 1945 is the return of cultural heritage taken to Taiwan raises an entirely different set of issues and would be best left to another book in the future.[41] Similar reasons apply to the ongoing illicit trafficking of stolen and smuggled cultural heritage in China. Although all these issues are of great importance for the management and protection of Chinese cultural heritage, they are beyond the discussion of this book, which primarily focuses on historically removed heritage.

Second, despite the different theories in terms of creating a new customary rule, this research adopts the ideas of Brownlie and Shaw, according to which the most crucial factor is the concurrence of specially affected states in that particular field. States whose interests are especially affected must belong to those endorsing the creation of the rule. In the field of restitution, specially affected states can be divided into two groups: current possessors, including the UK, the US, France, Japan, Germany, and Switzerland; and states of origin, such as China, Cambodia, Egypt, Greece, Italy, Turkey, and Peru. This book focuses on these specially affected states to argue that there is an increasing endorsement of the proposed customary rule.

Third, it should be further noted that what makes return legally complex is that it lies at the interface of a number of distinct branches of law: the law of war, private international law, human rights, cultural heritage law, and national laws (such as criminal law, property law, contract law, and tort law). These legal areas are quite different in nature, but form the basis for supporting the return of illegally removed heritage. This book will examine all the relevant laws that may form a basis for the return of wrongfully removed heritage.

Fourth, this book will not be limited to legal analysis, as the return of cultural heritage cannot be dealt with on a strictly legal argument alone. In the realm of cultural heritage, a wide range of guidelines, policies and other so-called soft laws have played an important role in facilitating the return of cultural heritage. Additionally, an increasing number of cultural objects have been returned to states of origin by private museums, non-governmental institutions, auction houses and individuals throughout the world. Although they do not constitute state behaviour and therefore cannot create customary international law, they are still worth discussing in this book, as the return of cultural heritage is not a theme that can be treated convincingly without a fully grounded engagement with ethics. The legal doctrinal discourse in this book is contextualised with reference to the moral arguments that support the return of wrongfully removed heritage.

41 For example, the return of cultural heritage to Taiwan is closely linked with the question as to whether "Taiwan is part of China's territory". The answer to this question is significant, as it will then determine the law applied to the question of removals' legality. According to the author, Taiwan is part of China's territory, which means the taking itself is an internal matter and should be governed by China's domestic law. However, others may have a different opinion and believe that Taiwan should be considered as an independent state. Therefore, the question of legality should be answered under the framework of public international law.

While discussing materials of both state practice and non-state practice, this book is significant and valuable to museums and art collectors in the event of buying and accepting art objects. First, this book deals with a large pool of repatriation cases and compares all available solutions, including litigation, negotiation, cooperation, buying-back, conditional return, art loan, donation, or simply stepping up the pressure. A problem-sensitive, practical approach is provided. Though this comparative study, the book provides a useful tool for a disputing party, including museums, art collectors, auction houses, and governments, to settle cultural disputes peacefully and to avoid unnecessary negative headlines, reputational damage or the impoverishment of their collections. In particular, through the systematic analysis of different branches of law in specially affected states, this book provides some suggestions on how museums, art collectors and auction houses should buy and accept foreign art, in case of getting embroiled in a dispute with a foreign government. Furthermore, from the perspective of cultural heritage law, this book is also structured on three categories of cultural heritage: (1) heritage looted during armed conflicts; (2) heritage stolen, illegally excavated, or illegally exported in peacetime; (3) and historically taken heritage. By examining the evolving cultural heritage law, this book is significant in suggesting the protection and management of cultural heritage, which will eventually have an impact on the art market, museums and art collections.

6. Chapter Summary

After this introductory chapter, the book is structured in the following ways. Chapter 2 investigates the long-lasting legal, moral and societal debates surrounding the allocation of cultural heritage. This chapter argues that although cultural heritage should be available to and protected by all humankind, it should be conducted in a reasonable way and respect the will of the people from states of origin. Cultural heritage that was removed against the will of the original owners should be returned due to the special and strong connection between states of origin and their cultural heritage.

Chapter 3 focuses on the legal grounds that exist for China to request the return of its cultural heritage in order to determine whether the taking of objects during 1840 to 1949 was prohibited under either China's national law or international law. This chapter concludes that China does not have a basis for the return of all removals that occurred between 1840 and 1945, and, in these cases, the customary rule may provide an answer. This chapter ends with a discussion about the definition of historically removed heritage and its return, which is the fundamental question that this book aims to resolve.

With regards to the creating of a new customary rule, there is considerable academic debate as to whether and when a new rule can be accepted as a customary rule. Chapter 4 explores the notion of customary international law and the process of creating a new customary rule. This chapter argues that the most crucial factor is the concurrence of "specially affected" states in the field of the removal and return of cultural heritage.

The following two chapters focus on the two premises needed to create the proposed customary rule: the return of looted heritage during wartime; and the return of stolen and illegally exported heritage in peacetime respectively. Chapter 5 examines the evolving international law and practice regarding the prohibitation of looting of cultural heritage during wartimes and the repatriation of removed arts after the end of war. This chapter argues that specially affected states have shown an increasing agreement that cultural heritage looted, stolen or illegally exported during wartime should be returned. However, the unresolved issues of war repatriations during the two world wars have constituted a powerful deterrent to the creation of the proposed customary rule.

Chapter 6 discusses the restitution of stolen and illegally exported arts taken during peacetime. This chapter examines international law, European law, as well as laws in the market states, including the US, Germany, Switzerland, the UK and the Netherlands. This chapter reaches the conclusion that state practice has shown a growing recognition that stolen and illegally exported cultural objects should be returned to states of origin. However, the lack of uniformity suggests that the proposed customary rule is at the very beginning of the process of its formation.

Chapter 7 focuses on the practice of individuals, private museums and auction houses, in order to explore whether there is increasing public endorsement for the return of wrongfully removed heritage and moral acknowledgment of claims by the states of origin. Although they do not constitute state behaviour, they are still a noteworthy issue, as public attitudes and ethical considerations generally precede the development of legal rules. In other words, they are important in suggesting whether the proposed customary rule is likely to come into existence. Additionally, the return of cultural heritage is not a theme that can be treated convincingly without a fully grounded engagement with ethics.

Chapter 8 first examines three return cases of historically removed heritage, which show that a dialogue about the future of historically removed objects is complicated and will not be a quick-fix. This concluding chapter then answers the final question as to whether a new rule of customary international law is emerging, to the effect that historically removed cultural heritage should be returned to states of origin; and, if such a rule is emerging, what are the likely limitations to this rule.

Bibliography

'China Condemns Christie's Auction', *The BBC News* February 26 2009 <http://news.bbc.co.uk/2/hi/asia-pacific/7911691.stm>

'China Condemns Christie's Sculpture Sale, Warns of "Serious Effects"', *Xinhua News* February 26 2009 <http://news.xinhuanet.com/english/2009-02/26/content_10900960.htm>

'China Tightens Control on Christie's After Auction', *The Xinhua News* February 26 2009 <http://news.xinhuanet.com/english/2009-02/26/content_10901300.htm>

'Chinese Experts Demand Return of Cultural Relics' in Lyndel Prott (ed), *Witnesses to History* (UNESCO, 2008) 119

'Culture Insider: Chinese Cultural Relics Lost Overseas', *China Daily* August 15 2014 <www.chinadaily.com.cn/culture/art/2014-08/15/content_18311574.htm>

'"Give Us Back Our Treasure": Chinese Demand Cameron Returns Priceless Artefacts Looted during 19th Century Boxer Rebellion', *Mail Online* December 4 2013 <www.dailymail.co.uk/news/article-2518111/China-demand-David-Cameron-return-Boxer-Rebellion-artefacts.html>

'UK Government Rejects Parthenon Marbles UNESCO Mediation', *Elginism* March 27 2015 <www.elginism.com/elgin-marbles/uk-government-rejects-parthenon-marbles-unesco-mediation/20150327/7859/>

'War Damage on Cultural Relics Commission under the Department of Education', *China Cultural Relics* August 22 2007 <www.xhgxt.com/html/View_9270.html>

Bator, Paul M., 'An Essay on the International Trade in Art' (1982) 34(2) *Stanford Law Review* 275

Beurden, Jos van, 'How to Break the Deadlock in the Debate About Colonial Acquisitions?' in Valentina Vadi and Hildegard Schneider (eds), *Art, Cultural Heritage and the Market: Ethical and Legal Issues* (Springer, 2014) 165

Bilefsky, Dan, 'Seeking Return of Art, Turkey Jolts Museums', *New York Times* September 30 2012 <www.nytimes.com/2012/10/01/arts/design/turkeys-efforts-to-repatriate-art-alarm-museums.html?pagewanted=all&_r=0>

Blake, Janet, *International Cultural Heritage Law* (Oxford University Press, 2015)

Changhong, Yan and Li Xia, 'A Review of Japan's Cultural Aggression against China during Anti-Japanese War' (in Chinese) (2005) 25(4) *Journal of South-Central University for Nationalities (Humanities and Social Sciences)* 12

Cuno, James, *Who Owns Antiquity?: Museums and the Battle over Our Ancient Heritage* (Princeton University Press, 2008)

Demetriou, Danielle, 'Japan Returns Looted South Korean Documents to Homeland', *Telegraph* December 6 2011 <www.telegraph.co.uk/news/worldnews/asia/japan/8937503/Japan-returns-looted-South-Korean-documents-to-homeland.html>

Fairbank, John King, *The Cambridge History of China Volume 10: Late Ch'ing 1800–1911, Part 1* (Cambridge University Press, 1978)

Gordley, James, 'The Enforcement of Foreign Law: Reclaiming One Nation's Cultural Heritage in Another Nation's Courts' in Francesco Francioni and James Gordley (eds), *Enforcing International Cultural Heritage Law* (Oxford University Press, 2013) 110

Gruber, Stefan, 'The Fight Against the Illicit Trade in Asian Cultural Artefacts: Connecting International Agreements, Regional Co-operation, and Domestic strategies' (2013) 3(2) *Asian Journal of International Law* 341

Kennedy, Randy and Hugh Eakin, 'The Met, Ending 30-Year Stance, Is Set to Yield Prized Vase to Italy', *New York Times* February 3 2006 <www.nytimes.com/2006/02/03/arts/03muse.html>

Kowalski, Wojciech, 'Types of Claims for Recovery of Lost Cultural Property' (2005) 57(228) *Museum International* 85

Liu, Zuozhen, *The Case for Repatriating China's Cultural Objects* (Springer, 2016)

Meyer, Karl, 'The Chinese Want Their Art Back', *New York Times* June 20 2015 <www.nytimes.com/2015/06/21/opinion/the-chinese-want-their-art-back.html?_r=0>

Peng, Lei, *A Research on Legal History of Return of Relics (in Chinese)* (Nanjing: Yilin Publishing, 2012)

Perez, Louis G., *Japan at War: An Encyclopedia* (ABC-CLIO, 2013)

Prott, Lyndel and Patrick O'Keefe, '"Cultural Heritage" or "Cultural Property"?' (1992) 1(2) *International Journal of Cultural Property* 307

Reppas, Michael, 'Deflowering of the Parthenon: A Legal and Moral Analysis on Why the Elgin Marbles Must be Returned to Greece' (1999) 9 *Fordham Intellectual Property, Media and Entertainment Law Journal* 911

Scott, David, *China and the International System, 1840–1949: Power, Presence, and Perceptions in A Century of Humiliation* (State University of New York Press, 2008)

Sheng, Gao, 'Recovering Illegally Removed Cultural Property and Improving Cultural Property Protection: A Chinese Perspective' (2009) (1) *Art Antiquity and Law* 1

Smith, Helena, 'Greece Drops Option of Legal Action in British Museum Parthenon Marbles Row', *Guardian* May 14 2015 <www.theguardian.com/artanddesign/2015/may/13/greece-drops-option-legal-action-british-museum-parthenon-marbles-row>

Stamatoudi, Irini A., *Cultural Property Law and Restitution: A Commentary to International Conventions and European Union law* (Edward Elgar Publishing, 2011)

Wang, Yunxia, *Cultural Heritage Law* (The Commercial Press, 2012)

Wong, Edward and Steven Erlanger, 'Frenchman Will Return to China Prized Bronze Artifacts Looted in 19th Century', *The New York Times* April 26 2013 <www.nytimes.com/2013/04/27/world/europe/frenchman-will-return-to-china-prized-bronze-artifacts-looted-in-19th-century.html>

Zhang, Yu, 'France Returning Treasure to China Sets Precedent for Further Restitutions', *Global Times* September 9 2015 <www.globaltimes.cn/content/941506.shtml>

2 States of Origin and Cultural Heritage

1. Introduction

There is little debate surrounding the unique importance of cultural heritage. The international debate; however, centres on who is entitled to possess cultural heritage and in what situation should items be returned to their place of origin.[1] Museums in the market states, private art dealers and collectors, and auction houses assert that cultural heritage is a part of a common human culture, whatever its place of origin. They argue that a cultural object is best appreciated when exhibited at a museum in a large international city, where it is easily accessed by the wider public, rather than the place of the artefact's origin. States of origin argue for the return on the basis that cultural heritage is an indispensable part of their history and identity, and that their people have an inalienable right to access the heritage created by their ancestors. However, many commenters assert that linking cultural heritage to a country of origin is problematic and flawed, arguing that the relationship is no more than a historical accident: "they just happen to have been found within its borders".[2] China's claims for its cultural heritage raise two additional questions: first, as China is a large multi-national state, composing of the Han Chinese majority and 55 additional ethnic groups, it is unlikely that many people from a minority dominated area, such as Tibet, would care about the return of the looted Summer Palace sculptures. Second, as many cultural treasures were destroyed during the Cultural Revolution, China's claims for return have been undermined, raising questions as to whether cultural heritage would be preserved if returned to China.[3]

1 For more discussions, see Lyndel Prott, 'The International Movement of Cultural Objects' (2005) 12(2) *International Journal of Cultural Property* 225; John Henry Merryman, 'Cultural Property Internationalism' (2005) 12(1) *International Journal of Cultural Property* 11; Eric Posner, 'The International Protection of Cultural Property: Some Skeptical Observations' (2007) 8(1) *Chicago Journal of International Law* 213.

2 James Cuno, *Who Owns Antiquity?: Museums and the Battle over Our Ancient Heritage* (Princeton University Press, 2008), 17.

3 It is generally agreed that the Cultural Revolution had its root in Mao's attempt to find an alternative path to socialism than the Soviets. The Cultural Revolution, usually called

As the primary purpose of this book is to argue for a new customary rule, which is created on the increasing recognition of the connection between states of origin and their cultural heritage, a chapter exploring this relationship is essential. Additionally, although a strong legal argument usually strengthens a recovery claim, it should be observed that many successful returns are not made strictly on legal analysis alone. The recognition and respect of states of origin's interests in their wrongfully removed cultural heritage has played an increasingly important role in resolving recovery disputes. Hence, before moving to strict legal analysis in the following chapters, this chapter investigates the long-lasting legal, moral, and societal debates surrounding the allocation of cultural heritage and argues that historically removed cultural heritage should be returned from moral and cultural perspectives.

Chapter 2 begins by stating that this book does not aim to empty the collections of current possessors, as cultural heritage from each state should be available to all humankind. It then explores the link between states of origin and cultural heritage, first by analysing the unique value of cultural heritage to states of origin, and then by exploring the determination of "states of origin". As China is used as a special case study in this book, the second part of this chapter explores the connection between China and its cultural heritage in order to justify China's assertion that its interests in cultural heritage taken during the period of 1840 to 1945 should be respected first. The last part of this chapter responds to the excuses used by current possessors to deny the return of cultural heritage, and argues that they cannot use these excuses to avoid dialogue around the issue of return, as these excuses are not defensible in every case. This chapter concludes that although cultural heritage should be available to and protected by all humankind, it should be conducted in a reasonable way and respect the will of people from the states of origin. Cultural heritage removed against the will of the original owners, in particular those stolen or looted in periods of colonialism or imperialism, should be returned due to the special and strong connection between states of origin and their heritage.

2. To Empty Our Museums?

One of the reasons recovery disputes remain unresolved is that many museums are worried that a successful case for the return of cultural heritage will result in an increasing number of recovery claims in the future, leading to the depletion of their collections.[4] This book does not argue for the removal of

---

the "10 years of chaos" in China, is the darkest age in modern Chinese history, during which many Chinese artefacts, monuments, and buildings were attacked and destroyed. For more discussion, see Roderick MacFarquhar and John King Fairbank, *The Cambridge History of China. Vol. 15, The People's Republic. Part 2, Revolutions within the Chinese Revolution, 1966–1982* (Cambridge University Press, 2008).

4 Elazar Barkan, 'Amending Historical Injustices: The Restitution of Cultural Property—An Overview' in *Claiming the Stones, Naming the Bones: Cultural Property and the Negotiation of National and Ethnic Identity* (Getty Research Institute, 2002) 16, 19.

every piece of Chinese artwork from, for example, the British Museum or the Louvre Museum. The intention is not to deprive the current holders of all the objects in their possession; instead, it is to highlight how a state's cultural heritage plays an indispensable role in linking the state's culture with the understanding of the history of the whole society. The world is comprised of many cultures, which are not confined to the political boundaries constructed by each state. While different cultural backgrounds shape our national identity, we also share some common natures and difficulties as human beings. Cultural heritage from each state forms an indispensable part of the whole picture of our international society and it is therefore important that it is accessible to all humankind.

As cultural heritage is not a renewable resource that belongs to all humankind, its protection is also the responsibility of the international community. In this regard, international support is particularly needed for those states that do not have adequate resources to protect their rich cultural heritage. Since 2001, the US Ambassadors Fund for Cultural Preservation has supported several projects to preserve Nepal's rich cultural heritage, including: the restoration of ancient and historical buildings; the conservation of rare manuscripts, museum collections, and important archaeological sites; and the documentation of vanishing traditional craft techniques and indigenous languages.[5] Especially during war, international cooperation is indispensable in requesting parties to respect cultural heritage. In 2002, UNESCO created the International Coordination Committee for the Safeguarding of Afghanistan' Cultural Heritage to coordinate all international efforts for the protection of cultural heritage.[6] In addition to wartime destruction, a state that is part of conflict and also rich in cultural heritage is usually a victim of illicit excavations, as well as the pillaging of museums, libraries, shops, and galleries. Pieces stolen and smuggled out are often damaged or lost, with few items ever returned to where they rightfully belong. In this regard, international organisations, including UNESCO, INTERPOL, the World Customs Organization, and governments and museums in the market states have worked together to fight against the illicit trafficking of cultural objects.[7]

However, if cultural heritage belongs to all humankind, what is the purpose of this book? Why is this research arguing for the creation of a new customary rule, which will eventually pave the way for the return of historically removed heritage? The reason is simple: although cultural heritage should be accessible

5 Bureau of Educational and Cultural Affairs Promoting Mutual Understanding, 'Ambassadors Fund for Cultural Preservation (AFCP): Nepal Projects' <http://eca.state.gov/cultural-heritage-center/gallery/ambassadors-fund-cultural-preservation-afcp-nepal-projects>.

6 Christian Manhart, 'UNESCO's Mandate and Recent Activities for the Rehabilitation of Afghanistan's Cultural Heritage' (2004) 86(854) *International Review of the Red Cross* 401, 409.

7 UNESCO, 'Help Stop the Destruction of Cultural Heritage in Syria and Iraq' <www.unesco.org/new/en/culture/themes/illicit-trafficking-of-cultural-property/awareness-raising-initiatives/help-stop-the-destruction-of-cultural-heritage-in-syria-and-iraq/>.

to all humankind, it does not contradict the recovery claims for historically removed heritage. By acknowledging our shared humanity and cultural difference, we should also acknowledge the special links between state of origin and cultural heritage. Cultural heritage is not merely an object; it serves as a link between the past and the future. It is instrumental in symbolising the history of a state and enhancing its national identity.

3. States of Origin and Cultural Heritage

In most recovery claims, cultural heritage has been frequently linked to the emotions of people from the state of origin. In the recovery of the Afo-A-Kom, the Cameroon Ambassador in Washington said that "it is beyond money, beyond value. It is the heart of the Kom, what unifies the tribe, the spirit of the nation, what holds us together."[8] However, many scholars view this link as problematic, arguing that cultural objects have no nationality.[9] Given these conflicting opinions, this section investigates the special values of cultural heritage, and explains the reasons for states of origin to insistently request their return.

3.1. Symbolising History

Many demands for return are often aimed at the "representatives", such as the Parthenon Marbles, which are important in symbolising the state's history. The Parthenon temple, built in the 5th century BC to honour Athena, is recognised as the greatest architectural achievement of that time and also one of the most recognised symbols of Greek civilisation. In most cases, claimed cultural objects are the last chance for a state of origin to learn about a particular period of history, because the objects were usually produced in an early time period with few copies available in the world. For example, the Benin bronzes claimed by Nigeria are the Benin equivalent of chronological records. Since each bronze head represented an Oba, they recorded dynasties' back to the 12th century. The refusal to return such cultural heritage is tantamount to separating a people from their history.[10]

In addition, the value of cultural heritage lies in its originality and antiquity. For example, the Dunhuang manuscripts provide scholars an independent look at Chinese history and civilisation.[11] The majority of historical materials

8 Patrick O'Keefe, 'Repatriation of Sacred Objects' in Lyndel Prott (ed), *Witnesses to History: A Compendium of Documents and Writings on the Return of Cultural Objects* (UNESCO, 2009), 229.

9 Cuno, *Who owns antiquity*, above n 2, 17; Merryman, *Internationalism*, above n 1, 12.

10 Folarin Shyllon, 'Unraveling History: Return of African Cultural Objects Repatriated and Looted in Colonial Times' in James A.R. Nafziger and Ann Nicgorski (eds), *Cultural Heritage Issues* (Martinus Nijhoff Publishers, 2009) 159, 163.

11 Translated by: Imre Galambos Rong Xinjiang, *Eighteen Lectures on Dunhuang* (Brill, 2013), 341.

from ancient China focus on the emperors and a limited group of top officials, and were produced by historians who served the bureaucracy. Despite their great historical and scholarly values, these materials were all compiled from the perspective of the central administration. In contrast, the Dunhuang manuscripts provide rich information on various strata of society and even recorded the script, such as Tibetan, which makes the manuscripts more authentic and at the same time more valuable than records written in Chinese.[12] Thus, it can be said that cultural heritage is important in symbolising the history of a nation and recording social, political, economic, and religious events in a chronological order.

3.2. Cultural Identity

While cultural heritage was not created for modern states, each cultural item connects a state's past to its future, providing an insight into the lives of its ancestors and the formation of its communities.[13] In addition, cultural heritage can represent times of victory, defeat, great suffering or important historical occasions, which can easily invoke feelings, such as pride, happiness, pity, and sorrow.[14] At the 2009 Paris auction, the Chinese Government urged Christie's to stop the auction, stating that it would seriously "hurt the national feelings of Chinse people".[15] One of the reasons is that China's highest culture had been ignored and violently smashed into pieces by the Western powers. The looting of the Summer Palace has become a source of bitterness for many Chinese, which is why related discussions easily become emotional and the reason that the Chinese businessman who successfully bid for the statues refused to pay as a patriotic act. This case clearly reflects the importance that societies attach to their cultural heritage. This sense of belonging passes from generation to generation, shaping the nature of a people as well as embodying the civilisation and development.

In addition, research has shown that in the process of globalisation, the more the world becomes global, the more people feel local.[16] As Annette Weiner said:

> Persons and groups need to demonstrate continually who they are in relation to others, and their identities must be attached to those ancestral connections that figure significantly in their statuses, ranks, or titles . . . To

12 Ibid, 6–7.

13 Tolina Loulanski, 'Revising the Concept for Cultural Heritage: The Argument for a Functional Approach' (2006) 13(2) *International Journal of Cultural Property* 207, 213.

14 Craig Forrest, *International Law and The Protection of Cultural Heritage* (Routledge, 2010), 4–5.

15 'China Condemns Christie's Auction', *The BBC News* February 26 2009 <http://news.bbc.co.uk/2/hi/asia-pacific/7911691.stm>.

16 Manuel Castells, *Power of Identity: The Information Age: Economy, Society, and Culture Volume II* (Wiley-Blackwell, 2009), xxiii.

> be able to keep certain objects that document these connections attests to one's power to hold oneself or one's group intact. For to give up these objects is to lose one's claim to the past as a working part of one's identity.[17]

In other words, people would like to embrace their cultural identity and difference. Notably, cultural heritage as an element of cultural identity has been reiterated in many legal instruments on cultural heritage. The 1970 UNESCO Convention states in the preamble that "cultural property constitutes one of the basic elements of civilization and national culture".[18]At the press conference on Re-building Cultural Heritage in Mali, the Director of the UNESCO Office in New York states that "a community's cultural heritage reflects its life, history and identity. Its preservation helps to rebuild broken communities, re-establish their identities, and link their past with their present and future".[19]

3.3. Who Is the "State of Origin"?

Despite the special connection between heritage and states of origin, difficulties arise in determining the state of origin. First, state border lines have changed and may continue to be altered, so it can become very problematic to identify the country of origin for some cultural objects.[20] If a cultural object stolen from former Yugoslavia, which has dissolved into six countries (seven, including Kosovo), is now being claimed by these countries, which state is entitled to possess the object? Second, the people who claim for the return of cultural heritage properly are not the descendants of the people who created the claimed items.[21] For example, modern day Iraqis have little in common with the people who lived in Mesopotamia thousands of years ago. Third, the history of a particular piece could be so complicated that it is difficult to establish the facts of its origin. When Italy claimed for the return of the Greek statue of the Victorious Youth from the Getty Museum, the main contentious points of this dispute were whether the statue was found in international waters and whether Italy is the real state of origin.[22]

17 Annette Weiner, 'Inalienable Wealth' in Simon Knell (ed), *Museums in the Material World* (Routledge, 2007) 253, 253.
18 Preamble of the 1970 UNESCO Convention.
19 UNESCO, 'Re-building Cultural Heritage in Mali' <www.unesco.org/new/en/unesco-liaison-office-in-new-york/about-this-office/single-view/news/re_building_cultural_heritage_in_mali/>.
20 Zuozhen Liu, *The Case for Repatriating China's Cultural Objects* (Springer, 2016), 130.
21 Posner, *Some Skeptical Observations,* above n 1, 223.
22 Alessandra Lanciotti, 'The Dilemma of the Right to Ownership of Underwater Cultural Heritage: The Case of the "Getty Bronze"' in Silvia Borelli and Federico Lenzerini (eds), *Cultural Heritage, Cultural Rights, Cultural Diversity: New Developments in International Law* (Martinus Nijhoff Publishers, 2012) 301, 302.

In fact, it is hard to determine a state of origin, owing to the conflicting interests and the overlapping claims for return. While this book does not aim to provide a universally agreed answer, a brief exploration of the determination is essential. This book first suggests that the place where the cultural object was found or excavated in modern times can be an important element in determining the state of origin, which has been endorsed by some national and international legislation. For example, the US Cultural Property Implementation Act (CPIA) applies to any object of archaeological and ethnological interest, which "was first discovered within the State Party".[23] Similarly, the Importation of Pre-Columbian Monumental or Architectural Sculpture or Murals Act (Pre-Columbian Act) defines the country of origin as "the country where such sculpture or mural was first discovered".[24]

However, questions still arise as there are other aspects of defining the value of cultural heritage to the state of origin that can impact on return claims. As China consists of Han Chinese and 55 other minority groups, many commentators argue that the Chinese Government's recovery claim cannot be justified as minority groups may not view the return of the Summer Palace sculptures as important. James Cuno, the former curator of the Art Institute of Chicago, reacts to China's recovery efforts with a sneer: "it is hard to imagine, when driving the long, straight, recently paved road from Urumqi to Turpan, that many people there cared about the Summer Palace sculptures when they were looted in the 1860".[25] In response, this book also suggests that, apart from location of discovery, each case has to be judged individually and the determination of a state of origin largely depends on the cultural connection between the requesting party and the item.[26] It is possible that Uighurs do not care about the looting of the Summer Palace, but Cuno has not elaborated on whether Uighurs care about their own Uighur cultural objects.[27] If a great Uighur palace were destroyed and plundered, would the Uighurs care about those looted objects? If Cuno explores this issue from the perspective of the Han Chinese instead of Uighurs, would he come to the same conclusion? For many Han Chinese, the intentional destruction of the Summer Palace is a mark of bitterness, because China's highest cultural achievement was violently smashed into pieces by Western powers. In Chinese discussion of the loss of cultural heritage, words such as grievance, pain, national disaster, and cultural tragedy are commonly used. Thus, in discussing the recovery of the Summer Palace sculptures, Han Chinese's opinions carry more weight than Uighurs' opinions. Similarly, if Uighurs argued for the return of their cultural heritage, their opinions and their feelings connected with that cultural object should be

23 Section 302 (2) of the CPIA.
24 Section 205(4) of the Pre-Columbian Act.
25 Cuno, *Who owns antiquity,* above n 2, 112–113.
26 Forrest, *International Law and Protection*, above n 14, 147.
27 Liu, *Repatriating China's Cultural Objects,* above n 20, 128.

evaluated first. The answer to determining a state of origin largely depends on the cultural connection between the requesting party and the heritage item.

After the analysis above, it is evident that the people with a special connection with the requested cultural object are very important to the claim for its return. But in practice, it is usually the government, not a particular group of people or an individual, that play an active role in pursuing the item's return. Regarding the role a state's government plays in the recovery, two further aspects need clarification. First, many countries that are rich in cultural heritage have enacted national ownership laws that vest ownership of archaeological resources and ancient monuments in the country.[28] So when a cultural object is stolen or illegally exported, a state and its government is the rightful plaintiff. Second, recovering a cultural object that has been scattered overseas can be very time consuming, expensive and diplomatically sensitive. A state government is usually in a better position to negotiate with current possessors, initiate a legal action, or place pressure by restricting archaeological excavation or refusing joint exhibition.

4. China and Its Cultural Heritage

As China has been used as a special case study in this book, the following section explores the connection between China and its cultural heritage in order to justify that its interests in cultural heritage taken from China between 1840 and 1945 should be respected first.

4.1. Strong National Identity as Chinese Throughout the History

Many Chinese people are very proud of their long history. Ask any Chinese person how long the country's history is, and they would be very proud to tell you that China has a 5,000-year history. Regardless of the preciseness, belonging to a long history has been instrumental in the construction of culture in China. This Chinese sensibility and the idea of being Chinese is the result of two main elements: the belief that China was the only true civilisation in ancient China, and strict political adherence to Confucian principles.[29] In the eyes of the ancient Chinese, the land where they lived was the only piece of land for humans. They called this land *tianxia* (all under heaven). Gradually, *tianxia* turned into a cultural concept. People at that time believed that only *tianxia* was the true culture, and people living outside *tianxia* were barbaric. The 17th century Chinese thinker Gu Yanwu draws a distinction between *guo* (state) and *tianxia*.[30] In the view of Gu Yanwu, state is a political concept,

28 State ownership law will be analysed in Chapter 6.

29 James Harrison, *Modern Chinese Nationalism* (Hunter College of the City University of New York, 1969), 3–14.

30 Liu, *Repatriating China's Cultural Objects*, above n 20, 150.

whereas *tianxia* is a cultural notion, which refers to Chinese cultural tradition and heritage. For Chinese people, the change of dynasties or government is not as profound as the ruin of Chinese cultural values.[31] For centuries, the meaning of being Chinese seemed simple and definite: a sense of belonging to a great civilisation and performing according to Confucian principles. The sense of belonging as Chinese is not just about the political understanding of a national state, but is foremost founded on the basis of belonging to a 5,000-year-old civilisation.

Reflected in the recovery, this sense of being Chinese extends to a strong recognition of Chinese cultural heritage. In ancient China, Chinese art, particularly painting and calligraphy, were intentionally considered a vital element of Chinese culture and also as a medium of consciousness. For example, one of the most important Chinese paintings, the Admonitions Scroll (also known as *Nüshi zhen tu*), which is currently exhibited in the British Museum, is a very important document with historical information. The scroll's full title, "Admonitions of the Instructress to the Court Ladies", indicates the work's moralising tone.[32] From the Han dynasty, Confucianism became orthodox in Chinese society. In Confucianism, a wife should submit to her husband. The scroll's protagonist is the court instructress, who advises the ladies of the palace on correct behaviour. The creation of the Admonitions Scroll was to spread the teaching of Confucianism. From this example, Chinese art is not just a form of artwork; it is also a cultural expression of social, political, economic, and religious events in a chronological order. Pursing the return of Chinese heritage removed during 1840 and 1945 is another form of pursuing the national identity of being Chinese.

4.2. Recognition and Appreciation of Chinese Culture

This sense of being Chinese also underpins the recognition and appreciation of Chinese culture by Chinese people throughout the country's long history. Evidence shows that traditional Chinese culture is an indispensable part of Chinese cultural heritage and has played an influential role in shaping the future of Chinese law.[33] According to China's Law on Protection of Cultural Relics, to determine whether an object falls within the scope of protection, the evaluation measures include that cultural relics have "historical value" or "great significance . . . for the preservation of historical data", or are produced

31 Martin Lu and Rosita Dellios, 'One Culture Two Systems: A Cultural Approach to Inter-Chinese Politics' 3(1) *Culture Mandala: The Bulletin of the Centre for East-West Cultural and Economic Studies* 18, 20.

32 Wu Hung, 'The Admonitions Scroll Revisited: Iconology, Narratology, Style, Dating' in Shane McCausland (ed), *Gu Kaizhi and the Admonitions Scroll* (British Museum Press, 2003) 89, 89–91.

33 Jianfu Chen, *Chinese Law: Context and Transformation* (Martinus Nijhoff Publishers, 2008), 9–10.

"dating from various historical periods".[34] The scope of protection under China's cultural heritage law is evidence of the recognition and respect of traditional legal culture from ancient China. Furthermore, Chinese state leaders borrow a lot of political norms from traditional Chinese cultures, such as "ruling the country by virtue [*Yide zhiguo*]" by Jiang Zeming, and the notion of the "harmonious society [*Hexie Shehui*]" by Hu Jintao.[35] Thus, it can be concluded that there is strong recognition of being Chinese and the importance of China's cultural heritage.

4.3. China's Recovery Efforts

During the period of 1840 to 1945, countless pieces of Chinese cultural heritage were destroyed and taken out of the country. However, the damage to Chinese cultural heritage tends to be forgotten by the international community: while the Nazi's looting of before and during the Second World War has been universally condemned, Japan's systematic plunder and destruction of China's cultural heritage during the same war is seldom discussed in literature. Despite the silence in the international community, the Chinese Government insists on asserting its interest over its wrongfully removed cultural heritage and has sought for the return of lost cultural heritage scattered overseas by all means in accordance with relevant international conventions and Chinese laws. After the Paris auction in 2009, the Summer Palace Administration began sending delegations of Chinese experts around the world to track down the treasures looted from the Summer Palace.

Apart from the Chinese Government, state-run companies, civil groups, and private collectors are endeavouring to bring Chinese antiquities back home. In April and May 2000, China Poly Group Corporation purchased the cow, monkey and tiger heads from the 12 Zodiacs. In September 2003, Dr Hung-San Ho bought the pig head and subsequently donated the bronze figure to the Poly Art Museum in Beijing.[36] However, the SACH does not encourage Chinese institutions and individuals to bid for any Chinese treasures "that have been plundered, stolen or illegally exported".[37] The reasons are multifaceted. First, China's repurchasing of lost cultural relics has the unfortunate side effect of pushing prices much higher than their normative value. Second, as commented by Song Xinchao, director of the Museum Department in SACH, "buying them back means we acknowledge they were taken out of

34 Article 2 of the Law of the People's Republic of China on Protection of Cultural Relics 2002.

35 Liu, Repatriating China's Cultural Objects, above n 20, 157.

36 'More Than 10 Million Chinese Cultural Relics Lost Overseas' (2007) *People's Daily* <http://english.people.com.cn/200701/30/eng20070130_345934.html>.

37 'The Efforts to Bid for or Purchase Any Chinese Treasures that Have Been Plundered, Stolen or Illegally Exported are not Encouraged', *Wenwu China* November 2 2010 <www.wenwuchina.com/news/list7/detail37/71320.html>.

our country legally. It will be a compromise to the wrong thing and even an indulgence in crimes."[38]

Another method of repossession is diplomatic negotiation between the current possessors and China. As the fastest developing economy entity, China plays an increasingly important role in the global and regional area, and this influence has helped to bring some cultural objects home, for example the two bronze statues that were returned to China by French businessman François-Henri Pinault.[39] After the statues' auction, the SACH announced new limits against Christie's. Specifically, the Chinese Government tightened the ownership control over all cultural relics that Christie's seeks to import or export. Interestingly, Christie's became the first foreign independent auction house in China in 2013 and it is worth noting that the Pinault Family is the controller of Christie's.[40] Although the agreement signed with the Chinese Government restricted the Christie's from dealing in Chinese cultural relics, this move still allows Christie's to sell directly to buyers from a growing class of wealthy collectors in China.[41] What also should be noticed is that by the end of 2011, China surpassed the US as the world's biggest art and auction market.[42] Over the past decade, China's art market has developed at an unprecedented rate. In a country that barely had an art market two decades ago, reported auction revenues for 2012 were up 900% from 2003, to $8.9 billion.[43] Speculation surrounding this donation also related to the French president's first visit to China with the purpose of strengthening diplomatic and trade relations with China.[44]

Apart from buying-back and diplomatic negotiation, it should be noted that China is getting more active in pursuing its lost cultural heritage. In

38 'Christie's Auction Controversy Reveals China's Dilemma In Retrieving Lost Relics', *Xinhua News* February 16 2009 <http://news.xinhuanet.com/english/2009-02/16/content_10829310.htm>.

39 Edward Wong and Steven Erlanger, 'Frenchman Will Return to China Prized Bronze Artifacts Looted in 19th Century', *The New York Times* April 26 2013 <www.nytimes.com/2013/04/27/world/europe/frenchman-will-return-to-china-prized-bronze-artifacts-looted-in-19th-century.html>.

40 Jane Perlez, 'Christie's Opens for Business in Mainland China With Its First Auction', *New York Times* September 26 2013 <http://artsbeat.blogs.nytimes.com/2013/09/26/christies-opens-for-business-in-mainland-china-with-its-first-auction/>.

41 According to Article 55(3) of China's Cultural Relics Protection Law, foreign companies and Chinese-foreign joint ventures are still prohibited from participating in the establishment of any shops or auction enterprises trading with "cultural relics".

42 However, since a peak in the art market in 2011, the total sales value in China has continued to decline. In 2015, China's art market represented 32% of the total global auction market and became the second-largest market globally in terms of total sales value for fine and decorative art. 'Global Chinese Art Auction Market Report 2015', *Artnet* <www.cn.artnet.com/en/chinese-art-auction-market-report/>, 8.

43 David Barboza, Graham Bowley and Amanda Cox, 'Forging an Art Market in China', *New York Times* October 28 2013 <www.nytimes.com/projects/2013/china-art-fraud/>.

44 Sonia Kolesnikov-Jessop, 'Toning Down the Bling Factor', *The New York Times* September 10 2012 <www.nytimes.com/2012/09/11/business/global/toning-down-the-bling-factor.html>.

August 2014, the China Federation of Demanding Compensation from Japan called on Japan to hand over a 1,300-year-old Tang dynasty stele from the North-Eastern city of Lushun.[45] This Tang dynasty stele carries considerable historical meaning and significance for defining a border for the Tang dynasty (618–906) and includes an inscription of 29 Chinese characters mentioning Tang emissary, Cui Xin, who gave instructions for two wells to be dug. However, the stele was looted by the Japanese military from Lushun, a North-Eastern city and then shipped to Tokyo as a trophy of Japan's victory over the Russians in 1905. Afterwards, the Tang-era stele was placed in the Imperial Palace in Tokyo. Chinese scholars have suggested that the stele be displayed in a place where the public can enjoy it, since it is not just Chinese people who cannot see the stele but Japanese, as well. However, Japan declined to move it maintaining that: "The Tang stele is Japan's national property and should be displayed within the Palace. Nobody was allowed to enter the Place unless permitted. Only pictures can be provided."[46] A Chinese civil group has finally asked Japan for the return of that cultural item. This is the first time a Chinese civil group has asked the Japanese imperial family for the return of a Chinese cultural item. In particular with Chinese cultural heritage looted during the Japanese Occupation, there is a strong indication that the Chinese Government has become frustrated with Japan's continued efforts to revise views of its history of military aggression and has sought to redress Japan's unlawful wartime acts. One obvious example is that, since July 2014, China began publicising the confessions of Japanese war criminals who were convicted by Chinese tribunals in the early 1950s, which carries strong evidential values from a legal perspective.[47] Previous complaints made by China against Japan were more in relation to diplomatic statements.[48]

Furthermore, on October 28 2016, China's State Cultural Relics Bureau published the amended Provisions on the Administration of Cultural Relic Auction (2016 Auction Provisions) to enhance its regulation of the art auction market.[49] The 2016 Auction Provisions are remarkable as, for the first time, they explicitly ban domestic auction houses from selling any cultural relics that have been "illegally looted in history". The previous Chinese law only stated that no stolen or smuggled cultural relics may be auctioned.[50] Accord-

45 Jane Perlez and Bree Feng, 'Chinese Group Calls on Japan to Hand Over Tang-Era Stele', *New York Times* August 21 2014 <http://sinosphere.blogs.nytimes.com/2014/08/21/chinese-group-calls-on-japan-to-hand-over-tang-era-stele/>.

46 Ibid.

47 State Administration of Cultural Heritage, 'Publication of Collective Documents on the Confessions of Japanese War Criminals by the State Archives Administration (Issue 2)' <www.sach.gov.cn/art/2017/7/21/art_722_142657.html>.

48 Austin Ramzy, 'Xi Condemns Efforts to Play Down Japan's Wartime Aggression', *New York Times* July 7 2014 <http://sinosphere.blogs.nytimes.com/2014/07/07/xi-condemns-efforts-to-play-down-japans-wartime-aggression/>.

49 Zhong, Hui, 'China's New Law on Art Auction' (2017) XXII(3) *Art Antiquity and Law* 220.

50 Article 14 of the 2016 Auction Provisions.

ing to a statement from the SACH on November 4 2016, China successfully prevented a Japanese auction house from selling looted Chinese cultural relics.[51] The disputed items were a few pieces of a mural and handwritten Buddhist manuscripts dating from the Tang Dynasty (618–907), which were obtained by Otani Kozui, a Japanese Buddhist and explorer, during his three expeditions to North-West China between 1902 and 1914. After learning the Japanese auction house planned to sell several looted Chinese cultural relics at the end of October, the SACH immediately contacted the auction company and urged for the sale to be stopped. Upon investigation, the company eventually decided to cancel the auction. In its statement, the SACH said:

> We consistently oppose to and denounce sales of illegally looted cultural relics. We hope that organizations and individuals honour the spirit of international conventions, respect the feelings of the people from the relics' original countries, while avoiding sales and commercial exploration of such relics.[52]

In view of the great amount of cultural relics lost overseas, both the Chinese Government and the general public are keen urgent to seek the return of its lost heritage. Cultural heritage is more than a product, but is also a connection surviving from a past age and linking to the future. It is instrumental in symbolising the history of a state and enhancing its national identity. The return of looted Chinese cultural relics is not just a redress for wrongful acts during the period of 1840–1945, but also a reunion for the integrity of China's cultural heritage.

5. Responses to the Popular Excuses Against Return

Despite the special connection between states of origin and cultural heritage, current possessors still refuse to return cultural heritage for different reasons. The following section responds to the popular excuses that current possessors have used to reject the recovery claims for cultural heritage. This section argues that current possessors cannot simply use these reasons to refuse to engage in dialogue around the issue of return, as they are not always defensible.

5.1. We Provide the Best Protection

Current possessors usually argue that most states of origin do not have adequate facilities to preserve cultural objects and that the possessor can provide the best facilities for protection. Particularly in response to China's recovery efforts, most possessors share the opinion that these cultural treasures would

51 'China Reserves Right to Recover Illegally Looted Cultural Relics', *Xinhua News* November 5 2016 <http://news.xinhuanet.com/english/2016-11/05/c_135806933.htm>.
52 Ibid.

not have survived the notorious Cultural Revolution if they had stayed in China. Although the Cultural Revolution has been a tragedy for all Chinese, it should not be used as a justification of the looting and theft of cultural objects that took place long before the Cultural Revolution. For recovery claims, each case has to be judged individually and the decision whether to return the object at issue should largely depend on whether the state of origin has the ability to ensure the item's protection and safety. In the case of cultural objects that are originally from Iraq, Syria or Afghanistan, return is inadvisable, as these countries currently do not have adequate facilities to ensure the safety of their cultural heritage. But if a state of origin has the ability to protect its cultural heritage, current possessors should not use this excuse to refuse to engage in dialogue around the issue of return.

In many cases, the states of origin have demonstrated that proper protection can be ensured after the return of the disputed objects. In the case of the Parthenon Marbles, the British Museum claims that the removal of the objects saved them from destruction, as they were not being protected at the time. However, times have charged. Greece has built the New Acropolis Museum to ensure that its collection is protected.[53] If the Marbles are returned to Greece, they can be viewed in their original context on the Acropolis mount, a hillside covered with art venerating the gods watching over Athens. In regards to Chinese cultural heritage, China has kept re-examining the Cultural Revolution and improved its domestic law to rectify the blatant shortcomings of the existing statutes and to enhance the legal protection of its heritage.[54] Similarly, many other states of origin have sought to protect their cultural heritage by declaring some or all of the cultural artefacts found within their territories to be property of the state. For example, the Mexican Federal Law of 1972 declares all pre-Columbian objects to be the property of the state and removes them from commerce and export.[55] However, such nationalisation, sometimes referred to as 'blanket' or 'umbrella' laws, has been criticised for its all-inclusive nature, which can create an economic incentive in art trafficking by increasing their value on the international market due to scarcity.[56] In the

53 Leila Amineddoleh, 'The British Museum Should Return The Parthenon Marbles To Greece', *Forbes* December 23 2014 <www.forbes.com/sites/realspin/2014/12/23/the-british-museum-should-return-the-parthenon-marbles-to-greece/>.

54 For more details about the law in China, see David Murphy, *Plunder and Preservation: Cultural Property Law and Practice in the People's Republic of China* (Oxford University Press, 1995); Sabine von Schorlemer, 'Legal Changes in the Regime of the Protection of Cultural Property in Armed Conflict' (2004) ix(1) *Art Antiquity and Law* 43.

55 MA Gonzalez, 'New Legal Tools to Curb the Illicit Traffic in Pre-Columbian Antiquities' (1973) 12(2) *Columbia Journal of Transnational Law* 316, 316.

56 Leslie Potter and Bruce Zagaris, 'Toward a Common US–Mexican Cultural Heritage: The Need for a Regional Americas Initiative in the Recovery and Return of Stolen Cultural Property' (1992) 5 *Transnational Law* 627, 670; Jamison Shedwill, 'Is the "Lost Civilization" of the Maya Lost Forever?: The US and Illicit Trade in Pre-Columbian Artifacts' (1992) 23(1) *California Western International Law Journal* 227, 251–252.

absence of import restrictions from other states, the art trade may simply shift to the black market. Additionally, the effectiveness of a state's ability to curb the illicit trade is also questioned:

> If cultural property laws were an effective means of protecting archaeological sites, we would see signs of their success surely by now: nearly 150 nation- states have such laws and many of them have had them for decades. But the looting continues and, in fact, has increased.[57]

However, this point is not entirely true. First, it has been proven that such strict ownership control, for example in Mexico, has had some success, especially in the sense of ensuring that objects of importance remain within the country.[58] Second, if the looting of sites and the trade in stolen arts were legitimised, the result would be more looting, not less, as there would no longer be any reason for restraint. Accordingly, more cultural heritage objects would find their way to the art dealers or collectors in art market states, as they are the ones who can afford the unbelievably high price of cultural heritage objects. Instead of being available to the public, cultural heritage objects will be possessed by private hands or only available to a small group of people. Third, the continuing theft or illicit trade of cultural heritage does not undermine the meaning and function of rigid legal control of cultural items. There is a need for international cooperation, particularly from the market states, to place import restrictions so market states do not become safe havens for dealing in unlawfully removed objects and illegally removed arts are returned to the applicable state of origin. In this respect, not all market states have adopted such measures, as they are worried that import restrictions would jeopardise their art markets. Last, it should be pointed out that it is not always guaranteed that current possessors can provide the best protection. For years, the British Museum argued that the risks involved in moving the Parthenon Marbles were too great because of their delicate nature, and that the carvings were safest in London. However, interestingly, the British Museum loaned one of the disputed Parthenon Marbles to Russia in 2014, despite Russia not having a good reputation for returning Nazi-looted arts to rightful owners, claiming that objects seized during the Second World War are classed as "compensatory restitution".[59] Thus, the British Museum has undercut its own argument with its actions. Similarly, possessing one of the most extensive Chinese collections in Europe, the KODE Museum, which returned seven of the Summer Palace columns in 2014, is never free of controversy. In January 2013, thieves made off with more than two dozen objects from the China collection. It was the

57 Cuno, *Who owns antiquity,* above n 2, 127.

58 Kifle Jote, *International Legal Protection of Cultural Heritage* (Juristforlaget, 1994), 155.

59 Helena Smith, 'Parthenon Marbles: Greece Furious over British Loan to Russia', *Guardian* December 6 2014 <www.theguardian.com/artanddesign/2014/dec/05/parthenon-marbles-greece-furious-british-museum-loan-russia-elgin>.

second theft from the collection, following a break-in in 2010, and led to the closure of the exhibit.[60]

5.2. *We Are the "Universal Museum"*

In addition to insecurity and political instability within states of origin, another reason why current museums do not contemplate the return of any part of their collections is the concept of the universal museum. In 2002, 18 major museums and research institutes in Europe and America, including the British Museum and the Louvre Museum, jointly signed the Declaration on the Importance and Value of Universal Museums (2002 Declaration).[61] According to the 2002 Declaration, these museums present their role as preserving cultural heritage and encouraging cultural pluralism, especially in allowing the artistic, scholarly and educational value of cultural heritage to be understood and appreciated on a global scale.[62] Thus, claims for recovery are not justified unless the law was breached when the objects were removed. However, the 2002 Declaration is never free from controversy. Many scholars criticise that the 2002 Declaration as a way of refusing to engage in dialogue around the issue of repatriation. George Abungu, the former Director General of the National Museums of Kenya, is quite right at revealing the nature of the 2002 Declaration: "it is signed principally by a group of large museums who want to create a different pedigree of museum, largely due to fears that materials held in their collections of which the ownership is contested, will face claims for repatriation".[63]

More importantly, despite the good intention of encouraging cultural pluralism, the effects of either the idea of universal museum or constantly rejecting the recovery claims are negative and dangerous. In fact, instead of understanding and tolerance, they provoke misunderstanding and resentment between different peoples. While millions of people visit the British Museum each year, it is still disheartening to view the Parthenon Marbles in London after learning that their removal damaged one of mankind's crowning achievements.[64] It is the same feeling for Chinese people when visiting the objects looted from the Summer Palace displayed in Western museums, where they would probably be reminded of the destruction of the Summer Palace, which is still a sore point in their collective memory. And they probably feel another

60 Bree Feng, 'Despite Frigid Relations, Chinese Relics Coming Home From Norway', *New York Times* February 12 2014 <http://sinosphere.blogs.nytimes.com/2014/02/09/despite-frigid-relations-chinese-relics-coming-home-from-norway/?_r=0>.

61 John Henry Merryman, *Imperialism, Art and Restitution* (Cambridge University Press, 2006), 15–33.

62 Irini A. Stamatoudi, *Cultural Property Law and Restitution: A Commentary to International Conventions and European Union law* (Edward Elgar Publishing, 2011), 23–24.

63 George Abungu, 'The Declaration: A Contested Issue' in Lyndel Prott (ed), *Witnesses to History* (UNESCO, 2009) 121, 121.

64 Amineddoleh, *British Museum Should Return Parthenon Marbles,* above n 53.

thing: *luohou jiuyao aida*, which means "if you are backward, you will be attacked".[65] In this case, it is questionable whether Chinese people can be convinced of the intention of the 2002 Declaration, such as encouraging cultural pluralism and enhancing mutual understanding, by seeing their looted cultural heritage displayed in the great universal museums. For some of them, to defend the colonial collections by using the idea of the universal museum, is an invention of the powerful countries to legitimise the acts of confiscating their treasure. The memories of departing from their treasures might stop people appreciating the great art from various civilisations, which goes against the good philosophical foundation of the universal museums.

5.3. Is It Necessary to Return Originals?

To defend their collection, opponents further question why the enjoyment of cultural heritage can only be acquired through originals rather than other alternatives, such as books, pictures, or reproductions. In this regard, Benjamin explains that even the most perfect reproduction lacks the presence of space and time.[66] The time element can only be brought out by chemical or physical analysis of originals, and the space element of an object has to be studied from the location of the originals.[67] Some cultural heritage can only have the fullest meaning and be appreciated sacredly in its original cultural setting. The British Museum aims to expose visitors to a variety of cultures and exhibit art in a broader context, providing a sense of a shared human cultural heritage. However, is this the best context for art? While millions of people visit the British Museum each year, they can only see random parts of the Parthenon along with a brief historical introduction, which is not equivalent to the original environment where the sculptures were created. Comparatively, the New Acropolis Museum is a mere 300 metres from the Acropolis, allowing the Parthenon Marbles to be seen as intended—basking in the Greek sunlight. The separation of cultural heritage from their original settings means the integrity of the whole will be destroyed. It is impossible to enjoy the original scene as its creators intended. An incomplete display of looted bits of cultural heritage is like a puzzle that is missing half its pieces.

To defend their possession, opponents also argue that art loan and exchange can be sufficient to allow people access to their cultural heritage.[68] A loan exhibition system seems to be a good choice; states of origin will have access to their cultural heritage. Loan exhibitions may also, to some extent, prevent museums and collectors from acquiring cultural heritage illegally, thus

65 Liu, *Repatriating China's Cultural Objects,* above n 20, 139.

66 Walter Benjamin, *The Work of Art in the Age of Mechanical Reproduction (transl. J.A. Underwood)* (Penguin, 2008), 5.

67 Liu, *Repatriating China's Cultural Objects,* above n 20, 120.

68 Posner, *Some Skeptical Observations,* above n 1, 223.

decreasing the demand for illegally taken cultural heritage.[69] However, the problem is that while art exchange occurs reciprocally between wealthy countries, poorer states are disadvantaged, with cultural resources flowing in one direction. It is far from an equal exchange. To negotiate for art loan and exchange, it also means that the fate of disputed cultural objects is left to the current possessors to decide. However, existing practices demonstrate that relying on another country's goodwill is unpredictable and unrewarding. For example, when Nigeria tried to borrow the Benin ivory pendant from the British Museum for a Pan-African and Black cultural festival in 1977, the Museum initially requested insurance for the mask, but eventually rejected the request.[70] In 2001, Robert Anderson, the director of the British Museum, admitted in an interview with *The Times* that there was never a chance of a loan, as visitors "expect to see these things on display in the British Museum".[71] More importantly, loan exhibition is ineffective and inadequate to prompt large-scale cultural heritage to be displayed in the states of origin. For example, the donation agreement with the KODE Museum only applies to the return of seven columns, despite the fact that the museum possesses one of the most extensive Chinese collections in Europe, with over 4,000 objects, including a collection consisting of 21 columns in total.[72]

6. Conclusion

Cultural heritage is a source of pride and identity for the nation's inhabitants, material evidence of the nation's civilization, and serves as a link between the past and the present.[73] While cultural heritage may be shared by all the people in the world, it should be conducted in a lawful way and respect the will of the people from the states of origin. Although return may be triggered by moral or cultural considerations, the available practice has made it very clear that ethical discourse is ineffective and inadequate to prompt large-scale recovery. Thus, states of origin need a stronger and legal argument to support their claims. In the recovery of cultural heritage, the first legal hurdle states

69 Sheng Gao, 'International Protection of Cultural property: Some Preliminary Issues and the Role of International Conventions' (2008) 12 *Singapore Year Book of International Law* 57, 62.

70 While the British Museum denied the request for art loan, the Museum had sold more than 30 of the controversial Benin pieces, primarily to Nigeria. Shyllon, *Return of African Cultural Objects,* above n, 162–165.

71 'Parthenon Echoes', *Guardian* March 28 2002 <www.theguardian.com/news/2002/mar/28/leadersandreply.mainsection>.

72 KODE Art Museums of Bergen, 'Chinese Pillars are Being Transferred' <http://kodebergen.no/en/article/chinese-pillars-are-being-transferred>; KODE Art Museums of Bergen, 'Often Asked Questions' <http://kodebergen.no/en/article/often-asked-questions>.

73 Kevin Jower, 'Comment: International and National Legal Efforts to Protect Cultural Property: The 1970 UNESCO Convention, the United States, and Mexico' (2003) 38 *Texas International Law Journal* 145, 145.

of origin should pass is the question of "legitimacy" and a requesting state should demonstrate when removal has been formally forbidden under either its national law or international law.

As this book uses China as a case study, the following chapter will focus on the legal grounds that exist for China to request the return of its cultural heritage. If the taking can be shown to be illegal, China will have a legal basis to claim for their return. This does not necessarily mean that China will take legal action against museums or art collectors, but it will provide China with a stronger argument, instead of merely an ethics discourse, in convincing the current possessors to return China's cultural heritage. Otherwise, claims for the return without a legal basis are usually silenced or, at best, discussed but very rarely facilitated.

Bibliography

'Ambassadors Fund for Cultural Preservation (AFCP): Nepal Projects (Bureau of Educational and Cultural Affairs Promoting Mutual Understanding <http://eca.state.gov/cultural-heritage-center/gallery/ambassadors-fund-cultural-preservation-afcp-nepal-projects>

'China Condemns Christie's Auction', *The BBC News* February 26 2009 <http://news.bbc.co.uk/2/hi/asia-pacific/7911691.stm>

'China Reserves Right to Recover Illegally Looted Cultural Relics', *Xinhua News* November 5 2016 <http://news.xinhuanet.com/english/2016-11/05/c_135806933.htm>

'Chinese Pillars are Being Transferred', KODE Art Museums of Bergen <http://kodebergen.no/en/article/chinese-pillars-are-being-transferred>

'Christie's Auction Controversy Reveals China's Dilemma In Retrieving Lost Relics', *Xinhua News* February 16 2009 <http://news.xinhuanet.com/english/2009-02/16/content_10829310.htm>

'The Efforts to Bid for or Purchase Any Chinese Treasures that Have Been Plundered, Stolen or Illegally Exported are not Encouraged', *Wenwu China* November 2 2010 <www.wenwuchina.com/news/list7/detail37/71320.html>

'Global Chinese Art Auction Market Report 2015', *Artnet* <www.cn.artnet.com/en/chinese-art-auction-market-report/>

'Help Stop the Destruction of Cultural Heritage in Syria and Iraq' (UNESCO) <www.unesco.org/new/en/culture/themes/illicit-trafficking-of-cultural-property/awareness-raising-initiatives/help-stop-the-destruction-of-cultural-heritage-in-syria-and-iraq/>

'More Than 10 Million Chinese Cultural Relics Lost Overseas' (2007) *People's Daily* <http://english.people.com.cn/200701/30/eng20070130_345934.html>

'Often Asked Questions' (KODE Art Museums of Bergen) <http://kodebergen.no/en/article/often-asked-questions>

'Parthenon Echoes', *Guardian* March 28 2002 <www.theguardian.com/news/2002/mar/28/leadersandreply.mainsection>

'Publication of Collective Documents on the Confessions of Japanese War Criminals by the State Archives Administration (Issue 2)' (State Administration of Cultural Heritage) <www.sach.gov.cn/art/2017/7/21/art_722_142657.html>

'Re-building Cultural Heritage in Mali', UNESCO, July 1 2014 <www.unesco.org/new/en/unesco-liaison-office-in-new-york/about-this-office/single-view/news/re_building_cultural_heritage_in_mali/>

Abungu, George, 'The Declaration: A Contested Issue' in Lyndel Prott (ed), *Witnesses to History* (UNESCO, 2009) 121

Amineddoleh, Leila, 'The British Museum Should Return The Parthenon Marbles To Greece', *Forbes* December 23 2014 <www.forbes.com/sites/realspin/2014/12/23/the-british-museum-should-return-the-parthenon-marbles-to-greece/>

Barboza, David, Graham Bowley and Amanda Cox, 'Forging an Art Market in China', *New York Times* October 28 2013 <www.nytimes.com/projects/2013/china-art-fraud/>

Barkan, Elazar, 'Amending Historical Injustices: The Restitution of Cultural Property—An Overview' in *Claiming the Stones, Naming the Bones: Cultural Property and the Negotiation of National and Ethnic Identity* (Getty Research Institute, 2002) 16

Benjamin, Walter, *The Work of Art in the Age of Mechanical Reproduction* (transl. J.A. Underwood) (Penguin, 2008)

Castells, Manuel, *Power of Identity: The Information Age: Economy, Society, and Culture Volume II* (Wiley-Blackwell, 2009)

Chen, Jianfu, *Chinese Law: Context and Transformation* (Martinus Nijhoff Publishers, 2008)

Cuno, James, *Who Owns Antiquity?: Museums and the Battle over Our Ancient Heritage* (Princeton University Press, 2008)

Feng, Bree, 'Despite Frigid Relations, Chinese Relics Coming Home From Norway', *New York Times* February 12 2014 <http://sinosphere.blogs.nytimes.com/2014/02/09/despite-frigid-relations-chinese-relics-coming-home-from-norway/?_r=0>

Forrest, Craig, *International Law and The Protection of Cultural Heritage* (Routledge, 2010)

Gao, Sheng, 'International Protection of Cultural Property: Some Preliminary Issues and the Role of International Conventions' (2008) 12 *Singapore Year Book of International Law* 57

Gonzalez, MA, 'New Legal Tools to Curb the Illicit Traffic in Pre-Columbian Antiquities' (1973) 12(2) *Columbia Journal of Transnational Law* 316

Harrison, James, *Modern Chinese Nationalism* (Hunter College of the City University of New York, 1969)

Hung, Wu, 'The Admonitions Scroll Revisited: Iconology, Narratology, Style, Dating' in Shane McCausland (ed), *Gu Kaizhi and the Admonitions Scroll* (British Museum Press, 2003) 89

Jessop, Sonia Kolesnikov, 'Toning Down the Bling Factor', *The New York Times* September 10 2012 <www.nytimes.com/2012/09/11/business/global/toning-down-the-bling-factor.html>

Jote, Kifle, *International Legal Protection of Cultural Heritage* (Juristforlaget, 1994)

Jower, Kevin, 'Comment: International and National Legal Efforts to Protect Cultural Property: The 1970 UNESCO Convention, the United States, and Mexico' (2003) 38 *Texas International Law Journal* 145

Lanciotti, Alessandra, 'The Dilemma of the Right to Ownership of Underwater Cultural Heritage: The Case of the "Getty Bronze"' in Silvia Borelli and Federico Lenzerini (eds), *Cultural Heritage, Cultural Rights, Cultural Diversity: New Developments in International Law* (Martinus Nijhoff Publishers, 2012) 301

Liu, Zuozhen, *The Case for Repatriating China's Cultural Objects* (Springer, 2016)

Loulanski, Tolina, 'Revising the Concept for Cultural Heritage: The Argument for a Functional Approach' (2006) 13(2) *International Journal of Cultural Property* 207

Lu, Martin and Rosita Dellios, 'One Culture Two Systems: A Cultural Approach to Inter-Chinese Politics' 3(1) *Culture Mandala: The Bulletin of the Centre for East-West Cultural and Economic Studies* 18

MacFarquhar, Roderick and John King Fairbank, *The Cambridge History of China. Vol. 15, The People's Republic. Part 2, Revolutions within the Chinese Revolution, 1966–1982* (Cambridge University Press, 2008)

Manhart, Christian, 'UNESCO's Mandate and Recent Activities for the Rehabilitation of Afghanistan's Cultural Heritage' (2004) 86(854) *International Review of the Red Cross* 401

Merryman, John Henry, 'Cultural Property Internationalism' (2005) 12(1) *International Journal of Cultural Property* 11

Merryman, John Henry, *Imperialism, Art and Restitution* (Cambridge University Press, 2006)

Murphy, David, *Plunder and Preservation: Cultural Property Law and Practice in the People's Republic of China* (Oxford University Press, 1995)

O'Keefe, Patrick, 'Repatriation of Sacred Objects' in Lyndel Prott (ed), *Witnesses to History: A Compendium of Documents and Writings on the Return of Cultural Objects* (UNESCO, 2009)

Perlez, Jane, 'Christie's Opens for Business in Mainland China With Its First Auction', *New York Times* September 26 2013 <http://artsbeat.blogs.nytimes.com/2013/09/26/christies-opens-for-business-in-mainland-china-with-its-first-auction/>

Perlez, Jane and Bree Feng, 'Chinese Group Calls on Japan to Hand Over Tang-Era Stele', *New York Times* August 21 2014 <http://sinosphere.blogs.nytimes.com/2014/08/21/chinese-group-calls-on-japan-to-hand-over-tang-era-stele/>

Posner, Eric, 'The International Protection of Cultural Property: Some Skeptical Observations' (2007) 8(1) *Chicago Journal of International Law* 213

Potter, Leslie and Bruce Zagaris, 'Toward a Common US-Mexican Cultural Heritage: The Need for a Regional Americas Initiative in the Recovery and Return of Stolen Cultural Property' (1992) 5 *Transnational Law* 627

Prott, Lyndel, 'The International Movement of Cultural Objects' (2005) 12(2) *International Journal of Cultural Property* 225

Ramzy, Austin, 'Xi Condemns Efforts to Play Down Japan's Wartime Aggression', *New York Times* July 7 2014 <http://sinosphere.blogs.nytimes.com/2014/07/07/xi-condemns-efforts-to-play-down-japans-wartime-aggression/>

Rong Xinjiang, Translated by: Imre Galambos, *Eighteen Lectures on Dunhuang* (Brill, 2013)

Schorlemer, Sabine von, 'Legal Changes in the Regime of the Protection of Cultural Property in Armed Conflict' (2004) ix(1) *Art Antiquity and Law* 43

Shedwill, Jamison, 'Is the "Lost Civilization" of the Maya Lost Forever?: The US and Illicit Trade in Pre-Columbian Artifacts' (1992) 23(1) *California Western International Law Journal* 227

Shyllon, Folarin, 'Unraveling History: Return of African Cultural Objects Repatriated and Looted in Colonial Times' in James A.R. Nafziger and Ann Nicgorski (eds), *Cultural Heritage Issues* (Martinus Nijhoff Publishers, 2009) 159

Smith, Helena, 'Parthenon Marbles: Greece Furious over British Loan to Russia', *Guardian* December 6 2014 <www.theguardian.com/artanddesign/2014/dec/05/parthenon-marbles-greece-furious-british-museum-loan-russia-elgin>

Stamatoudi, Irini A., *Cultural Property Law and Restitution: A Commentary to International Conventions and European Union Law* (Edward Elgar Publishing, 2011)

Weiner, Annette, 'Inalienable Wealth' in Simon Knell (ed), *Museums in the Material World* (Routledge, 2007) 253

Wong, Edward and Steven Erlanger, 'Frenchman Will Return to China Prized Bronze Artifacts Looted in 19th Century', *The New York Times* April 26 2013 <www.nytimes.com/2013/04/27/world/europe/frenchman-will-return-to-china-prized-bronze-artifacts-looted-in-19th-century.html>

Zhong, Hui, 'China's New Law on Art Auction' (2017) XXII(3) *Art Antiquity and Law* 220

3 Availability of a Legal Basis for the Return of China's Cultural Heritage

1. Introduction

While stating that China would continue to seek the return in accordance with relevant international conventions and Chinese laws, the Chinese Government did not refer to any specific law that would entitle China to claim for the return of the disputed art treasures. However, the question of legality is the first obstacle standing in the way of recovery and China needs to prove that the taking of the heritage was illegal according to the contemporaneous law. For example, two bronze statues, which were part of an ensemble of 12 bronze Chinese zodiac heads from a water clock fountain in the Summer Palace, disappeared after the Palace was torched and destroyed by British and French troops in 1860. In this case, China needs to prove that the behaviour of the British and French troops was a clear violation of international law, according to which the destruction or seizure of an occupied state's property was prohibited. Otherwise, even though the taking was morally wrong, it was perfectly legal and, therefore, the current possessors are under no legal obligation to return the statues to China. However, if the taking can be shown to be illegal, China will have a legal basis to claim for their return. This does not necessarily mean that China will take legal action against museums or art collectors, but it will provide China with a stronger argument, instead of merely an ethics and moral discourse, in convincing the current possessors to return China's cultural heritage. Thus, the first central question at the basis of this book is whether China has a legal basis for the return of its cultural heritage taken between 1840 to 1945. To answer the question of legality, this chapter examines the law relevant to the removal of Chinese cultural heritage that occurred between 1840 and 1945.

In terms of the availability of a legal basis, it is timely to identify two types of removal that will be discussed in the following section. This book divides the removal of Chinese cultural heritage into two categories: (1) cultural heritage taken either during or as a result of war or occupation, such as the looting of the Summer Palace, the pillage of Beijing by the Eight-nation Alliance and the Japanese Occupation; (2) cultural heritage taken by individuals during both times of war and peace, represented by the marble columns donated by the KODE museum and the Dunhuang manuscripts. The rationale behind these two categories is that the legality of removal will be determined by different bodies of law. As armed conflicts should be identified as conduct of two or more states in nature, the first category of removal will be determined by public international law, specifically the law of war. Given that the practice of looting an enemy's property as war booty existed since a very early time, the core question to address is when the law of war prohibited such looting. If it can be shown that the taking occurred after the ratification of an international convention, China will have a legal basis to request the return of their goods and seek to invoke state responsibility. When pursuing the return of Chinese heritage, China can argue that, according to international law, a state is responsible for its conduct and any breaches of its international obligations.[1] In particular, with regards to restitution, a state responsible for an internationally wrongful act is under an obligation to make restitution, that is, to reestablish the situation that existed before the wrongful act was committed.[2]

Regarding the second category, China's domestic law will be invoked in establishing that China has sufficient interests in claiming for the return of the Chinese cultural relics taken by individuals during times of war and peace. As the period of 1840 and 1945 covers two China's dynasties, the Qing Dynasty (1644–1912) and the Republic of China (1912–1949), the second part of this chapter examines the relevant law enacted in these two dynasties respectively. Further, as many cultural relics have been in the possession of foreign museums or private dealers for many years, recovery claims are normally directed to the competent authorities in the place where the objects are found and, thus, disputes often involve more than one legal system.[3] In cases of cross-border disputes, private international law will be applied to determine classification, standing, time limitations, applicable law and the non-application of foreign laws for public policy reasons.[4]

The first part of Chapter 3 deals with destruction and looting during times of war and belligerent occupation and focuses on the 1899 Hague Convention, the earliest instrument entitling China to claim for the return of its cultural heritage looted during armed conflicts. Next, it turns to China's domestic law and argues that the Qing Code and state ownership provisions of Chinese law between 1912 and 1949 form a legal basis for China to assert its interests in removed heritage. For a better explanation, Chinese ancient law, Chinese history

1 Anthony Aust, *Handbook of International law* (Cambridge University Press, 2005), 21; Mark W. Janis, *International law* (Wolters Kluwer Law & Business, 5th ed, 2012), 5.

2 Article 35 of the United Nations, 'Responsibility of States for Internationally Wrongful Acts' <http://legal.un.org/ilc/texts/instruments/english/draft_articles/9_6_2001.pdf>.

3 Norman Palmer, 'Fetters and Stumbling Blocks: Impediments to the Recovery and Return of Unlawfully Removed Cultural Objects—A Common Law Perspective' in Lyndel. V. Prott (ed), *Realising Cultural Heritage Law: Festschrift for Patrick O'Keefe* (Institute for Art and Law, 2012) 97, 98–99.

4 Lyndel Prott, 'Problems of Private International Law for the Protection of the Cultural Heirtage' in Hague Academy of International Law (ed), *Collected Courses of the Hague Academy of International Law* (Nijhoff, 1989) 215, 223.

and traditional Chinese culture and recovery cases occurred in the Republic of China are examined in this part. After examining the relevant law, this chapter moves on to conclude the availability of a legal basis for the recovery of China's cultural heritage. This chapter then concludes that China does not have a basis for the return of all removals that occurred between 1840 and 1945, and in these cases, the customary rule may provide an answer. This chapter ends with a discussion about the definition of "historically removed heritage" and its return, which is the fundamental question that this book aims to resolve.

2. Taking by States During Armed Conflicts

Traditionally, there has been no rule preventing the destruction and seizure of an enemy's property, meaning that a victor was legitimately allowed to take property, including cultural treasures, from the defeated.[5] Even though it was morally wrong, the taking itself was perfectly legal. However, starting from the beginning of the 19th century, codification efforts have been made to humanise the laws of war.[6] The earliest rule on the protection of cultural heritage from the direct and indirect effects of armed conflict is the Lieber Code, drafted for the use of the Union Army in the American Civil War. The Lieber Code stated that in no way could churches, museums or institutions of learning "be seized, sold, given away, wantonly destroyed, damaged, or privately appropriated".[7] Subsequent regulations, including the Brussels Declaration 1884 and the Oxford Manual 1880, also endorsed the opinion that property related to religion, charity, education, art and science should be protected.[8] However, these instruments did not apply to the looting of Chinese cultural

5 No consideration was given to the protection of cultural property during warfare until the 16th century when international jurists gradually realised that cultural objects should be respected and protected during warfare. Emer de Vattel, Bela Kapossy and Richard Whatmore, *The Law of Nations* (Liberty Fund, 2008), 293.

6 For more discussion about the evolving law of war, see Roger O'Keefe, *The Protection of Cultural Property in Armed Conflict* (Cambridge University Press, 2006); Jiri Toman, 'The Hague Convention—A Decisive Step Taken by the International Community' (2005) 57(4) *Museum International* 7; Leon Friedman, *The Law of War: A Documentary History* (Random House, 1972), 99; Chris Afjochnick and Roger Normand, 'The Legitimation of Violence: A Critical Historical of the Laws of War' (1994) 35(1) *Harvard International Law Journal* 49; Anthi Helleni Poulos, 'The 1954 Hague Convention for the Protection of Cultural Property in the Event of Armed Conflict: An Historic Analysis' (2000) 28(1) *International Journal of Legal Information* 1; Dietrich Schindler and Jiri Toman, *The Laws of Armed Conflicts: A Collection of Conventions, Resolutions, and Other Documents* (Martinus Nijhoff Publishers, 2004), 3–20; Geoffrey Best, *Humanity in Warfare: The Modern History of the International Law of Armed Conflicts* (Weidenfeld and Nicolson, 1980), 160–161.

7 Article 36 of the Instructions for the Government of Armies of the United States in the Field (Lieber Code).

8 Article 8 of the Project of an International Declaration concerning the Laws and Customs of War (Brussels Declaration) and Article 24 of the Law on Laws of War on Land (Oxford Manual).

heritage on the grounds that they were either a foreign national law or merely guidelines. Despite their limited application, they have nevertheless paved the way for the incorporation of the idea of prohibiting looting and the destruction of cultural heritage in international conventions.[9]

The earliest legal instrument entitling China to claim for the return of its cultural relics looted during the Japanese Occupation is the 1899 Hague Convention on the Laws and Customs of War on Land.[10] A number of provisions in the 1899 Hague Convention were revised and merged into the 1907 Hague Conventions on the Laws and Customs of War on Land (1907 Hague Convention).[11] The 1899 and 1907 Hague Conventions effectively codified the customary international law of war at that time, including those on the protection of cultural heritage, which had been developed since the Napoleonic wars.[12] Further, a number of provisions under the 1899 Hague Convention can be used as the legal basis for China to argue that the removal of its cultural heritage was illegal.

The overarching rule as to the treatment of enemy property in the course of hostilities is embodied in Article 23(g), which states that it is forbidden to destroy or seize the enemy's property, "unless such destruction or seizure be imperatively demanded by the necessities of war". In other words, during hostilities, monuments and buildings dedicated to art and science ought not to be attacked or bombarded, unless necessary for military reasons.[13] Accordingly, China can argue that Japan's notorious "Three Alls Campaign"—"Burn all, loot all, and kill all"—was a clear violation of the 1899 Hague Convention, because it sought to destroy and loot all property, including China's cultural treasures, without distinguishing whether it was militarily necessary. During the Second Sino-Japanese War, public museums, libraries, imperial palaces and private houses were all targets of pillage for Japanese troops.

The 1899 Hague Convention also included two articles specifically designed to provide protection for cultural heritage. Article 27 provides that in sieges and bombardments,

> All necessary steps should be taken to spare as far as possible edifices devoted to religion, art, science, and charity, hospitals, and places where the sick and wounded are collected, provided they are not used at the same time for military purposes.[14]

9 Kifle Jote, *International Legal Protection of Cultural Heritage* (Juristforlaget, 1994), 43.
10 Convention (II) with respect to the Laws and Customs of War on Land (1899 Hague Convention).
11 Convention (IV) Respecting the Laws and Customs of War on Land and its annex: Regulations concerning the Laws and Customs of War on Land (1907 Hague Convention).
12 Craig Forrest, *International Law and The Protection of Cultural Heritage* (Routledge, 2010), 67.
13 O'Keefe, *Protection of Cultural Property*, above n 6, 24.
14 Compared to the 1899 Hague Convention, the only innovation of Article 27 of the 1907 Hague Convention was the inclusion of 'historic monuments' among the several types of property to be spared in bombardment.

Article 27 subjects protection to the precondition that the cultural heritage is being used for "military purposes", rather than "military necessity". In the latter situation, it could still be destroyed if it "served to obstruct a line of attack, or . . . to provide a shelter to which the enemy might retire, or in order to impede the enemy's advance, or the like" for the purpose of "military necessity".[15] However, according to Article 27, the use of cultural heritage for military purposes is not a breach of the Convention, which means the destruction of heritage can only be justified in the case of direct bombardment rather than in a broader sense of military necessity.[16] Otherwise, had this phrase not been emphasised, damage to cultural heritage, whether by way of accident or direct targeting, would have been subject to military necessity and, thus, should be allowed on a legal basis. Through the restriction of the targeting of cultural heritage, the Convention limits the lawfulness of attacks to very exceptional situations where a waiver can be invoked in the case of "military purposes". Further, despite the precondition of "military purposes",[17] destruction is not necessarily justified in all circumstances: refer the general restriction embodied in Article 23(g), which states that the destruction of enemy property is only justified when damaged by the necessity of war.[18] In other words, any bombardment directed at or likely to cause avoidable incidental injury to churches, art galleries, museums and historical monuments was prohibited, unless such attack was demanded by the purposes of war.[19]

Accordingly, it can be argued that the manner in which Japan launched the 1939 carpet bombing of Chongqing, with two days of air raids, was a clear violation of the 1899 Hague Convention. Described by survivors as "a sea of fire", it was reported that 741 historical sites, more than 15,000 paintings and over 3,000,000 books were damaged or destroyed. China can argue that these heritage sites were undefended during the bombardment and the destruction caused to privileged buildings and historical sites was not an unavoidable incident of the bombardment.[20]

The second special provision of the 1899 Hague Convention is Article 56, which deals with the protection of cultural heritage in occupied territory:

> The property of the communes, that of religious, charitable, and educational institutions, and those of arts and science, even when State

15 O'Keefe, *Protection of Cultural Property*, above n 6, 25–26.

16 Forrest, *International Law and Protection*, above n 12, 69; Stanislaw E. Nahlik, 'International Law and The Protection Of Cultural Property In Armed Conflicts' (1975) 27 *Hastings Law Journal* 1069, 1073.

17 While the term "military purposes" is not specifically defined, it was generally agreed that it included the use of buildings as offices and quarters for soldiers, or as signalling stations or observation posts to help target artillery. James Edward Edmonds and Lassa Oppenheim, *Land Warfare* (HM Stationery Office, 1912), 136.

18 O'Keefe, *Protection of Cultural Property*, above n 6, 24.

19 Ibid, 25–26.

20 'War Damage on Cultural Relics Commission under the Department of Education', *China Cultural Relics* August 22, 2007 <www.xhgxt.com/html/View_9270.html>.

> property, shall be treated as private property. All seizure of, destruction or wilful damage done to institutions of this character, historic monuments, works of art and science, is forbidden, and should be made the subject of legal proceedings.

Accordingly, the obligation to protect both movable and immovable cultural heritage in occupied territory is absolute; no exception is given for military purposes.[21] The reason for this is that, as cultural heritage is under the control of an occupying force, it no longer constitutes any threat to military operation. Thus, there is no need for a military necessity exemption to ensure a successful military outcome.[22] Further, Article 56 states that all cultural objects, including state property, are to be treated as private property and hence can neither be confiscated (Article 46) nor pillaged (Article 47) by occupying forces. Thus, it can be concluded that the 1899 Hague Convention placed an explicit prohibition on any seizure of cultural heritage as war booty.[23] Accordingly, in a recent claim for the return of a 1,300-year-old Tang Dynasty stele, which is currently in the Imperial Palace in Tokyo, China should have had a stronger argument for the recovery (see Chapter 1). This Tang Dynasty stele was shipped by the Japanese military as a trophy of Japan's victory over the Russians in 1905, despite the fact that the plundering of the enemy's cultural heritage is clearly prohibited pursuant to the Hague Convention.

The states that invaded China in the early 20th century and took China's cultural heritage, such as the US, the UK, Japan, Germany, and France, all ratified the 1899 Hague Convention in 1900. Accordingly, they were obliged to follow the provisions of the Convention, particularly on the subject of the protection of cultural heritage and the prohibition of looting the enemy's property. Based on the 1899 Hague Convention, China should have a legal basis for the recovery of its cultural heritage taken during the events that occurred after 1899, represented by the pillage of Beijing by Eight-Nation Alliance (1900) and the Japanese Occupation (1931–1945). During the pillage of Beijing, the destruction and pillage of Chinese cultural relics was massive, represented by the burning of the Hanlin Academy and the looting of its

21 Nahlik, *International Law and The Protection Of Cultural Property,* above n 16, 1074.

22 Forrest, *International Law and Protection,* above n 12, 69.

23 William Gerald Downey, 'Captured Enemy Property: Booty of War and Seized Enemy Property' (1950) 44(3) *The American Journal of International Law* 488, 497; L. H. Woolsey, 'The Forced Transfer of Property in Enemy Occupied Territories' (1943) 37(2) *The American Journal of International Law* 282, 285; Loukis G. Loucaides, 'The Protection of the Right to Property in Occupied Territories' (2004) 53(3) *The International and Comparative Law Quarterly* 677, 679; Adriaan Bos, 'The Importance of the 1899, 1907 and 1999 Hague Conferences for the Legal Protection of Cultural Property in the Event of Armed Conflict' (2005) 57(4) *Museum International* 32, 36.

prominent collection, the Yongle Encyclopedia.[24] The Yongle Encyclopedia preserved textual information from roughly 8,000 texts of all kinds from pre-Qin times to the early Ming Dynasty, covering all that had ever been written on Confucian canon, history, philosophy and the arts and sciences. However, many copies met an unfortunate fate, as only 400 out of 11,095 volumes are extant. The volumes have been distributed among more than 30 collections in eight countries, including the Library of Congress in the US, the British Library, the Bodleian Library in Oxford and the School of Oriental and African Studies of the University of London.[25] Based on the 1899 Hague Convention, China is entitled to claim for the return of Yongle Encyclopedia from the known possessors.

Despite the illegality of the taking by Japanese troops, securing the return is still problematic due to the 1972 Joint-Statement between China and Japan. Article 5 reads that "the Government of the People's Republic of China declares that in the interest of the friendship between the Chinese and the Japanese peoples, it renounces its demand for war reparation from Japan".[26] It is generally agreed that under the 1972 Joint Communique, the Chinese Government renounced its right for reparations. The question then becomes whether, when the state renounced its claims for war reparations against Japan in a peace treaty, individuals still have a means to vindicate their rights to request restitution. Additionally, even if individuals' rights were not extinguished by the 1972 Joint Communique, it is unclear whether there remains the right to request restitution of looted cultural relics. Conversely, the Japanese Government has insisted that the matter of war reparations from the Second World War has been settled pursuant to the 1972 Joint Communique.[27]

However, for any taking that occurred before the 1899 Hague Convention, represented by the looting of the Summer Palace during the Second Opium War (1856–1860), China does not have a legal basis for the reovery on the grounds that there was no law determining that such conduct was illegal. Although return in some cases may still be triggered by business or diplomatic

24 The Hanlin Academy was an academic and administrative institution founded in the 8th century Tang China. In the Qing Dynasty, Hanlin Yuan developed a huge collection of 'the quintessence of Chinese scholarship' dating from different historical period.

25 'Experts Urge Collectors To Share World's Earliest Encyclopedia', *China.org.cn* April 17 2002 <http://china.org.cn/english/PP-e/31248.htm>.

26 'Joint Communique of the Government of Japan and the Government of the People's Republic of China' (1972) *Ministry of Foreign Affairs of Japan* <www.mofa.go.jp/region/asia-paci/china/joint72.html>.

27 The private claims against Japan's unlawful acts are a completely different issue from the war reparations claimed by states. This book does not aim to resolve the issue arising out of private claims. For more discussion, see Hui Zhong, 'Can Chinese Individuals Request the Restitution of Chinese Cultural Relics in Japan?: A Revisit under International Law' (2017) 10(1) *Journal of East Asia & International Law* 179.

considerations, claims for the return without a legal basis are usually silenced or, at best, discussed only but very rarely facilitated.

3. Taking by Individuals During Times of War and Peace

One of the early misunderstandings about China's feudal society is that there was no law in traditional China.[28] Conversely, traditional Chinese law has a long history from rich sources. While far from perfect, the basic idea running through the traditional Chinese legal system is that cultural heritage, particularly publicly owned and stated-owned heritage, should be protected. With regards to the second category of taking, Chinese domestic law contemporaneous to the taking is the governing law, namely the law in the Qing Dynasty (1644–1911) and the Republic of China (1912–1949).[29]

3.1. Law in the Qing Dynasty (1644–1911)

Inheriting the Great Ming Code,[30] the Great Qing Code[31] was a sophisticated structure, regulating all of the major aspects of the social affairs in the Qing Dynasty, such as political, economic, military, familial, ritual, international and legal relations. As will be shown, the Qing Code is very clear in: (1) prohibiting looting and theft; (2) protecting imperial palaces and public monuments; and (3) exercising jurisdiction over foreigners. All of these provisions are strong evidence to support China's interests in its removed heritage. However, the central question remains as to whether the Qing Code would be recognised and enforced by a foreign forum in cross-border disputes.

28 Geoffrey MacCormack, *The Spirit of Traditional Chinese Law* (University of Georgia Press, 1996), xiii–xiv.

29 Hui Zhong, 'Legal Protection of Chinese Cultural Relics: A Justification for the Return' (2015) XX(1) *Art Antiquity and Law* 47, 67–68.

30 The Great Ming Code *(Da Ming lu)* reached its final form in 1397. The Great Ming Code represents a break with the past, following the alien-ruled Yuan dynasty and the flourishing of culture under the Ming, the last great Han-ruled dynasty. It was also a model for the Qing Code, which followed it, and is a fundamental source for understanding Chinese society and culture. Yonglin Jiang, *The Great Ming Code: Da Ming Lü* (University of Washington Press, 2005).

31 For more details about the Qing Code, see George Thomas Staunton, *Ta Tsing Leu Lee: Being the Fundamental Laws, and a Selection from the Supplementary Statutes, of the Penal Code of China* (Cambridge University Press, 2012); Qingqi Zhu, Derk Bodde and Clarence Morris, *Law in Imperial China: Exemplified by 190 Ch'ing Dynasty Cases* (Harvard University Press, 1967), 56–63; Yanping Wang and John W. Head, *Law Codes in Dynastic China: A Synopsis of Chinese Legal History in the Thirty Centuries from Zhou to Qing* (Carolina Academic Press, 2005), 192–212; Geoffrey MacCormack, *Traditional Chinese Penal Law* (Edinburgh University Press, 1990), 210–230.

3.1.1. Prohibiting Looting and Theft

The basic idea running through China's ancient law is that punishment should ensue when property is unlawfully acquired. In the Tang Dynasty (618–907 AD), the concept of *tsang* ('illicit goods') is one of the key notions used by Tang legislators in constructing a remarkably precise and integrated set of rules. In its broadest sense, *tsang* expresses "either property that the law treats as having been unlawfully acquired and with respect to which it establishes a penalty, or property that has been lost destroyed, or damaged as a consequence of someone's unlawful act".[32] These fundamental principles were inherited in the following instruments, including the Qing Code.[33] Section CCLXIX, Stealing in General, clearly prohibits robbery and theft, as "any person found guilty of an attempt to steal should be punished".[34] Regarding the term of "any person", the Qing Code states that when a theft was actually committed, that is to say, possession obtained of the property intended to be stolen, all of the parties concerned, whether sharers or not in the plunder, shall be punished in proportion to the amount of the largest sum stolen by any one individual.

3.1.2. Special Protection of Imperial Palaces and Public Monuments

In China's feudal society, public monuments and imperial palaces, for example the Summer Palace and the Forbidden City, were usually rich in priceless cultural relics. Such relics also appeared in various forms throughout China, for example, well-known architectural masterpieces, cave paintings, old temples and palaces in historical cities. As per the Qing Code, public monuments and imperial property were under absolute priority and special protection. For example, any person guilty of "defacing or destroying any of the public monuments and buildings, which have been erected in honour and commemoration

32 The Tang dynasty is generally considered to have been the most prosperous period of Chinese civilisation, a time of both financial and intellectual growth. The Tang Code with Commentary, also known as Tang Lü Shu Yi, was passed in 653, and served as the foundation for the legal codes for the following dynasties. Wuji Zhangsun, *Tang Lü Shu Yi* (Taiwan shang wu yin shu guan, 1965); Zhu, Bodde and Morris, *Law in Imperial China,* above n 31, 58.

33 The Great Ming Code, the precedent of the Qing Code, clearly prohibited looting and theft of cultural property, including 'sacred objects of the spirits such as sacrificial utensils and curtains that are devoted to the Great Sacrifices, or sacrificial offerings such as jade, silk, livestock, and vessels' (Article 280 Stealing Sacred Objects of the Spirits Devoted to the Great Sacrifices of Great Ming Code), imperial decrees (Article 281 Stealing Imperial Decrees), property from the Palace Treasury (Article 283 Stealing Property from the Palace Treasury), and plants and trees within the Imperial Mausoleum (Article 286 Stealing Plants or Trees within the Imperial Mausoleum).

34 Section CCLXIX Stealing in General.

of particular individuals and events" should be punished.[35] The Qing Code also explicitly prohibited "shooting arrows or bullets or throwing tiles or stones at the Imperial Ancestral Temple or at imperial palaces or halls".[36] Additionally, all persons found guilty of stealing, or attempting to steal, the property of the government, deposited in the public treasuries and storehouses, or in the Imperial Palace shall be punished for their offences.[37] In particular, stealing sacred objects from the imperial palace would receive the most severe punishment in the Qing Dynasty. Section Sacrilege reads that "all persons guilty of stealing the consecrated oblations offered up by the Emperor to the spirits of Heaven and Earth, or any of the sacred utensils, cloths and precious stones used on such occasions, shall whether principals or accessories to the offence, in all cases", shall be sentenced to death.[38] Third, entering the imperial palaces, ancestral temple or imperial mausoleums required special permission issued from the government.[39] Thus, it can be concluded that imperial property and public monuments in the Qing Dynasty were under special protection and any attempt to destroy or steal items from these places was clearly prohibited.

However, a notable drawback of this limited protection was that privately owned cultural relics were ignored. From the late 16th century, the majority of valuable cultural relics were in the hands of Chinese private art collectors, as the possession and collection of art works has become an indispensable pastime for upper class. Compared with imperial property, a large number of priceless cultural relics owned by private art collectors were not under special protection. The limited scope of protection may hinder the realisation of the good intentions enunciated in the Qing Code. However, while privately owned cultural objects were not particularly emphasised under the Qing Code, reference should be made to the restrictions embodied in the general provisions of prohibiting looting and theft.

3.1.3. Jurisdiction Over Foreigners

Despite the protection of cultural heritage, the question that should be raised here is whether China has the jurisdiction over foreign individuals to commence legal proceedings. After China's defeat in the First Opium War, the country was forced to open its gates and Chinese treasures were suddenly exposed and attractive to Western society. Due to the strong demand, many foreigners had a hand in collecting Chinese arts and taking them overseas, even though such behaviour was prohibited by the Qing Code.

35 Section CCCLXXVI Defacing or Destroying Public Monuments.
36 Section CXCII Shooting or throwing missile weapons towards an Imperial Palace.
37 Sections CCLXV Theft of Public Property and CCLX Stealing from an Imperial Palace.
38 Section CCLVII Sacrilege of Qing Code.
39 Sections CLXXXIII Unauthorized entering the Imperial Temple and CLXXXIV Unauthorized entering the Imperial Palace.

The first laws to regulate the behaviour of foreigners can be found in the early Tang Dynasty at a time when there were communities of Arab traders in Canton. With the view to allowing foreign traders a certain degree of freedom and autonomy in the resolution of disputes, the relevant provisions regarding legal jurisdiction over foreigners provided that:

> With respect to offences committed by aliens in China, if the offence involves only persons of the same nationality, the case shall be decided according to the laws of their own country.
>
> Where the offence involves persons of different nationalities, the case shall be decided according to the Tang Code.[40]

The Ming Dynasty adopted the principle of unlimited territorial jurisdiction such that "in all cases where persons beyond the pale of civilisation commit crimes, they shall all be judged in accordance with the *Code*".[41] The Qing Government argued that, since aliens have attached themselves to the empire, when they commit offences they should be punished in the same way as ordinary Chinese subjects. Therefore, the Qing Code retained the Ming alien jurisdiction regulation, stating that "all foreigners who come to submit themselves to the government of the empire, shall, when guilty of offences, be tried and sentenced according to the established laws".[42] The jurisdiction over foreigners also applied to the law regarding cultural relics in the Qing law. This is a very important factor in protecting Chinese cultural relics, as it was a precondition to start legal proceedings against foreigners under Chinese law.

Accordingly, Auriel Stein came into possession of a significant collection from the Mogao Grottoes, and it is highly doubtful as to whether this collection was obtained legally (see Chapter 1). First, the Mogao Grottoes were imperial palaces, as is evidenced by the governmental funding and the special guardian sent by the Qing Government. Second, there are no documents to show that Auriel Stein obtained any official permission to enter the Mogao Grottoes, meaning his entering was already a breach of the Qing Code. Third, after illegally entering the Mogao Grottoes, Auriel Stein acquired some 7,000 complete manuscripts, 6,000 fragments and several cases of paintings, embroideries and other artefacts, which was equivalent to theft pursuant to the section on Stealing from an Imperial Palace.

40 Jerome Alan Cohen, R. Randle Edwards and Fu-mei Chang Chen, *Essays on China's Legal Tradition* (Princeton University Press, 1980), 224.

41 Article 36 Committing Crimes by Persons beyond the Pale of Civilization of Great Ming Code.

42 Section XXXIV Offences committed by Foreigners of Qing Code. However, as a result of the Treaty of Bogue, which had granted foreign powers extraterritoriality, China gradually lost its jurisdiction over foreigners. Therefore, foreigners were exempt from Chinese law and judged by their own national law in criminal cases on Chinese soil. Jonathan D. Spence, *The Search for Modern China* (W.W. Norton & Company, 2013), 160–161.

3.1.4. Renovation of Codes of Law in the Early 20th Century

After the First Opium War, Western science and technology, particularly in relation to the production of weapons, was introduced in China.[43] However, following China's defeat by Japan in the Sino-Japanese war of 1895, the Qing Government realised that the manufacture of tools was not the essential aspect of Western advantages. A thorough reform of all aspects of the political, economic structure, culture and ideology was required, particularly in the legal area.

Reforms were made to the Chinese codes of law in two stages, which were carried out almost simultaneously: revising the old law with a focus on abolishing the cruel punishments that then existed and making new codes in line with Western laws.[44] The first stage of the reform was to respond to Western criticism on the cruelty of certain provisions in the Qing Code and to pave the way for the transition from ancient Chinese law to modern Western law. This change was done swiftly and by 1910 the Qing Code had been completely revised, abolishing cruel punishment. In the second stage, the Qing reforms began a process of the Westernisation of Chinese law. Several new codes were drafted and issued, including criminal and civil procedural law, civil law, General Principles for Merchants, Company Law, and Bankruptcy Law, as well as the Law for the Organization of the Courts, to name a few. Many foreign codes were translated into Chinese. Thus, with borrowings from Western legal instruments, the renovation of the legal codes in the early 20th century paved the way for Western legal ideas and systems to be further studied, developed and adopted in China. In the field of cultural heritage, official documents began adopting legal terms from the Western legal system, including state-owned property, and movable and immovable property.

3.1.5. Questions Arising Out of the Enforcement of the Qing Code

Although the Qing Code is strong evidence to support China's assertion, it is not guaranteed that China can obtain the return of its removed heritage by solely relying on the Qing Code. If seeking the return of heritage lost overseas through litigation, China needs to file a claim for the return in the

43 In the second half of the 19th century, the Qing authority launched the Self-Strengthening Movement of 1860–1894, the Hundred Days' Reform in 1898 and the Xinzheng for the purpose of maintaining the ruling dynasty and solving the national crisis. For example, the Xinzheng, also known as New Polices, launched in the early 20th century, comprised many projects of Western learning and was most reflected in education. Students were sent abroad on an unprecedented scale. Xi Wang and Frederic Wakeman, *China's Quest for Modernization: A Historical Perspective* (Institute of East Asian Studies, University of California, Berkeley, 1997), 150–155; Meribeth Cameron, *The Reform Movement in China, 1898–1912* (AMS Press, 1974) 172.

44 Jianfu Chen, *Chinese Law: Context and Transformation* (Martinus Nijhoff Publishers, 2008), 25.

possessing state or in an intermediary jurisdiction, arguing that the taking was a breach of the Qing Code. At this point, the available judicial practice has shown that the first legal hurdle is to demonstrate that the Qing Code is sufficiently clear in declaring national ownership over claimed objects.[45] However, the issue that arises here is that the bulk of the Qing Code's provisions were phrased with harsh punishment inserted. Thus, despite the clear intention to protect China's cultural heritage, it is unclear whether the Qing Code should be viewed as ownership law or merely penal law. Only foreign ownership law enjoys extra-territorial effects, while it is generally agreed that a court will not enforce a foreign state's penal law.[46] Thus, the obstacle standing in the way of recovering China's cultural heritage taken during the Qing Dynasty is the understanding and interpretation of the Qing Code.

With regards to understanding foreign law, available state practices have shown the difficulty of proof, as well as the difficulty of convincing the court that a foreign law is sufficiently clear enough in declaring state ownership. The case of *Peru v Johnson* is a good illustration of this point.[47] This case concerned 89 pre-Columbian artefacts seized by US customs from art collector Benjamin Johnson that were claimed by the Peruvian Government. One of central questions of the case is whether the Government of Peru was the owner of the items at the time of their removal. An important issue is whether the concept of ownership taken by the court in *Peru v Johnson* is too narrow with regards to items of cultural importance.[48] Despite expressing considerable sympathy for the plight of Peru over its problem with the looting of archaeological sites, the court was not persuaded that the relevant Peruvian legislation suggested a sufficient basis for proving the taking as illegal. It was decided that "the laws of Peru concerning its artefacts could reasonably be considered to have no more effect than export restrictions" and that since "export restrictions constitute an exercise of the police power of a state they don't create ownership in the state". As a result, Peru's claim was denied and this was affirmed by the Court of Appeals in 1990. If the *Peru v Johnson* decisions were the standard for the interpretation of a foreign law, it would be very difficult to persuade a foreign court to accept the Qing Code as ownership law, not only because it did not clearly assert China's state ownership interests, but also because many provisions in the Code contained harsh punishments.

However, to understand Chinese ancient law, it is inappropriate to apply contemporary Western liberal conceptions and assumptions about law and

45 For further discussion, see Chapter 6.

46 For example, in the *Ortiz*, the English court affirmed that it would not entertain a suit brought by a foreign sovereign, directly or indirectly, to enforce its penal, revenue or other public laws. *Attorney General of New Zealand v Ortiz* [1982] 3 All ER 432

47 *Government of Peru v Johnson* (720 F Supp 810, CD Cal 1989). Apart from the reason that Peruvian laws at the time of the alleged export were not specific enough to confer ownership on the State, the court also found that the plaintiffs had not been able to prove that the objects in question came from Peru.

48 Janet Blake, *International Cultural Heritage Law* (Oxford University Press, 2015), 57.

justice to a foreign system and traditions that preceded the Western liberal tradition itself.[49] The understanding of a foreign legal system must be assessed together with its historical and cultural context. Assuming that it would satisfy the requirements of an equivalent legal test of ownership, it should be accepted that the Qing Code did suggest a sufficient basis for proving ownership rights. In other words, as long as the central idea running through the Qing Code is to ensure the state control over China's cultural heritage, it is reasonable for the Qing Code to be accepted as ownership law. The circumstance that a provision is found within a law, which contains criminal sanctions, such as penalties, does not mean that the provision itself is automatically penal in nature.

The reason that ancient Chinese law appeared in the form of harsh punishments is that traditional Chinese society was largely influenced by the writings of traditional schools of philosophy.[50] While *Ru Jia* (Confucianism)[51] and *Fa Jia* (Legalism)[52] initially played a significant role in influencing China's legal traditions and the development of law, the theory of *Yin-Yang* became the dominant force after the Han Dynasty (206 BC).[53] The theory of *Yin-Yang* created a theoretical foundation for the harmonisation between Confucianism and Legalism through the justification of the supplementary function of punishment in governing a state, with *li*, being *Yang*, as the first instrument, and punishment, being *Yin*, as a supplementary tool for governing a state.[54] Thus, law in the traditional society increasingly became an administrative tool

49 MacCormack, *The Spirit of Traditional Chinese Law*, above n 146, xiii; H.C. Darby, 'The Chinese Legal and Political system: Historical Background' in Kathryn Bernhardt and Philip C. C. Huang (eds), *Civil law in Qing and Republican China* (Stanford University Press, 1994), 12–14.

50 Yulan Feng and Derk Bodde, *A Short History of Chinese Philosophy* (Free Press, 1966).

51 The starting point of Confucianism was its emphasis on the educational function of morality (*li*) in governing a state. Confucianists believed that people were educable and by education through *li* an ideal social order can be created on the basis of virtue (*de*). Regarding the role of law (*fa*), Confucianists strongly opposed the Legalists who emphasised the necessity of using severe punishment for maintaining a desired social order. Zhu, Bodde and Morris, *Law in Imperial China*, above n 31, 20–21; Chen, *Chinese Law*, above n 44, 10–14.

52 In strong contrast to the Confucian conception that all men are educable, Legalists believed that man was naturally evil. Their main concern was thus primarily with evil behaviour, and the primary function of law in their conception was to prevent evil, not to encourage good behaviour. Thus, Legalism was primarily associated with the concept of punishment, indeed, severe punishment. One of the most famous Legalists, Han Fei Zi, once said that: "It is by means of strict penalties and heavy punishments that the affairs of state are managed." Shang Yang, whose reform helped the Qin State to conquer other states and unify China, said that "nothing is more basic for putting an end to crimes than the imposition of heavy punishment". Chen, *Chinese Law*, above n, 14–16; Feng and Bodde, *History of Chinese Philosophy*, above n 50, 162.

53 Feng and Bodde, *History of Chinese Philosophy*, above n 50, 191–206.

54 At the same time, Confucianism was gradually accepted in a dominant position to unify state ideology and was to remain the state orthodoxy in China for nearly 2,000 years. However, Confucianism was now very different from that of previous periods, having absorbed many ideas from Legalism. Law in the traditional society increasingly became

for determining and maintaining social order, with the state at the centre. The first consequence of focusing on maintaining the social order is that law in traditional Chinese society was first and foremost a political tool, operating in a vertical direction, with its primary concern being state interests, rather than on a horizontal plane between individuals.[55] The second consequence is that the sophisticated and complex bureaucracy established and developed since the Qin period (221 BC to 206 BC) facilitated the development of a system of administrative law, with its primary focus being punishment rather than adjudication.[56] Thus, it can be noted that the Chinese concept of *Fa Zhi* (literally means 'rule of law') came to be associated with harsh despotism, heavy reliance on force and oppressive demands on the people by an interventionist state.[57] The traditional Chinese legal system was mainly conceived as a penal law, operated in a vertical direction and used as a supplementary means for maintaining a hierarchical social relationship that continued for centuries. On the other hand, it can be noted that the fundamental idea running through the development of law as an administrative tool for maintaining social order is to ensure that the state is at the centre and its interests are supreme and protected. Such priority can be reflected in the protection of public monuments and imperial palaces. Together with the historical and cultural background, law in traditional Chinese society can be understood as conferring similar state ownership rights, assuming that it would satisfy the requirements of an equivalent legal test of ownership. However, no case has been brought in reliance on the Qing Code.

Although it might be problematic to have the Qing Code recognised and enforced by a foreign court, it should be admitted that the Qing Code clearly addressed the protection of Chinese cultural relics and the state interests throughout its legal system, particularly through the prohibition of looting and theft of cultural heritage, and the special protection of public monuments and imperial palaces. Accordingly, China can argue that the Qing Code did provide a legal basis for the return of Chinese cultural heritage lost overseas because of individual illegal behaviour in the Qing Dynasty.

3.2. Law in the Republic of China (1912–1949)

After the Xinhai Revolution of 1911, led by Sun Yat-sen, who overthrew the Empire of Qing, 2,000 years of Chinese feudal monarchy came to an end and the Republic of China replaced the Qing Government as the governing force until 1949.[58] Soon after taking power, the newly established government

---

an administrative tool for determining and maintaining social order, with the state at its centre. Chen, *Chinese Law*, above n 44, 18.

55 Zhu, Bodde and Morris, *Law in Imperial China*, above n 31, 10–13.

56 Chen, *Chinese Law*, above n 44, 21.

57 Ibid, 19.

58 During the Republic of China, 1911 to 1928, the Peiyang Government was the ruling governmental authority of China, which was usually collectively referred to as a series of

published a series of documents to address urgent questions emerging at that time, including preserving heritage sites, regulating the art market through restrictions on foreign buying and preventing the outflow of art objects. The most significant contribution made during the Republic of China was the state ownership provisions of Chinese law, by which China has a stronger legal argument for the return of its illegally removed heritage.

3.2.1. Preserving the Longmen Grottos: The Gap in Law

On February 26v1914, the Chinese Minister of the Interior wrote to the chief governor in the Henan Province criticising its failure to protect the Longmen Grottoes.[59] On March 11 1916, the Minister issued an Administrative Order to all provincial governments, emphasising the importance of preserving cultural relics. The Minister pointed out that the destruction, either intentional or through negligence, of cultural relics and historical sites had become a national issue, as destruction occurred in both culturally rich provinces, such as the Henan and Shanxi provinces, as well as in some remote areas. Further, the Minister argued that the lack of governmental protection was the main reason for the destruction:

> If the government failed to take care of our ancient objects, individuals would take advantage of this gap to acquire, to sell or to transfer. Therefore, the authority in localities should pass legislation to preserve ancient objects. Anyone who privately acquires, sells, transports, or destroys cultural items should be subject to punishment.[60]

Although the 1916 Administrative Order was not binding, it can be viewed as a starting point for the Government of the Republic of China to combatting the continuous loss of its cultural relics and to enhance state control over Chinese heritage through an effective legal regime.

The 1916 Administrative Order also urged the Government of the Republic of China to take action to preserve cultural relics. With strong interests in preserving its cultural relics, the Government of the Republic of China constructed a legal regime to deal with the massive destruction and loss of its relics. The main applicable laws, including the 1916 Provisional Measures of Preserving Antiquities, the 1928 Regulations on the Preservation of Historical Sites and Ancient Objects, and the 1930 Law on the Preservation of Ancient Objects, contained provisions designed as both preventive and protective. In

---

military powers ruling from Beijing. In 1928, the Nationalist Government led by the Nationalist Party, reunified and governed the country until the defeat against the Communist Party in the Civil War in 1949.

59 Second Historical Archives, *A Collective Documents about the Republic of China, Volume 3, Culture* (Jiangsu Phoenix House, 1999), 190.

60 Zhong, *A Justification for the Return*, above n 27, 54.

the first half of the 20th century, modern Chinese cultural heritage law developed to address urgent questions emerging at that time for better preservation. One example that best reflects the development of Chinese cultural heritage law in the Republic of China was the evolving understanding of the definition of cultural relics and the scope of protection.

3.2.2. What Shall We Protect?

In October 1916, the newly established Peiyang Government opened investigations to record all cultural relics across the country.[61] According to the Registration Form and the Manual published by the Ministry of the Interior, the scope of protection included a list of 12 sub-items for consideration: Buildings, Historic Sites, Statues, Stones, Potteries, Plants, Documents, Weapons, Clothes, Sculptures, Instruments, and Groceries.[62] Under each sub-item, the Manual listed possible items that could fall into the category. For example, the sub-item of Buildings contained city walls, border crossings, dams, bridges, temples, gardens, monasteries, towers, pavilions, and all other ancient buildings. Such detailed categorisation was necessary to provide clear guidelines to investigate and record all cultural relics nationwide, since Chinese cultural relics appear in various forms. More importantly, this nationwide investigation was thought to be a reaction to the limited scope of protection in the Ming and Qing laws, which covered only public monuments and imperial palaces.

One notable point in this nationwide investigation was the differentiation between state-owned and privately-owned cultural relics. The Manual provides that "first priority should be given to stated-owned and publicly-owned items. All information about name, date, location, preservation and notes in the registration form should be provided".[63] The reasons behind this priority could first be that there was insufficient funding or professionals to track all cultural relics around the whole country. Secondly, privately owned cultural relics were generally held by the upper classes who understood the unique values contained in their collection and had the ability to preserve them. However, questions may arise with regards to the ambiguity of the term "first priority", since it was not clear whether this provision was designed for restoration or merely registration. There was no further information as to how registration information would be used or how such priority would help the government to provide an enhanced preservation of stated-owned cultural relics.

Later in the same year, the Provisional Measures on the Preservation of Ancient Objects were published. The 1916 Provisional Measures included five categories: Ancient Tombs, Historical Sites, Stone Carvings and Murals, Trees, and Art Works. Under each sub-item, the Manual listed possible items that could fall into the category. For example, the category of Historical Sites

61 Second Historical Archives, *Culture* (Volume 3), above n 59, 197.
62 Ibid, 200–201.
63 Article 1 of the Manual.

contained "Sites of ancient culture, ancient architectural structures, cave temples, bridges, lakes or typical buildings that are related to major historical events, or famous personalities, or are highly memorable, all shall be well be well preserved."[64] The category of Art Works included "valuable works of art, important documents dating from earlier periods, manuscripts, books and materials that are of historical, artistic or scientific value should be preserved".[65]

The 1928 Regulations were a modified copy of the 1916 Provisional Measures. The protection covered a similar scope to that of the 1916 Provisional Measures, but with the addition of Ancient Cities, which was a category that included not just the cultural relics or historical sites themselves, but also the unique role they played in history. For example, other than the rich cultural relics represented by the Terracotta Warriors, the City of Xi'an has enjoyed a prestigious historical reputation as it served as the capital city for 13 dynasties, and is generally viewed as the cradle of China's ancient civilisation.

Through the developing legal system, it can be noted that the scope of protection had been extended from merely public monuments and imperial property to a wide range of cultural relics, including plants, documents, weapons, and tombs. A possible reason for China's expansive definition was that it had a greater need for protection from the massive outflow of cultural relics and their destruction. After the First Opium War, when China was forced to open its gates, the country's rich cultural relics were at risk due to escalating international demand and a lack of regulations in the art market. For example, local populations would engage in excavations of buried cultural relics without taking the necessary care to prevent damage. A great demand for China's rich cultural relics, in turn, created an urgent need to foster greater protection over these objects.

However, the legal system at this stage of development did not really focus on the intrinsic historical and cultural values of cultural relics, since the laws merely described the possible items to determine the scope of protection. Neither the 1928 Regulations nor the 1916 Provisional Measures explained what features suggested that cultural relics deserved greater protection than ordinary property. In addition, the provisions were highly subjective, including words such as "valuable" and "highly memorable". The 1916 Provisional Measures stated that "valuable works of art, important documents dating from earlier periods, manuscripts, books and materials that are of historical, artistic or scientific value should be preserved".[66] While valuable art works were to be protected by the law, there was no guidance on how to achieve this.

On June 2 1930, the Law on the Preservation of Ancient Objects was published by the Nationalist Government, and was generally viewed by international scholars as the earliest known enactment in the area.[67] The definition

64 Article 2 of the 1916 Provisional Measures.

65 Article 5 of the 1916 Provisional Measures.

66 Article 2 of the 1916 Provisional Measures.

67 David Murphy, *Plunder and Preservation: Cultural Property Law and Practice in the People's Republic of China* (Oxford University Press, 1995), 81.

of cultural relics was first significantly codified in the 1930 Law: Article 1 designated cultural relics as "all ancient objects related to archaeology, history, palaeontology and other cultures".[68] The Interim Rules for the Scope and Types of Ancient Objects specified the protected scope by providing three criteria: first, the relic must have been produced from an earlier period; second, there must be only limited copies available; and third, the item must have great scientific, historical or artistic value.[69] This significant change from simple descriptions to establishing precise criteria to determine the scope of protection reflected the fact that Chinese cultural heritage law had begun to acknowledge the unique values of cultural relics as a reflection of a society's beliefs, religions, ideologies and values. Each cultural item is more than a just product, it is also a connection surviving from a past age and a link to the future.

3.2.3. State Interests in Chinese Cultural Relics

In 1913, the Department of Revenue issued a memorandum to the Ministry of the Interior, addressing the gap in the legal system to the effect that "there was no legal basis for the Customs to forbid the export of cultural relics".[70] In response, the President published the first order, restricting the export of cultural relics, which required the Ministry of the Interior and the Department of Revenue to stem the tide of antiquities being taken out of the country.[71] The former took charge of the preservation of antiquities located within China, including making records, taking protective measures against damage or destruction and preparing copies of original items. The Department of Revenue was primarily responsible for export control, ensuring that Chinese cultural relics would not be exported or taken out of the country temporarily.

With regards to the legal basis for the recovery, the 1916 Provisional Measures stated that "sites of ancient culture, ancient architectural structures, cave temples, bridges, lakes or typical buildings that are related to major historical events, or famous personalities, or are highly memorable, all shall be preserved".[72] Although the words 'should be preserved' are ambiguous as to what is specifically involved in preserving these privileged objects, the subsequent development of Chinese cultural heritage law and practice suggest that the government interpreted the term rather broadly. This protection includes not only the traditional protection against destruction or theft, but also the intention that Chinese cultural relics were owned by the state, which is reflected in the following repatriation cases.

On October 20 1927, a case was reported to the Ministry of Interior relating to the archives of the Grand Secretariat. These archives were originally

68 Article 1 of the 1930 Law.

69 Article 2 of the 1935 Interim Rules.

70 Second Historical Archives, *Culture (Volume 3),* above n 59, 185–186.

71 Ibid, 185.

72 Article 2 of the 1916 Provisional Measures.

stored at the Grand Secretariat Storehouse in the Qing imperial palace, but had been shipped to Japan.[73] The Tianjing Supervisory Commission for the Customs and Excise Department issued a letter to the Ministry of the Interior, reporting that over 40 boxes of the archives of the Grand Secretariat held by Luo Zhenyu would be sold to a Japanese national.[74] The Commission suggested that the Ministry of the Interior inform other customs authorities to inspect carefully in case the archives were transported to Japan, as Article 5 of the Provisional Measures required "valuable works of art, important documents dating from earlier periods, manuscripts, books and materials that are of historical, artistic or scientific value should be preserved".[75] Similar restrictions were applied to the category of Stone Carvings and Murals.[76]

In another case, in July 1926, the China Japanese Association planned to donate four pieces of Han Brick and one piece of plaster model to the School of Architecture of Kyoto University. In this instance, the Japanese Embassy wrote to the tax office and asked to simplify the customs processing of these items that were to be shipped to the City of Tianjing immediately.[77] These pictorial bricks had patterns or a scene made by pressing and moulding, which were a decorative component of the buildings from the Warring States period to the Yuan Dynasty, containing a history of more than ten centuries.[78] According to the letter, the China Japanese Association planned to donate four pieces of Han Brick and one piece of plaster model to the School of Architecture of Kyoto University. However, the Ministry of the Interior explicitly rejected the request, stating that "according to the Provisional Measures 1916, the four pieces of Han bricks requested from the Japan Embassy are precious cultural relics and should not be allowed for export". Thus, it can be concluded that the government was very clear that Chinese cultural relics that fall within the protected categories, such as art works, stone carvings and murals, should be maintained within the country. The above cases illustrate that, pursuant to the Provisional Measures of 1916, any damage, destruction or sale of cultural items without permission was prohibited.[79]

Law 1930 took a step forward in declaring China's state interests in its heritage: Article 2 stated that "apart from privately-owned cultural relics, all

73 Second Historical Archives, *Culture (Volume 3)*, above n 59, 254
74 These archival materials include imperial decrees, edicts, memorials, tribute document, examination questions and papers, rosters of successful examination candidates, documents from the offices of the Grand Secretariat, documents from the offices for book compilation, general administrative activities and legal cases. The Academia Sinica Graduate Institute of History, 'The archives of the Grand Secretariat' <http://archive.ihp.sinica.edu.tw/mctkm2/index.html>.
75 Article 5 of the 1916 Provisional Measures.
76 Article 3 of the 1916 Provisional Measures.
77 Second Historical Archives, *Culture (Volume 3)*, above n 59, 255.
78 National Museum of China, 'Pictorial Bricks' <http://en.chnmuseum.cn/Default.aspx?TabId=557&HotType=46&AspxAutoDetectCookieSupport=1>.
79 Article 3 of the 1916 Provisional Measures.

cultural relics should be preserved by the Central Ancient Objects Preservation Commission".[80] The Central Ancient Objects Preservation Commission, which belonged to the Ministry of Interior, was the government's enforcing agent in dealing with all of the issues related to Chinese cultural relics, for example, the recovery of illegally removed cultural relics, the examination of application for cultural exchange overseas and the approval of conducting archaeological excavation in China.[81] Accordingly, all cultural relics, except those privately-owned objects, should be under the preservation and control of the Government. Moreover, Article 7 of Law 1930 reaffirmed that all cultural relics remaining underground or exposed were owned by the state. In conclusion, the law in the Republic of China not only prohibited any destruction or removal without permission, but also emphasised state interests in the cultural relics found within the territories.

3.2.4. Preventing Heritage Being Taken Out of the Country

Apart from the special protection of state interests in cultural relics, Chinese individuals were restricted when selling cultural relics to foreigners. The most well-known case was the return of a series of cultural relics taken from Jvlu Country, Hebei Province.[82] In 1921, it was reported to the Ministry of the Interior that the local governor of Jvlu Country had privately sold more than 10,000 cultural relics to foreigners. The disputed cultural relics had been found by locals in Jvlu Country since 1920, but were privately appropriated by the local governor. According to the report, representatives from Jvlu Country wanted the Ministry of the Interior to trace the cultural relics held by the governor that were recorded in the accompanying attachment, which contained the name, number of pieces, whether they had been found on private or state-owned land, their market value and detailed descriptions. In its response, the Ministry of the Interior wrote that "all ancient objects remaining underground should be preserved by the local governments. Unless proved to be legally privately owned items, all ancient objects remaining underground are owned by the State." The Ministry of the Interior emphasised that individuals were not allowed to sell cultural relics to foreigners unless they had express permission to do so, and requested the provincial governor bring all the unlawfully obtained objects back into the state's hands.

The restriction placed on Chinese individuals was confirmed by Article 7 of the Law 1930, which clearly prohibited Chinese individuals from selling cultural relics to foreigners in order to reduce the chance of Chinese arts being

80 Article 2 of the 1930 Law.

81 All institutions engaged in archaeological excavations were subject to examination by the Central Ancient Objects Preservation Commission. For those that may conduct archaeological excavations, the Department of Education and the Ministry of the Interior shall issue an authorisation certificate. Article 3 of the Regulations for Excavations 1935.

82 Second Historical Archives, *Culture (Volume 3)*, above n 59, 244.

taken out of the country. Article 13 of the Law 1930 further established that any transfers or sales of cultural relics were allowed only within China.[83] The reason for this is that while it was forbidden to sell cultural relics to foreigners, the law did not prevent Chinese citizens from taking cultural relics out of the country. Therefore, the Law 1930 put a total stop to any form of transfers, sales, smugglings or any act of removal directed at taking cultural relics out of the country.

The only exception to this prohibition was for research purposes, which required compliance with a very strict application process.[84] First, only academic organisations directly under the central or local governments were eligible, meaning that individuals were not allowed to apply. Secondly, eligible academic organisations were required to submit an application to the Central Ancient Objects Preservation Commission for further examination, verification, and supervision.[85] Final approval of an application for export was made by the Central Preservation Commission. After approval, a temporary export permit would be issued jointly by the Department of Education and the Ministry of the Interior. Thirdly, cultural relics taken out of the country were to be returned to their place of origin within two years.[86] In this regard, the academic institution that submitted the application for the export would be responsible for ensuring the return and for any damage or loss incurred during the traveling overseas.[87] However, there were no clear guidelines for the Central Commission to make a decision on granting permission as to whether and when a cultural item, especially those priceless and vulnerable items, could travel outside the country. On the other hand, it should be emphasised that the law at this stage had developed to address the important issue of illicit trafficking of Chinese arts and to maintain cultural relics within the country.

3.2.5. Regulating Archaeological Excavations

After the fall of the Qing Dynasty and in the absence of strong political control after the Revolution of 1911, separationist warlord regimes fought ceaseless wars against one another. In the chaos of war, grave robbers were extremely active. Tomb guards left by former Qing governments were no longer paid wages, so they often stole, or helped steal, the objects they were supposed to be guarding.[88] Illicit excavation not only caused a loss of cultural objects but also the destruction of large numbers of archaeological and historical sites.

83 Articles 6 and 13 of the Law 1930.
84 Article 13 of the Law 1930.
85 Article 13 of the Law 1930; Articles 5, 6, 7, 8 and 9 of the 1935 Regulations on the Passport for Taking Ancient Objects out of the Country.
86 Article 13 of the 1930 Law.
87 Article 10 of the 1935 Regulations on the Passport.
88 'The Qing East Imperial Tombs', *Chinaorg* <www.china.org.cn/english/features/atam/115430.htm>.

In this regard, another aspect of the legal protection for cultural relics in the Republic of China is ensuring state interests during archaeological excavations.

Article 7 the Law 1930 explicitly declared state ownership over all cultural relics remaining underground or exposed. Any relics found must be immediately reported to the government, meaning that the results of any unauthorised excavations constituted stolen property. By this provision, China may be able to claim the cultural relics that were illegally taken through tomb robbery. For example, the East Tombs, 125 kilometres outside of Beijing, are the largest and most complex of imperial tombs in China, among which the most magnificent are the Yuling mausoleum of Emperor Qian Long and the Dingling mausoleum of Emperor Dowager Ci Xi.[89] However, these underground palaces were later found to have been blown open and many precious articles were cut off and stolen.

Apart from bringing all cultural relics under state control, the Law 1930 also elevated the standards for those organisations eligible for conducting archaeological excavations. First, only Chinese academic institutions directly under the central and local governments were able to conduct excavations, meaning that individuals were completely ruled out for engaging in excavations. This provision is of great significance to the protection of Chinese cultural heritage, as individuals usually lack the necessary knowledge to recognise the value of ancient objects or may cut off a smaller piece from a larger artwork in order to obtain transportable parts for sale on the international art market. Secondly, foreigners or foreign organisations were prohibited from participating in excavations unless granted special permission from the Central Preservation Commission.[90] The 1931 Detailed Rules on the Implementation explicitly stated that "no matter for what reasons, no foreigners may conduct any archaeological excavations within China. Only financial support from foreigners can be accepted after the approval from the Central Preservation Commission".[91] However, the Regulations for the Archaeology Excavation 1935 allowed Chinese domestic academic institutions to apply for permission to allow foreign nationals or foreign organisations to participate in excavations on the basis of providing "special help".[92] To define the term special help, the Regulations on Foreigner or Foreign Organisation's Participation in Archaeological Excavations set out these restrictions: "first, foreigner and foreign organisation can only participate excavation when it is necessary, and secondly, any foreign participant shall be under the supervision of Central Preservation Commission and shall follow the excavation plan provided by the academic institutions".[93] However, there was no guidance on how to determine the phrase "when it

89 Ibid.
90 Article 10 of the 1930 Law.
91 Article 13 of the 1931 Detailed Rules on the Implementation.
92 Article 6 of the 1935 Regulations for Excavations.
93 Articles 1, 4 and 6 of the 1935 Regulations on Foreigner or Foreign Organisation's Participation.

is necessary". Thirdly, the intention to ensure China's state interests in its heritage are reflected in the following aspects: While foreigners were allowed to engage in archaeological work with permission, only Chinese academic institutions had the right to publish any discoveries during the excavations.[94] Any exports of the discoveries were subject to submitting reports for approval through academic institutions.[95]

In conclusion, the law in the Republic of China developed to address the urgent questions that occurred at the time, for example, declaring state ownership over cultural relics, preventing Chinese cultural relics from being taken out of the country, regulating archaeological excavations and restricting foreign engagement in any activity that may lead to the loss of Chinese cultural relics. Although the law was far from perfect, it nevertheless established a legal basis for China to argue that the removal of its cultural relics by individuals during times of war and peace without permission was illegal. More importantly, the law in the Republic of China had developed to be in line with modern cultural heritage law, meaning that it is less problematic being recognised and enforced by a foreign court.

4. Return of Historically Removed Heritage

4.1. Was All of China's Cultural Heritage Removed Illicitly?

Based on the above analysis, it is necessary to come to a conclusion on the availability of a legal basis for China's cultural heritage. If the taking can be shown to be illegal, China will have a stronger argument for convincing the current possessors to return China's cultural heritage, instead of merely an ethics and moral discourse.

4.1.1. Cultural Heritage Taken During Armed Conflicts

With regards to the first category of taking, the removal of China's cultural heritage during armed conflicts, the answer to the question of legality varies in three specific situations. First, for removals that occurred after the enactment of the 1899 Hague Convention, China has a legal basis for the return on the grounds that the taking of an enemy's property as war booty had been formally forbidden. However, this is not clear cut: even though the looting of Chinese cultural heritage during the Japanese Occupation was a breach of international law, the Chinese Government has renounced its demands for war reparations pursuant to the 1972 Joint Statement. The question then becomes whether, since the Chinese Government renounced its claims for war reparations in a peace treaty, Chinese individuals still have a means to vindicate their

94 Article 9 of the1935 Regulations on Foreigner or Foreign Organisation's Participation.
95 Article 8 of the 1935 Regulations on Foreigner or Foreign Organisation's Participation.

rights to request restitution.[96] Japan consistently insists that the 1972 Joint Statement has closed the door on the past and no individual claims may now be brought forward. However, this point is not entirely clear or true, given that an increasing number of claims have been filed by private individuals against Japan's actions during the Second World War. On the other hand, even if individuals' rights were not extinguished by the 1972 Joint Statement, it is unclear whether there remains the right to request restitution of looted cultural relics. Because individuals are not usually considered capable of bringing international claims against states, it is unclear whether individuals have the standing as direct beneficiaries for war damages and can assert the treaty rights of state parties for the return of China's cultural heritage. In addition, the issue of a statute of limitations is still another legal hurdle for all post-war compensation claims. All these legal issues have made it difficult to resolve private claims. Thus, the return of Chinese cultural heritage taken during the Japanese Occupation represents the second category of taken of Chinese cultural heritage, a special issue for cultural items taken during armed conflicts. Third, any removals that occurred before the enactment of the 1899 Hague Convention were perfectly legal on the grounds that there was no law regulating such taking as illegal.

4.1.2. Cultural Heritage Taken by Individuals During Times of War and Peace

With regards to the loss of cultural heritage through individual illegal acts during both times of war and peace, the Qing Code and state ownership provisions of Chinese law between 1912 and 1949 suggest a legal basis for return. However, legal issues arising from private international law, such as characterisation of dispute, proof of title, conflict of laws in time and place, public policy, limitation law, and others, may prevent China from obtaining recovery through civil litigation.[97]

In the case of the 2009 Paris auction, a group of lawyers and the Association for the Protection of Chinese Art in Europe filed suit in Paris seeking to enjoin the auction. The injunction was denied on the grounds that the Association did not have standing to file the motion because it did not have a direct relationship with the bronze heads. However, even though the Chinese Government or the Summer Palace Administration can act as the plaintiff to commence the legal proceeding, the legal answer may not support recovery claims. First, there are time limitations for bringing a suit. Current possessors may argue that the Chinese Government has been aware of the removal for

96 This book does not aim to the recovery claims filed by Chinese individuals, as they raise an entirely different set of issues For more discussion, see Zhong, *Chinese Individuals Request,* above n 27, 179–196.

97 For more discussion, see Chapter 4, Zuozhen Liu, *The Case for Repatriating China's Cultural Objects* (Springer, 2016).

nearly 100 years, and it never filed lawsuits, for example, against the British Museum for the return of the Dunhuang manuscripts. The statute of limitations may stop any lawsuit from moving forward. Second, jurisdictions differ in allocating rights and obligations between bona fide purchasers and victims of theft. In general, civil law systems favour possessors of property, in so far as a bona fide purchaser may obtain valid title even from a thief. Thus, it is problematic to recover China's cultural heritage from current possessors in civil law systems, for example, a French institution that hold many Chinese cultural heritage removed during the respective era. Even though English common law gives priority to an original owner, the claim seeking recovery of the Dunhuang manuscripts could probably still be barred by the six-year limitation period within the English statute of limitations. Third, although the Qing Code clearly addressed the protection of Chinese cultural relics and state interests throughout its legal system, it is unclear whether the Qing Code can be recognised and enforced by a foreign court as no case has been brought forward that relies on the Qing Code. In conclusion, the Qing Code and state ownership provisions of Chinese law between 1912 and 1949 suggest a legal basis for China to argue that the unauthorised removal of its cultural relics by individuals during times of war and peace was illegal and that these items should therefore be returned. However, bringing cultural heritage home through civil litigation can be legally complex due to the various questions arising out of private international law.

In conclusion, China does not have a legal basis for the return of all items removed between 1840 and 1945, and in these cases, the customary rule may provide an answer. This book argues that a new customary international law is emerging, according to which the interests of states of origin in their wrongfully removed heritage should be prioritised. This proposed customary rule supports the return of historically removed heritage, including Chinese cultural heritage that was lost overseas between 1840 and 1945. But what constitutes historically removed heritage? What is the difference between historically removed heritage, wrongfully removed heritage and illegally removed heritage? Before moving to the legal analysis for the proposed customary rule, a section exploring the determination of historically removed heritage is necessary.

4.2. Defining Historically Removed Heritage

Several features distinguish historically removed heritage. First, historically removed heritage is the "representative" of a state of origin, such as the imperial treasures from China, the Parthenon Marbles from Greece, the Koh-i-Noor Diamond from India, and the Rosetta Stone from Egypt, which are important in symbolising the state's history and enhancing the national identity. In other words, this book only focuses on those representative heritage objects that have special cultural and historical meaning for the states of origin and their people. It does not aim to return every piece of cultural object removed in history to its state of origin. For China, it is impossible to recover all its heritage taken during the period of 1840–1945, nor does China have the ability to do that. But China can try to recover the heritage items that have special value or importance, such as the Dunhuang manuscripts, the Admonitions Scroll and the imperial treasures taken from the Summer Palace. As a representative, historically removed heritage often has strong emotional and cultural connections with its state of origin. One reason for this is that historically removed heritage was usually created in a very early time period. For example, the Parthenon temple was built in 5th century BC to honor Athena and is regarded as the highest architectural achievement of the Ancient Greeks. Additionally, they often symbolise times of victory, defeat, great suffering, or important historical events in the development of a state, and can easily invoke emotions in people, such as pride, happiness, pity, and sorrow. This was clearly illustrated when the Cameroon Ambassador requested the return of the Afo-A-Kom, stating that "it is beyond money, beyond value. It is the heart of the Kom, what unifies the tribe, the spirit of the nation, what holds us together."[98] Similarly, in the Paris auction case in 2009, a Chinese businessman placed the winning bid, but then refused to pay as a 'patriotic' act. Convinced that he had fulfilled his duty as a Chinese citizen, he further stated that "these cultural relics belong to China . . . they were looted by the West in time of war and illegally taken abroad".[99] These cases reflect that the true value of cultural heritage goes beyond an economic value. They are considered material evidence of a nation's civilisation and an ideal means to enhance national identity and memory.

However, the central question that makes return problematic is that there is no convincing evidence to prove a country's legal title over a disputed item. The difficulties in this regard are various. A lot of historically removed heritage, such as the Parthenon Marbles, were taken during historical events occurring before the promulgation of international conventions or domestic ownership laws. In other words, due to the lack of law regulating such taking as illegal, enforceable legal action is not an option, resulting in an unsatisfying outcome both legally and ethically. Thus, the second important feature is the lack of a legal basis stating that the taking was illegal.

Third, although there may not be a strict legal basis for a claim, the takings can be viewed as morally wrong because of the manner in which they were acquired. The takings usually fail to comply with present legal standards, or the process of removal destroyed fragile objects and jeopardised the object's physical integrity. For example, the Summer Palace bronze heads were taken

98 Patrick O'Keefe, 'Repatriation of Sacred Objects' in Lyndel Prott (ed), *Witnesses to History: A Compendium of Documents and Writings on the Return of Cultural Objects* (UNESCO, 2009), 229.

99 Roland Arkell, 'Christie's Face Chinese Threats as Buyer Refuses to Pay', *Antiques Trade Gazette* March 9 2012 <www.antiquestradegazette.com/news/2009/mar/09/christie%E2%80%99s-face-chinese-threats-as-buyer-refuses-to-pay/>.

when invaders torched or levelled as many as 200 buildings. It is clear that the taking itself jeopardised the Summer Palace's integrity, which means that what these objects can tell us about the past is limited to the information intrinsic within the object itself, rather than from the object's full associated and original context. Therefore, the third feature of historically removed heritage is that although the taking was legal, it was morally wrong.

It is clear that the most important difference between historically removed and illegally removed heritage is that the state of origin does not have a legal basis, but rather a strong ethics discourse to claim for the return of historically removed heritage. Historically removed heritage can only be viewed as wrongfully taken heritage, but not as illegally removed heritage. Comparatively, the term of wrongfully taken heritage has a much broader understanding, as it can be legally wrong or morally wrong. In other words, it includes both illegally removed heritage and historically removed heritage. For example, the Summer Palace sculptures can be described as historically removed heritage or wrongfully taken heritage, but not illegally removed heritage.

5. Conclusion

In the absence of mandatory obligations, current possessors are under no legal obligation to relinquish their collections, since contested materials were taken out of a state of origin without violating any relevant law at the time of the acquisition. In other words, claims for return without a legal basis are usually silenced, or at best discussed, but very rarely successful. However, worldwide in the past two decades an increasing number of cultural relics have been returned to the original states by individuals, museums, and countries. In particular, many claims that had been largely unsuccessful in the late 20th century have now been successfully negotiated and settled. This fact strongly contributes to the idea of the proposed customary rule, according to which the interests of states of origin in their wrongfully removed heritage should be prioritised. The proposed customary rule will create a legal basis not only for China, but also for other original states with similar difficulties in claiming for the return of their historically removed heritage.

Bibliography

'Experts Urge Collectors To Share World's Earliest Encyclopedia', *China.org.cn* April 17 2002 <http://china.org.cn/english/PP-e/31248.htm>

'Joint Communique of the Government of Japan and the Government of the People's Republic of China' (1972) *Ministry of Foreign Affairs of Japan* <www.mofa.go.jp/region/asia-paci/china/joint72.html>

'The Qing East Imperial Tombs', *Chinaorg* <www.china.org.cn/english/features/atam/115430.htm>

'Responsibility of States for Internationally Wrongful Acts' (United Nations) <http://legal.un.org/ilc/texts/instruments/english/draft_articles/9_6_2001.pdf>

'War Damage on Cultural Relics Commission under the Department of Education', *China Cultural Relics* August 22 2007 <www.xhgxt.com/html/View_9270.html>

Afjochnick, Chris and Roger Normand, 'The Legitimation of Violence: A Critical Historical of the Laws of War' (1994) 35(1) *Harvard International Law Journal* 49

Arkell, Roland, 'Christie's Face Chinese Threats as Buyer Refuses to Pay', *Antiques Trade Gazette* March 9 2012 <www.antiquestradegazette.com/news/2009/mar/09/christie%E2%80%99s-face-chinese-threats-as-buyer-refuses-to-pay/>

Aust, Anthony, *Handbook of International Law* (Cambridge University Press, 2005)

Best, Geoffrey, *Humanity in Warfare: The Modern History of the International Law of Armed Conflicts* (Weidenfeld and Nicolson, 1980)

Blake, Janet, *International Cultural Heritage Law* (Oxford University Press, 2015)

Bos, Adriaan, 'The Importance of the 1899, 1907 and 1999 Hague Conferences for the Legal Protection of Cultural Property in the Event of Armed Conflict' (2005) 57(4) *Museum International* 32

Cameron, Meribeth, *The Reform Movement in China, 1898–1912* (AMS Press, 1974)

Chen, Jianfu, *Chinese Law: Context and Transformation* (Martinus Nijhoff Publishers, 2008)

China, National Museum of, 'Pictorial Bricks' <http://en.chnmuseum.cn/Default.aspx?TabId=557&HotType=46&AspxAutoDetectCookieSupport=1>

Cohen, Jerome Alan, R. Randle Edwards and Fu-mei Chang Chen, *Essays on China's Legal Tradition* (Princeton University Press, 1980)

Darby, H.C., 'The Chinese Legal and Political system: Historical Background' in Kathryn Bernhardt and Philip C. C. Huang (eds), *Civil law in Qing and Republican China* (Stanford University Press, 1994)

Ding, James, 'China' in James A.R. Nafziger and Robert Kirkwood Paterson (eds), *Handbook on the Law of Cultural Heritage and International Trade* (Edward Elgar Publishing, 2014) 107

Downey, William Gerald, 'Captured Enemy Property: Booty of War and Seized Enemy Property' (1950) 44(3) *The American Journal of International Law* 488

Edmonds, James Edward and Lassa Oppenheim, *Land Warfare* (HM Stationery Office, 1912)

Feng, Yulan and Derk Bodde, *A Short History of Chinese Philosophy* (Free Press, 1966)

Forrest, Craig, *International Law and The Protection of Cultural Heritage* (Routledge, 2010)

Friedman, Leon, *The Law of War: A Documentary History* (Random House, 1972)

Graduate Institute of History, The Academia Sinica 'The archives of the Grand Secretariat' <http://archive.ihp.sinica.edu.tw/mctkm2/index.html>

Janis, Mark W., *International Law* (Wolters Kluwer Law & Business, 5th ed, 2012)

Jiang, Yonglin, *The Great Ming Code: Da Ming Lü* (University of Washington Press, 2005)

Jote, Kifle, *International Legal Protection of Cultural Heritage* (Juristforlaget, 1994)

Liu, Zuozhen, *The Case for Repatriating China's Cultural Objects* (Springer, 2016)

Loucaides, Loukis G., 'The Protection of the Right to Property in Occupied Territories' (2004) 53(3) *The International and Comparative Law Quarterly* 677
MacCormack, Geoffrey, *The Spirit of Traditional Chinese Law* (University of Georgia Press, 1996)
MacCormack, Geoffrey, *Traditional Chinese Penal Law* (Edinburgh University Press, 1990)
Murphy, David, *Plunder and Preservation: Cultural Property Law and Practice in the People's Republic of China* (Oxford University Press, 1995)
Nahlik, Stanislaw E., 'International Law and The Protection of Cultural Property in Armed Conflicts' (1975) 27 *Hastings Law Journal* 1069
O'Keefe, Patrick, 'Repatriation of Sacred Objects' in Lyndel Prott (ed), *Witnesses to History: A Compendium of Documents and Writings on the Return of Cultural Objects* (UNESCO, 2009)
O'Keefe, Roger, *The Protection of Cultural Property in Armed Conflict* (Cambridge University Press, 2006)
Palmer, Norman, 'Fetters and Stumbling Blocks: Impediments to the Recovery and Return of Unlawfully Removed Cultural Objects—A Common Law Perspective' in Lyndel. V. Prott. (ed), *Realising Cultural Heritage Law: Festschrift for Patrick O'Keefe* (Institute for Art and Law, 2012) 97
Poulos, Anthi Helleni, 'The 1954 Hague Convention for the Protection of Cultural Property in the Event of Armed Conflict: An Historic Analysis' (2000) 28(1) *International Journal of Legal Information* 1
Prott, Lyndel, 'Problems of Private International Law for the Protection of the Cultural Heirtage' in Hague Academy of International Law (ed), *Collected Courses of the Hague Academy of International Law* (Nijhoff, 1989) 215
Schindler, Dietrich and Jiri Toman, *The Laws of Armed Conflicts: A Collection of Conventions, Resolutions, and Other Documents* (Martinus Nijhoff Publishers, 2004)
Second Historical Archives, *A Collective Documents about the Republic of China, Volume 3, Culture* (Jiangsu Phoenix House, 1999)
Spence, Jonathan D., *The Search for Modern China* (W.W. Norton & Company, 2013)
Staunton, George Thomas, *Ta Tsing Leu Lee: Being the Fundamental Laws, and a Selection from the Supplementary Statutes, of the Penal Code of China* (Cambridge University Press, 2012)
Toman, Jiri, 'The Hague Convention—A Decisive Step Taken by the International Community' (2005) 57(4) *Museum International* 7
Vattel, Emer de, Bela Kapossy and Richard Whatmore, *The law of Nations* (Liberty Fund, 2008)
Wang, Xi and Frederic Wakeman, *China's Quest for Modernization: A Historical Perspective* (Institute of East Asian Studies, University of California, Berkeley, 1997)
Wang, Yanping and John W. Head, *Law Codes in Dynastic China: A Synopsis of Chinese Legal History in the Thirty Centuries from Zhou to Qing* (Carolina Academic Press, 2005)
Woolsey, L. H., 'The Forced Transfer of Property in Enemy Occupied Territories' (1943) 37(2) *The American Journal of International Law* 282
Zhangsun, Wuji, *Tang Lü Shu Yi* (Taiwan shang wu yin shu guan, 1965)

Zhong, Hui, 'Can Chinese Individuals Request the Restitution of Chinese Cultural Relics in Japan?: A Revisit under International Law' (2017) 10(1) *Journal of East Asia & International Law* 179

Zhong, Hui, 'Legal Protection of Chinese Cultural Relics: A Justification for the Return' (2015) XX(1) *Art Antiquity and Law* 47

Zhu, Qingqi, Derk Bodde and Clarence Morris, *Law in Imperial China: Exemplified by 190 Ch'ing Dynasty Cases* (Harvard University Press, 1967)

4 Customary International Law

1. Introduction

This book argues that a new customary rule is emerging, which requires the interests of the states of origin to be prioritised in regards their wrongfully removed heritage. This proposed customary rule supports the return of historically removed heritage. However, there is a considerable academic debate as to whether and when a rule could be viewed as a new customary rule.[1] Although this chapter does not aim to resolve this debate, certain questions still need to be raised and answered, such as: what is necessary for a new rule to be established? What evidence constitutes state practice? Regarding the quantity of state practice, how much and how long should it have been established? How is it determined that the performance of a state is the result of legal obligation not merely courtesy? How does the persistent objector doctrine affect this rule? Through answering these questions, this chapter provides a brief introduction to the creation of customary law.

This chapter starts with a brief introduction to customary international law. It then moves on to analyse the two elements of customary law: state practice and *opinio juris*. With regards to state practice, this chapter argues that the creation of a new customary rule depends on the practice of the "specially affected states". It is essential that the states whose interests are specially affected by the proposed customary rule should be in favour of the creation of this rule. The types of materials and evidence that constitute state behaviour

1 Malcolm N. Shaw, *International Law* (Cambridge University Press, 2014); Ian Brownlie and James Crawford, *Brownlie's Principles of Public International Law* (Oxford University Press, 2012); Brian D. Lepard, *Customary International Law: A New Theory with Practical Applications* (Cambridge University Press, 2010); Michael Akehurst, *A Modern Introduction to International Law* (Allen and Unwin, 1987); Anthony A. D'Amato, *The Concept of Custom in International Law* (Cornell University Press, 1971); Karol Wolfke, *Custom in Present International Law* (Martinus Nijhoff Publishers, 1993); Jorg Kammerhofer, 'Uncertainty in the Formal Sources of International Law: Customary International Law and Some of Its Problems' (2004) 15(3) *European Journal of International Law* 523; Eric Heinze and Malgosia Fitzmaurice, *Landmark Cases in Public International Law* (Kluwer Law International, 1998).

will also be analysed. In respect to *opinio juris*, this chapter argues that it is not necessary to demonstrate the existence of *opinio juris* before a customary rule can be established. This chapter concludes that the most crucial factor in creating the proposed customary rule is the concurrence of specially affected states in the field of removal and return of cultural heritage.

2. An Important Source of International Law

Customary law is traditionally recognised as one of the most important sources of international law, along with international conventions, general principles of law recognised by civilized nations and, as subsidiary means, judicial decisions and the teachings of highly qualified publicists. The classical definition of custom appears in Article 38(1) of the Statute of the International Court of Justice (ICJ): "international custom, as evidence of a general practice accepted as law". However, customary law is never free of controversy. Because its creation is mysterious and slow in accommodating the evolution of international law, some scholars deny that customary law can be a significant source.[2] Other writers suggest that customary law should be abandoned or at least redefined, because it is too difficult to determine its existence.[3]

Despite assertions of its diminishing value, customary law helps to resolve disputes. The ICJ and its predecessor, the Permanent Court of International Justice (PCIJ), have held or suggested a vast array of norms, which have now entered the realm of customary law.[4] In the realm of international humanitarian law, many judgements by the ICJ have concluded that essential norms governing the use of force in armed conflicts have attained the status of customary law.[5] Similarly, many crimes under international law are defined primarily by customary law.[6] In regards to cultural heritage protection, the ICRC Custom-

2 Ingrid Doimi di Delupis, *The Concept of International Law* (Norstedts, 1987), 112–116; W. Friedmann, *The Changing Structure of International Law* (Stevens, 1964), 121–123.

3 Hilary C. M. Charlesworth, 'Customary international law and the Nicaragua case' (1991) 11 *Australian Yearbook of International Law* 1,1; N. C. H. Dunbar, 'The Myth of Customary International Law' (1978) 8 *Australian Year Book of International Law* 1, 18–19; J. Patrick Kelly, 'The Twilight of Customary International Law' (2000) 40(2) *Virginia Journal of International Law* 449, 540.

4 Lepard, *CIL: A New Theory,* above n 1, 4–6.

5 These norms include a general prohibition of the use of non-defensive force by one state against another (see, e.g., *Nicaragua Case*, 1986 ICJ Rep 14, 98–101, paras 187–190; *Wall Advisory Opinion*, 2004 ICJ Rep 136, 171, para. 87), states' right of self-defence against armed attacks by other states (see *Nicaragua Case*, 1986 ICJ Rep 14, 94, para. 176 holding that the "right of self-defence" is "of a customary nature"), and a principle resolving disputes between states peacefully (see *Nicaragua Case*, 1986 ICJ Rep 14, 145, para. 290 (affirming that the "principle that the parties to any dispute . . . should seek a solution by peaceful means" has the status of customary law).

6 Jean-Marie Henckaerts and Louise Doswald-Beck, *Customary International Humanitarian Law, Volume 1* (Cambridge University Press, 2005); Antonio Cassese, *International Criminal Law* (Oxford University Press, 2008), 17–20.

ary Law Study found the following rules regarding cultural heritage to be customary:

> Rule 38. Each party to the conflict must respect cultural property:
>
> A. Special care must be taken in military operations to avoid damage to buildings dedicated to religion, art, science, education or charitable purposes and historic monuments unless they are military objectives.
> B. Property of great importance to the cultural heritage of every people must not be the object of attack unless imperatively by military necessity.[7]
>
> Rule 39. The use of property of great importance to the cultural heritage of every people for purposes which are likely to expose it to destruction or damage is prohibited, unless imperatively required by military necessity.[8]
>
> Rule 40. Each party to the conflict must protect cultural property:
>
> A. All seizure of or destruction or wilful damage done to institutions dedicated to religion, charity, education, the arts and sciences, historic monuments and works of art and science is prohibited.
> B. Any form of theft, pillage or misappropriation of, and any acts of vandalism directed against, property of great importance to the cultural heritage of every people is prohibited.[9]

In addition, customary law has played an important role in developing treaty law. It is clear that differences exist between treaty law and customary law. Treaties are written conventions and bind only those states that have expressed their consent to uphold them, usually through ratification.[10] By contrast, customary law is unwritten and binds states generally whether or not they have formally consented to the rules. Unlike the explicit agreement in treaties, a state could only persistently object to a customary rule in the process of formation. However, despite the difference, the distinction is not that strict: customary law can be embodied in a treaty, or treaty provisions may become customary law.[11] More importantly, once a treaty is recognised as customary,

7 Henckaerts and Doswald-Beck, *Customary Rule (Volume 1),* above n 6, 127–130.
8 Ibid, 131–132.
9 Ibid, 132–135.
10 Bing Bing Jia, 'The Relations between Treaties and Custom' (2010) 9(1) *Chinese Journal of International Law* 81.
11 See *Continental Shelf Case (Libya v Malta)*, 1985 ICJ Rep 13, 29–30, para. 27 (holding that "multilateral conventions may have an important role to play in recording and defining rules deriving from custom or indeed in developing them"); *Nicaragua Case*, 1986 ICJ Rep 14, 95, paras 187–190 (holding that customary law is an extremely important and separate source, "even if two norms belonging to two sources of international law

it is binding on all states, irrespective of their participation in the treaty. All states have to ensure that a contemplated course of conduct is consistent with their international legal obligation, even though a state may argue that it has not signed and ratified the convention. For example, at the Nuremberg War Crimes Trial, the belligerents in the Second World War argued that they were not party to the Hague Convention 1907 and therefore not legally bound. However, the court decided that the Hague Convention 1907 is customary and thus binding on all states. Therefore, customary law is an important source of international law.

However, before a customary rule exists, it first needs to be created. It is generally agreed that the existence of a customary rule requires two elements: state practice and *opinio juris*. In order to create a new rule of customary law, it is necessary to demonstrate that, first, there is sufficient and uniform state practice and, second, there is a belief, *opinio juris*, that this practice is rendered obligatory because it is required by a rule of law. In the 1969 *North Sea Continental Shelf* case, the ICJ confirmed these two elements by stating that "not only must the acts concerned amount to a settled practice, but they must also be such, or be carried out in such a way, as to be evidence of a belief that this practice is rendered obligatory by the existence of a rule of law requiring it".[12] The following section explores how state practice and *opinio juris* can be used to create the proposed customary law for the return of historically removed heritage.[13]

3. State Practice

State practice, described as the objective or material element, lies at the centre of the formation of customary law. There are numerous points to consider concerning the nature of a particular state practice, including its duration, consistency, repetition, and generality. Although some time will normally elapse

---

appear identical in content, and even if the states in question are bound by these rules both on the level of treaty law and on that of customary international law").

12 *North Sea Continental Shelf Cases,* 1969 ICJ Rep 43, para. 74. See also, e.g., *Continental Shelf Case (Libya v Malta)*, 1985 ICJ Rep 13, 29–30, para. 27 (holding that customary international law must be "looked for primarily in the actual practice and *opinio juris* of States").

13 However, the relationship between state practice and *opinio juris* has been disputed by different writers, basically according to whether the theoretical approaches favour either the element of state practice or the requirement of *opinio juris*, or both or neither. The two main philosophical concepts of international law are naturalism and positivism. However, from the 20th century onward opinions have diversified, and one can further identify realist thoughts advanced by the New Haven School of International Law, or the so-called New Approaches to International Law, which encompass, for example, critical Legal Studies theory. Birgit Schlütter, *Developments in Customary International Law: Theory and the Practice of the International Court of Justice and the International ad HOC Criminal Tribunals for Rwanda and Yugoslavia* (Martinus Nijhoff Publishers, 2010), 15–70; Wilfrid E. Rumble John Austin, *Austin: The Province of Jurisprudence Determined* (Cambridge University Press, 1995).

before there is sufficient practice to satisfy these criteria, no precise amount of time is required. The essence of custom is the concurrence of specially affected states in that particular field. States whose interests will be affected by the proposed new rule should support its creation.

3.1. Uniform State Practice

Theoretically, state practice is supposed to be general in the sense that it is practised by all or almost of all the states of the world. But in practice, it is impossible to achieve complete uniformity in the international community. With regards to consistency or uniformity, it should be noted that while a new rule does not need to be entirely accepted worldwide, a sufficient quantity of state practice is required before determining a rule to be a customary rule.

The requirement of uniform state practice is emphasised in numerous court decisions investigating whether a norm rises to the level of customary international law.[14] In the *North Sea Continental Shelf* case, the ICJ ruled that "virtually uniform" state practice was required. The reason for applying such strict formula in this case is because the equidistance rule argued for by the Netherlands and Denmark involved the transformation into custom of a treaty provision that altered existing customary international law, and because of the short period in which it was asserted that the principle had been generated.[15] But in other court decisions, it is clearly suggested that the qualification of virtually uniform is not a question of repetition of identical conduct, but only of similar conduct. In the *Fisheries* case, the ICJ was presented with a situation regarding a ten-mile closing line for bays. The court reaffirmed that uniformity among the states is required before a customary rule could come into existence:

> The Court deems it necessary to point out that although the ten-mile rule has been adopted by certain States both in their national law and in their treaties and conventions, and although certain arbitral decisions have applied it as between these States, other States have adopted a different limit. Consequently, the ten-mile rule has not acquired the authority of a general rule of international law.[16]

In addition, the court held that minor inconsistencies do not prevent the creation of a customary rule, after considering that "too much importance need not be attached to a few uncertainties or contradictions, real or apparent" in a state's practice when making an evaluation.[17] In other words, it is

14 See, e.g., *Asylum Case (Colombia v Peru)*, 1950 ICJ Rep 266, 277–278 (holding that the practice was not sufficiently uniform to establish a regional customary law allowing a host state to qualify political offences for the purpose of diplomatic asylum).

15 Charlesworth, *CIL and the Nicaragua case*, above n 3, 7.

16 *Fisheries Case (UK v Norway)*, 1951 ICJ Rep 116, 131.

17 *Fisheries Case (UK v Norway)*, 1951 ICJ Rep 116, 138.

enough for the practices to be sufficiently similar. Likewise, in the *Continental Shelf* cases, the ICJ ruled that although the various proclamations of such a zone were not identical, they were sufficiently similar for the court to reach this conclusion. Thus, the concept of the exclusive economic zone has become part of customary law.[18] Contrary practice, at first sight, appears to undermine the uniformity of the practice concerned.[19] However, if this contrary practice is condemned by other states or denied by the government itself, this practice tends to reinforce, not weaken, the existence of the rule. Through such condemnation or denial, the projected customary rule is actually confirmed. In summary, uniformity is not a question of repetition of identical conduct, but only of similar conduct.[20]

3.2. Specially Affected States

However, it is still unclear how to define the uniformity of state practice, as no one can delimit the quantity of states or put a precise figure on the extent of participation needed to create a new customary rule. The debate is whether the practices of some states should be given more emphasis than others or if all states should be treated equally. Based on the principle of state equality, every state is entitled to be considered equal in value to other states.[21] A contrary view is that the practice of more powerful states ought to be given greater weight in determining the existence of a new customary rule, since more powerful states have greater opportunities to influence the development of customary law.[22]

Despite differing opinions, there is increasing agreement that a proposed new customary rule should be widely accepted by those states directly involved in the relevant activities. In the *North Sea Continental Shelf* cases, the ICJ remarked that state practice, particularly that of states whose interests are "specially affected", had to be "both extensive and virtually uniform in the sense of provision invoked".[23] That is to say, it is not simply a question of how many states support the creation, but also *which* states.[24] This consideration

18 *Continental Shelf Case (Libya v Malta)*, 1985 ICJ Rep 13, 33, para. 34 (holding that the institution of the exclusive economic zone "is shown by the practice of States to have become a part of customary law").

19 Henckaerts and Doswald-Beck, *Customary Rule (Volume 1)*, above n 6, xliii.

20 H. Meijers, 'How is International Law Made?—The Stages of Growth of International Law and the Use of its Customary Rules' (1978) 9 *Netherlands Yearbook of International Law* 3, 14.

21 Georg Schwarzenberger, *International Law: As Applied by International Courts and Tribunals* (Stevens, 1957), 35.

22 Michael Byers, *Custom, Power and the Power of Rules: International Relations and Customary International Law* (Cambridge University Press, 1999), 37.

23 *North Sea Continental Shelf Cases*, 1969 ICJ Rep 43, para. 74.

24 International Committee of the Red Cross, 'Assessment of Customary International Law' <https://ihl-databases.icrc.org/customary-ihl/eng/docs/v1_rul_in_asofcuin>; Henckaerts and Doswald-Beck, *Customary Rule (Volume 1)*, above n 6, xliv.

has two implications: first, a new, proposed customary rule does not need to be accepted worldwide, but it must be accepted by the states whose interests are specially affected. For example, in the *Legality of Nuclear Weapons* case, the ICJ made its decision by referring to the practice of certain nuclear-weapon states, not to the practice of the entire international community.[25] Similarly, in the *Asylum* case, a regional or local customary rule was addressed, and the ICJ decided that while

> the issue involved here dealt with a regional custom pertaining only to Latin America and it may be argued that the same approach need not necessarily be followed where a general custom is alleged . . . the Columbian Government must prove that the rule invoked by it is in accordance with a constant and uniform usage practiced by the states in question.[26]

In other words, while the practice does not need be to worldwide, the states whose interests will be specially affected should reflect a consistent and uniform agreement of the proposed rule.

Second, if specially affected states do not accept the new rule, it cannot be recognised as a rule of customary international law. What is implied is that the absence or contradiction of practice by other states does not prevent the creation of a new customary rule. But if several specially affected states join each other in opposing the emergence of a new customary rule, the rule would not be created even if is otherwise extensively supported.[27] The criterion for the creation of a new customary rule depends not on a precise number or percentage of states, but on the degree of representativeness of the practice.[28] The states whose interests are specially affected should be in favour of creating the proposed new rule as a customary rule.[29]

Deciding who is specially affected varies according to specific circumstances.[30] With respect to any rule of international humanitarian law, countries that participated in an armed conflict are specially affected. In the area of humanitarian aid, states whose population requires aid and states that frequently provide aid are considered specially affected. For the proposed customary rule in this book, specially affected states include two different groups: first, the current possessing states, including the UK, the US, France, Japan, Germany, and Switzerland. These states usually have large

25 *Nuclear Weapons Advisory Opinion*, 1996 ICJ Rep 226, 263 (holding that "Nor can [the Court] ignore that practice referred to as 'policy of deterrence', to which an appreciable section of the international community adhered for many years.") Peter Malanczuk and Michael Barton Akehurst, *Akehurst's Modern Introduction to International Law* (Routledge, 1997), 42.

26 *Asylum Case (Colombia v Peru)*, 1950 ICJ Rep 266, paras 276–277.

27 Kammerhofer, *Uncertainty in Formal Sources,* above n 1, 290.

28 Henckaerts and Doswald-Beck, *Customary Rule (Volume 1),* above n 6, xxxviii.

29 Shaw, *International Law,* above n 1, 57.

30 *Assessment of CIL,* above n 24.

collections of foreign cultural heritage, but are reluctant to return these items to the states of origin. The second group is the opposite side, and includes China, Cambodia, Egypt, Greece, Italy, Turkey, South Korea, and Peru. These states, referred to as states of origin, are rich in cultural heritage, but also victims of removals that occurred during the periods of colonialism or imperialism, and/or the ongoing illicit trafficking of stolen and smuggled cultural heritage. To argue for the proposed customary rule, the crucial factor is the concurrence of specially affected states in the field of removal and return of cultural heritage. The states of origin may propose ideas and exert pressure but, without the agreement of the possessing states, it cannot amount to a customary rule.

However, although special attention is given to the practice of these specially affected states, it does not mean practice of other less affected states is not relevant. Based on the assumption that the new rule exists, the proposed customary rule that this book is discussing can be applied to all states, rather than limited to a regional area or a few particular states. The performance of states outside the scope of specially affected states discussed above should also be taken into account, but with less importance.

3.3. Evidence of State Practice

While the most crucial factor is the concurrence of specially affected states, it is unclear what types of state action count as state practice. Anthony D'Amato rejects claims or statements as the material component of custom due to its weak predictive power: "a claim is not an act . . . for a state has not done anything when it makes a claim; until it takes enforcement action, the claim has little value as a prediction of what the state will actually do".[31] In his opinion, the crucial material component is "what [the] state would actual do". Michael Akehurst; however, argues that if state practice only consists of what states do, it would be too restrictive, especially if a state is forbidden from performing certain acts.[32] To determine what type of material should be considered, this book adopts the opinion that any evidence that can reflect the performance of a state or indicate what states will do in practice should be considered as constituent elements of state practice. In this regard, Ian Brownlie provides a list of the material sources for customary law:

> Diplomatic correspondence, policy statements, press releases, the opinions of official legal advisers, official manuals on legal questions, e.g. manuals of military law, executive decisions and practices, orders to naval forces etc., comments by governments on drafts produced by the International Law Commission, state legislation, international and national

31 D'Amato, *Concept of CIL,* above n 1, 88.
32 Malanczuk and Akehurst, *Akehurst's Modern Introduction,* above n 25, 28.

> judicial decisions, recitals in treaties and other international instruments, a pattern of treaties in the same form, the practice of international organs, and resolutions relating to legal questions in the United Nations General Assembly.[33]

Thus, any type of evidence, not merely physical acts of state, but also claims, declarations, national laws, and judgments, should be considered. In this regard, three further aspects necessitate clarification. First, it should be noted that what makes return legally complex is that it lies at the interface of a number of distinct branches of law: public international law, private international law, cultural heritage law, and national laws (such as criminal law, property law, and contract law). These legal areas are quite different in nature, but form the basis for supporting the return of illegally removed heritage. Thus, this book examines different branches of law in specially affected states, which can be considered as relevant evidence for the formation of customary rules.

Second, recovery disputes are important materials, as they suggest whether the existing international or national legal system is sufficient in resolving cultural disputes, and how law can play a better role in the future. To argue for the proposed customary rule, recovery disputes actually contain a wide scope: settled or unsettled; and resolved by the court or outside the court through other means, such negotiation, arbitration, or mediation. In addition, not only the result of each case, but also the opinions expressed by the judges, the response from each party, and the impact on the future development of law and practice, are relevant in creating the proposed customary rule. These materials contribute to either supporting or objecting to the creation of the proposed customary rule.

Third, any state consists of government departments and individuals who are office-holders within government institutions, for example, legislative institutions, courts, diplomatic agents, state's legal officers, and political leaders.[34] They determine, enunciate and carry out the policy decisions ascribed to the state and thus, exert influence on the process of law making. Therefore, any acts and statements by government entities or individuals should also be taken into consideration.

3.4. Time Requirement

Although some time will normally elapse before there is sufficient practice to satisfy the criteria for customary law, no precise amount of time is required. International courts do not emphasise the time element in determining the existence of a new customary rule. For example, in the *North Sea Continental Shelf* cases, the ICJ decided that "the passage of only a short period of time

33 Brownlie and Crawford, *Brownlie's Principles,* above n 1, 6–7.
34 Shaw, *International Law,* above n 1, 58.

was not necessarily a bar to the formation of a new rule of customary international law", as long as the state practice is extensive and virtually uniform.[35] In other words, the court placed more weight on the uniformity of state practice than the duration. A short period can be balanced by the generality and consistency of state practice.

In fact, in certain particular circumstances such as continental shelf and airspace, a customary rule has emerged from fairly quick maturation of practice.[36] Decisions depend on the specific situation and the nature of the practice in question. A new rule may quickly come into existence even on the basis of one particular act of practice, if supported by general acceptance as law.[37] A long period of state practice is not necessary. As commented by Malcolm Shaw, the duration and generality of a practice may be less important than the states favouring the formation of a new customary rule in any given field.[38]

4. *Opinio Juris*

To create a new customary rule, it is important that states view their behaviours as an aspect of legality.[39] If such behaviour is motivated only by courtesy, convenience or tradition, but not a sense of legal duty, the state practice only remains a practice.[40] However, the problem is the burden of proof. The idea of *opinio juris* is mysterious because it refers to an attitude that states have toward a behavioural regularity.[41] It needs to distinguish behaviour motivated by law from behaviour undertaken because of other reasons, from ideological support to political concern. In this regard, although independent evidence was suggested, such as a statement made by a high-level official, the ratification of a treaty that contains a norm similar to the customary law in question, or an attitude of approval toward a General Assembly resolution, questions still exist as the application for using such evidence is unsettled.[42] More questionably, if it calls for behaviour in accordance with law, how can a new customary rule be

35 *North Sea Continental Shelf Cases,* 1969 ICJ Rep 43, para. 74.
36 Brownlie and Crawford, *Brownlie's Principles,* above n 1, 7.
37 Matthias Weller, 'Immunity For Artworks on Loan? A Review of International Customary Law and Municipal Anti-Seizure Statutes in Light of the Liechtenstein Litigation' (2005) 38(4) *Vanderbilt Journal of Transnational Law* 997, 1006.
38 Shaw, *International Law,* above n 1, 57.
39 See, e.g., *North Sea Continental Shelf Cases,* 1969 ICJ Rep 43, para. 74 (holding that "state practice . . . should have been both extensive and virtually uniform . . . and should moreover have occurred in such a way as to show a general recognition that a rule of law or legal obligation is involved"); *SS "Lotus" Case,* 1927 PCIJ 28 (holding that "only if such abstention were based on their being conscious of a duty", it would not amount to a custom).
40 Brownlie and Crawford, *Brownlie's Principles,* above n 1, 8.
41 Jack L. Goldsmith and Eric A. Posner, *The Limits of International Law* (Oxford University Press, 2005), 24.
42 Ibid, 24.

created since that obviously requires action different from or contrary to what until then is regarded as law.[43]

With regards to *opinio juris*, Malcolm Shaw argues, correctly in my view, that

> one has to treat the matter in terms of a process whereby states behave in a certain way in the belief that such behaviour is law or is becoming law. It will then depend upon how other states react as to whether this process of legislation is accepted or rejected.[44]

It is assumed that a state acts in the belief that it is in accordance with the law or the action contains the beginnings of a new law. If other states follow, it is vindicated and a new rule of customary law is established. If other states reject the proposition, then the projected rule cannot be recognised as a new customary rule and the original rule stands, reinforced by state practice and common acceptance. Thus, it is not necessary to demonstrate the existence of the subjective element before a customary rule can be established.[45]

It should be summarised that the tendency is not to look for direct evidence of a state's psychological convictions, but to infer *opinio juris* indirectly from the actual behaviour of states.[46] The reasons are multifaceted: first, it is difficult to strictly separate state practice and legal conviction, since an act can reflect both practice and legal conviction in some situations.[47] As the International Law Association has pointed out, the ICJ

> has not in fact said in so many words that just because there are (allegedly) distinct elements in customary law the same conduct cannot manifest both. It is in fact often difficult or even impossible to disentangle the two elements.[48]

Second, there is a clear tendency that both international and national courts have focused more on the uniform state practice in investigating whether a norm rises to the level of customary international law.[49] They do not always put

43 Shaw, *International Law*, above n 1, 62.
44 Ibid, 87.
45 Lepard, *CIL: A New Theory*, above n 1, 24.
46 Malanczuk and Akehurst, *Akehurst's Modern Introduction*, above n 25, 44.
47 This is particularly true when involving verbal acts, such as military manuals, which should be viewed as state practice and also reflect the legal conviction of the state involved at the same time. Jean-Marie Henckaerts, 'Study on Customary International Humanitarian Law: A Contribution to the Understanding and Respect for the Rule of Law in Armed Conflict' (2005) 87(857) *International Review of the Red Cross* 175, 182; Internaitonal Law Association, 'Formation of Customary (General) International Law' <www.ila-hq.org/en/committees/index.cfm/cid/30>.
48 Henckaerts, *Study on Customary International Humanitarian Law*, above n 47, xxxiii.
49 See also, e.g., *Fisheries Case (UK v Norway)*, 1951 ICJ Rep 116; *Barcelona Traction, Light and Power Company, Limited, case (Belgium v Spain)*, 1970 ICJ Rep 3; *Polyukhovich v Commonwealth ("War Crimes Act Case")*, [1991] HCA32 (14 August 1991),

as much emphasis on the element of *opinio juris*, but sometimes simply refer to the practice of states, without any reference to the subjective element.[50] In fact, in the ICJ's Advisory Opinion regarding the *Legality of Nuclear Weapons*, the court admitted that if states are clearly divided on whether a certain conduct constitutes the expression of the *opinio juris*, then it is impossible to find evidence of *opinio juris*:

> the members of the international community are profoundly divided on the matter of whether non-recourse to nuclear weapons over the past 50 years constitutes the expression of an *opinio juris*. Under these circumstances, the Court does not consider itself able to find that there is such *opinio juris*.[51]

Third, even if evidence of *opinio juris* is nevertheless required, uniform practice is the best evidence.[52] In the *North Sea Continental Shelf* case, the court held that "the general practice of states should be recognized as prima facie evidence that it is accepted as law".[53] Therefore, the idea of *opinio juris* is really a conclusion about a practice's status as international law.[54]

Opinio juris plays an important role in situations where the practice is ambiguous, in order to decide whether or not that practice counts towards the formation of custom. This is often the case with omissions, when states fail to act or react with unclear intentions. A related question is whether silence or omission constitutes state practice. As remarked in the *Gulf of Maine* case, silence was clearly defined as "equivalent to tacit recognition manifested by unilateral conduct which the other party may interpret as consent" and founded upon the principles of good faith and equity.[55] When states fail to protest the behaviour of other states, it may be an indication that such behaviour is accepted as legitimate. A failure to act or react can create obligations for the silent states and thus, should be viewed as relevant practice.[56] However, in the *Lotus* case, the court held that "only if such abstention were based on their (the states) being conscious of having a duty to abstain would it be possible to speak of

---

para. 28 (holding that affirmed that "an *opinio juris* supportive of a postulated rule of customary international law must explain and inform the practice of States in order to show that that practice is 'accepted as law' ").

50 Nout van Woudenberg, *State Immunity and Cultural Objects on Loan* (Martinus Nijhoff Publishers, 2012), 45.

51 *Nuclear Weapons Advisory Opinion*, 1996 ICJ Rep 226, 254–255, para. 70.

52 Lepard, *CIL: A New Theory*, above n 1, 24.

53 *North Sea Continental Shelf Cases*, Dissenting Opinion of Judge Lachs, 1969 ICJ Rep 219, 231

54 Goldsmith and Posner, *Limits of International Law*, above n 41, 24.

55 ICJ, *Delimitation of the Maritime Boundary in the Gulf of Maine Area (Canada v United States of America)*, Judgment, October 12 1984, 1984 ICJ Rep 305.

56 Wolfke, *Custom in Present International Law*, above n 1, 61; Michael Akehurst, 'Custom as a Source of International Law' (1975) 47(1) *British Yearbook of International Law* 1, 10.

an international custom".[57] This means that a rule prohibiting certain actions cannot be inferred merely because states do not participate in that activity.[58] This decision asserts a cap in the discussion of silences being viewed as state practice, because except for tacit agreement, silence may also stem from lack of time or lack of an interest.[59]

5. Dissenting States

A customary rule binds all states, even if the state did not participate in the rule's creation. However, this should not be confused with a persistent objector.[60] A state may be exempt from the customary rule if it has persistently objected to that rule in the formation period.[61] The persistent objector rule only applies when the rule of custom is still emerging. A dissenting state needs to unequivocally and consistently refuse to accept the rule. Evidence of objects must be clear, and repeated as often as circumstances require because there is a presumption of acceptance that needs to be rebutted.[62] It is worth noting that if several specially affected states join each other in opposing the emergence of a new customary rule, the rule would not be created even if it is otherwise extensively supported.[63]

Additionally, some scholars argue that persistent objector should be abandoned from international law making. First, there is no clear clarification or explanation regarding the application for this exception or its boundaries.[64] Second, there is a lack of actual examples of states claiming to object persistently to a putative customary rule.[65] Only in two cases, the *Asylum* case and the *Fisheries* case, has the ICJ indirectly mentioned the persistent objector, and in both cases the Court did not conclude that any customary rule already existed. In the *Fisheries* case, the ICJ held that any ten-mile rule

57 In the *Lotus* case, France disputed Turkey's right to prosecute for a collision on the high seas. France argued that the absence of such prosecutions proved a prohibition under customary international law to prosecute, except by the flag state of the ship on board that the wrongful act took place. The court, however, disagreed because it was not clear whether other states had abstained from prosecuting because they thought they had no right to do so or because of some other reason, for example, lack of interest or belief that a court of the flag state is a more convenient forum. *SS "Lotus" Case*, 1927 PCIJ 28.
58 Shaw, *International Law*, above n 1, 64.
59 Brownlie and Crawford, *Brownlie's Principles*, above n 1, 8; Woudenberg, *State Immunity*, above n 50, 45.
60 Shaw, *International Law*, above n 1, 64–65.
61 Ted L. Stein, 'The Approach of the Different Drummer: The Principle of the Persistent Objector in International Law' (1985) 26(2) *Harvard International Law Journal* 457; David A. Colson, 'How Persistent Must the Persistent Objector Be?' (1986) 61(3) *Washington Law Review* 957.
62 Woudenberg, *State Immunity*, above n 50, 45.
63 Kammerhofer, *Uncertainty in Formal Sources*, above n 1, 290.
64 Lepard, *CIL: A New Theory*, above n 1, 37.
65 Stein, *Persistent Objector*, above n 61, 458–463.

concerning the closure of bays, even if it existed in customary international law, "would appear to be inapplicable as against Norway inasmuch as she had always opposed any attempt to apply it to the Norwegian coast".[66] Thus, due to the ambiguity and uncertainty, scholars such as Jonathan Charney have argued that "the persistent objector rule has no legitimate basis in the international legal system".[67] The persistent objector may play a more important role in the future, but greatly depends on the specific circumstances of each case. This chapter does not aim to resolve the debate whether the persistent objector should be abandoned in the process of law-making, but will discuss when specially affected states clearly oppose the creation of the proposed customary rule.

6. Conclusion

While a new customary rule does not require worldwide acceptance, it has to be endorsed by the states whose interests will be affected by the proposed customary rule. For the proposed customary rule regarding the return of cultural heritage, the most important condition is that specially affected states, particularly the current possessing or market states, should be in favour of recognising states of origin's interests in their historically removed heritage and supporting the return of such items. Thus, the central question at the basis of this research is whether there is increasing recognition of states of origin's interests.

In practice, throughout the world in the past two decades, an increasing number of cultural heritage objects have been returned to the states of origin by governments, museums, and individuals. In particular, many claims that had been largely unsuccessful in the late 20th century have now been successfully negotiated and settled. On one hand, it should be admitted that the fundamental reason for the successful repatriation is that the states of origin generally have a legal basis and strong evidence to convince the courts that the disputed objects were illegally removed. On the other hand, these returning cases are important evidence in respect to states of origin's interests in their wrongfully taken heritage. Thus, the crux of this research is to link the return of illegally taken heritage to historically removed heritage. In this regard, the increasing recognition of the interests of states of origin in regard to their wrongfully taken cultural heritage is the bridge between illegally removed heritage and historically removed heritage.

The following two chapters will examine the return of two types of illegally removed heritage: first, the return of heritage looted during armed conflicts; and, second, return of stolen and illegally exported heritage. These two types of removals are known as the two the main causes of the impoverishment of

66 *Fisheries Case (UK v Norway)*, 1951 ICJ Rep 116, 131.

67 JI Charney, 'The Persistent Objector Rule and the Development of Customary International Law' (1985) 56(1) *British Yearbook of International Law* 1, 21.

the countries of origin of such property. While examining the law and returning cases in each specially affected state, this book also aims to answer the question as to whether there is increasing recognition of states of origin's interests in their wrongfully taken heritage. This recognition is significant in not only illegally taken heritage and historically removed heritage, but also supporting the creation of the proposed customary rule.

Bibliography

'Assessment of Customary International Law' (International Committee of the Red Cross <https://ihl-databases.icrc.org/customary-ihl/eng/docs/v1_rul_in_asofcuin>

Akehurst, Michael, 'Custom as a Source of International Law' (1975) 47(1) *British Yearbook of International Law* 1

Akehurst, Michael, *A Modern Introduction to International Law* (Allen and Unwin, 1987)

Brownlie, Ian and James Crawford, *Brownlie's Principles of Public International Law* (Oxford University Press, 2012)

Byers, Michael, *Custom, Power and the Power of Rules: International Relations and Customary International Law* (Cambridge University Press, 1999)

Cassese, Antonio, *International Criminal Law* (Oxford University Press, 2008)

Charlesworth, Hilary C. M., 'Customary international law and the Nicaragua case' (1991) 11 *Australian Yearbook of International Law* 1

Charney, J. I., 'The Persistent Objector Rule and the Development of Customary International Law' (1985) 56(1) *British Yearbook of International Law* 1

Colson, David A., 'How Persistent Must the Persistent Objector Be?' (1986) 61(3) *Washington Law Review* 957

D'Amato, Anthony A., *The Concept of Custom in International Law* (Cornell University Press, 1971)

Doimi di Delupis, Ingrid, *The Concept of International Law* (Norstedts, 1987)

Dunbar, N. C. H., 'The Myth of Customary International Law' (1978) 8 *Australian Year Book of International Law* 1

Friedmann, W., *The Changing Structure of International Law* (Stevens, 1964)

Goldsmith, Jack L. and Eric A. Posner, *The Limits of International Law* (Oxford University Press, 2005)

Heinze, Eric and Malgosia Fitzmaurice, *Landmark Cases in Public International Law* (Kluwer Law International, 1998)

Henckaerts, Jean-Marie, 'Study on Customary International Humanitarian Law: A Contribution to the Understanding and Respect for the Rule of Law in Armed Conflict' (2005) 87(857) *International Review of the Red Cross* 175

Henckaerts, Jean-Marie and Louise Doswald-Beck, *Customary International Humanitarian Law, Volume 1* (Cambridge University Press, 2005)

ILA, 'Formation of Customary (General) International Law' (International Law Association, 2000) <www.ila-hq.org/en/committees/index.cfm/cid/30>

Jia, Bing Bing, 'The Relations between Treaties and Custom' (2010) 9(1) *Chinese Journal of International Law* 81

John Austin, Wilfrid E. Rumble, *Austin: The Province of Jurisprudence Determined* (Cambridge University Press, 1995)

Kammerhofer, Jorg, 'Uncertainty in the Formal Sources of International Law: Customary International Law and Some of Its Problems' (2004) 15(3) *European Journal of International Law* 523

Kelly, J. Patrick, 'The Twilight of Customary International Law' (2000) 40(2) *Virginia Journal of International Law* 449

Lepard, Brian D., *Customary International Law: A New Theory with Practical Applications* (Cambridge University Press, 2010)

Malanczuk, Peter and Michael Barton Akehurst, *Akehurst's Modern Introduction to International Law* (Routledge, 1997)

Meijers, H., 'How is International Law Made?—The Stages of Growth of International Law and the Use of its Customary Rules' (1978) 9 *Netherlands Yearbook of International Law* 3

Schlütter, Birgit, *Developments in Customary International Law: Theory and the Practice of the International Court of Justice and the International Ad Hoc Criminal Tribunals for Rwanda and Yugoslavia* (Martinus Nijhoff Publishers, 2010)

Schwarzenberger, Georg, *International Law: As Applied by International Courts and Tribunals* (Stevens, 1957)

Shaw, Malcolm N., *International Law* (Cambridge University Press, 2014)

Stein, Ted L., 'The Approach of the Different Drummer: The Principle of the Persistent Objector in International Law' (1985) 26(2) *Harvard International Law Journal* 457

Weller, Matthias, 'Immunity For Artworks on Loan? A Review of International Customary Law and Municipal Anti-Seizure Statutes in Light of the Liechtenstein Litigation' (2005) 38(4) *Vanderbilt Journal of Transnational Law* 997

Wolfke, Karol, *Custom in Present International Law* (Martinus Nijhoff Publishers, 1993)

Woudenberg, Nout van, *State Immunity and Cultural Objects on Loan* (Martinus Nijhoff Publishers, 2012)

5 Return of Cultural Heritage Looted during Armed Conflicts

1. Introduction

In ancient times, the rule of war decreed "to the victor go the spoils". The destruction and seizure of an enemy's property, including cultural objects, was an inevitable consequence of war.[1] At this stage, states of origin's interests in their wrongfully removed cultural heritage were completely overlooked. However, as the law of war has evolved, the rules regarding the treatment of cultural heritage during armed conflicts includes two dimensions: first, each party in the conflict must respect and protect cultural property. Any deliberate destruction of cultural objects that is not a military objective is widely regarded as unlawful and is condemned. The second dimension is that an occupying state not only needs to prohibit looting and illegal export of cultural property from an occupied state, but also needs to return such property after the end of the war.

These two progresses are significant in creating the proposed customary rule, but with different levels of value. With regards to the first dimension, states of origin can benefit as their heritage can be protected from destruction. But this protection is usually made on the consideration that "cultural heritage is of great importance for all peoples of the world" rather than just states of origin.[2] However, the second dimension provides strong evidence to support the creation of the proposed customary rule, not only because return is an indispensable part of seeking redress for the unlawful acts committed during wars, but also because it is a form of recognising the links between states of origin and their heritage. In this regard, it should be noted that the state practice of war repatriation has been consistent for a period of approximately 200 years.[3] It is clearly established that the requirements for an occupying power to prevent the illicit export of cultural heritage from occupied territory

1 Jiri Toman, 'The Hague Convention—A Decisive Step Taken by the International Community' (2005) 57(4) *Museum International* 7, 8.
2 Preamble of the 1954 Hague Convention.
3 Wayne Sandholtz, 'Plunder, Restitution, and International Law' (2010) 17(2) *International Journal of Cultural Property* 147, 168.

and return illicitly exported property to the competent authorities of the occupied territory have attained the status of customary law.[4]

Chapter 5 focuses on the state practice related to the return of cultural heritage looted during armed conflicts. The first part explores the early precedents and post-war settlements following the First World War (WWI) and the Second World War (WWII), which include the repatriation of cultural objects that were taken illegally during conflicts. The second part examines both international and national laws that contain clear legal obligations on wartime restitution. Lastly, this chapter analyses the international reactions to the recent regional conflicts in the Middle East. This chapter concludes that while the state practice of returning cultural heritage looted during armed conflicts is generally consistent and uniform, the unresolved issue of cultural heritage taken during WWII constitutes a deterrent to the uniformity of state practice. Despite the inconsistency, the state practice and evolving rules regarding the treatment of cultural objects during wars clearly reflect the respect and recognition being shown to countries of origin when their cultural heritage has been impacted by armed conflicts. This respect and recognition serves as an important premise in creating the proposed customary rule.

2. Early Precedents

Looking back through history, conquered property belonged to the victor. The significance of spoils of war is not limited to economic value, but is also concerned with the symbolic dimension of war, where the victors demonstrated their superiority over the vanquished.[5] However, starting from the 17th century, state practice can be found in which the international community began to condemn taking spoils during or at the close of armed conflicts.[6] As early as 1648, the Peace of Westphalia treaties contained previsions stipulating the return of cultural objects that had been seized during the Thirty Years War (1618–1648).[7] At the end of the 18th century, Sweden, in compliance with the treaty, returned 133 Bohemian archival records taken during the war.[8] During the military hostilities between the US and England in 1812, a shipment of paintings and prints bound from Italy to the Academy

4 Jean-Marie Henckaerts and Louise Doswald-Beck, *Customary International Humanitarian Law, Volume 1* (Cambridge University Press, 2005), 135.

5 Alessandro Chechi, *The Settlement of International Cultural Heritage Disputes* (Oxford University Press, 2014), 258.

6 For a general discussion, see Wayne Sandholtz, *Prohibiting Plunder: How Norms Change* (Oxford University Press, 2007), 69; Adam Roberts, *Documents on the Laws of War* (Oxford University Press, 2000), 53; Alwyn V. Freeman, 'General Note on the Law of War Booty' (1946) 40(4) *The American Journal of International Law* 795, 795–796; William Gerald Downey, 'Captured Enemy Property: Booty of War and Seized Enemy Property' (1950) 44(3) *The American Journal of International Law* 488, 488–489.

7 Article CXIV of the Treaty of Westphalia.

8 Toman, *A Decisive Step,* above n 1, 7.

of Arts in Philadelphia was seized by a British ship. Nearly 200 years ago, the judge ordered the return of the paintings as follows:

> The arts and sciences are admitted amongst all civilized nations as forming an exception to the severe rights of warfare, and as entitled to favour and protection. They are considered not as the peculium of this or of that nation, but as the property of mankind at large, and as belonging to the common interests of the whole species.[9]

During the Napoleonic Wars, Napoleon systematically removed art treasures from countries occupied by France.[10] After Waterloo, the Allies, including England, Austria, Spain, the German states, ordered the return of their stolen artworks "without any diplomatic negotiations", arguing that "systematic looting of art by a conquering army was contrary to principles of justice and to the rules of modern warfare".[11] However, France asserted that as a "right of conquest . . . has been admitted by all nations in all times", the art objects shall belong to France. In the end, the pro-restitution position prevailed. It was affirmed at the Congress of Vienna that there could be no right to conquest that would permit the French to retain the plundered art and that these cultural objects had to be returned. All of these early state practice examples not only reflect that art plundered as spoils of war was no longer universally accepted, but also laid the groundwork for the incorporation of these ideas in legally binding rules among states.[12]

3. Post-War Settlements Following WWI and WWII

Pursuant to the Hague Conventions 1899 and 1907, any seizure of cultural heritage as war booty is explicitly prohibited.[13] However, although Article 3 establishes that a belligerent party should be liable to pay compensation for any breaches of the Conventions, the Conventions do not expressly include an obligation for return. On the other hand, state practice in the aftermath of the two world wars confirms that the Hague Conventions can be used as a mechanism for states of origin to demand the return of cultural objects looted during armed conflicts.[14]

9 Sandholtz, *Prohibiting Plunder*, above n 6, 69.
10 M. Cherif Bassiouni, 'Reflections on Criminal Jurisdiction In International Protection of Cultural Property' (1983) 10(2) *Syracuse Journal of International Law and Commerce* 281, 288.
11 Sandholtz, *Plunder, Restitution, and International Law*, above n 3, 151.
12 Kifle Jote, *International Legal Protection of Cultural Heritage* (Juristforlaget, 1994), 43.
13 Articles 27 and 56 of the Hague Conventions 1899 and 1907.
14 Wojciech Kowalski, *Art Treasures and War: A Study on the Restitution of Looted Cultural Property Pursuant to Public International Law* (Art, Antiquity and Law, 1998), 77–87.

3.1. The First World War

The First World War witnessed widespread damage and destruction to cultural heritage, including the bombing of the Rheims Cathedral and the burning of the library at Louvain. All the peace treaties signed at the conclusion of WWI provided for the return of any cultural heritage unlawfully removed during the war from occupied states. With regards to the settlements with Germany, an extensive list of claims was issued by France and Belgium. Under the 1919 Treaty of Versailles, Germany had to hand over to France not only the "trophies, archives, historical souvenirs or works of art" removed during WWI, but also those taken in the Franco-Prussian War (1870–1871).[15] Further, the Treaty broadened these provisions via the inclusion of "restitution in kind" for lost or destroyed cultural heritage.[16] For the cultural losses in Belgium, Germany was obliged to furnish the University of Louvain with specific "manuscripts, incunabula, printed books, maps and objects of collection corresponding in number and value to those destroyed in the burning by Germany of the Library of Louvain".[17] Moreover, Belgium was compensated for its losses in artistic patrimony with famous Flemish paintings, which had been legally acquired by German public collections in the 19th century.[18]

Treaties with Austria and Hungary also included regulations on the restitution of artworks.[19] Thus, it can be noted that the treaties at the end of WWI provided for the repatriation of objects removed during and, in some instances, well before the war. The post-war settlements contributed to the consistent state practice of restitution, and the recognition of states of origin's interests in cultural heritage wrongfully removed during wartime.

3.2. The Second World War

During WWII, German forces systematically pillaged art treasures and, in particular, looted Jewish properties in Germany and occupied territories throughout Europe.[20] Faced with the massive losses, the Allied Powers, including the UK, the US, France, and the Soviet Union, were planning for the return of looted cultural heritage as early as 1942, when the war was still happening. The general policy for post-war restitution was the Inter-Allied Declaration of the Allied Nations against Acts of Dispossession Committed in Territories

15 Article 245 of the 1919 Treaty of Versailles.

16 Sandholtz, *Plunder, Restitution, and International Law,* above n 3, 156–157.

17 Article 246 of the 1919 Treaty of Versailles.

18 Andrzej Jakubowski, *State Succession in Cultural Property* (Oxford University Press, 2015), 63.

19 Lyndel Prott, 'The History and Development of Processes for the Recovery of Cultural Heritage' in Lyndel Prott (ed), *Witnesses to History* (UNESCO, 2008) 2, 3–4.

20 Lynn H. Nicholas, *The Rape of Europa: The Fate of Europe's Treasures in the Third Reich and the Second World War* (Vintage, 1995).

under Enemy Occupation or Control, also known as the Declaration of London (the Declaration). The Declaration declared the Allies' intention of doing everything in their power to reverse all acts of property acquisition property, including cultural objects, which occurred in the territories occupied by Germany and their allies. This Declaration was an especially important precedent because it recognised that the principle of unconditional restitution was applicable to all property deriving from occupied countries.[21]

Immediately after WWII, measures were taken to implement the Declaration. In Germany, the Allied Powers issued laws on restitution for their respective zones of occupation, which overrode provisions of the German Civil Code that would protect a good faith purchaser and defeat restitution.[22] For example, in the US zone, Law No. 59 Restitution of Identifiable Property (s.3.75(2)) provided that "property shall be restored to its former owner or to his successor in interest in accordance with the provisions of this Law No. 59, even though the interest of other persons who had no knowledge of the wrongful taking must be subordinated".[23] Therefore, the general principle of restitution asserted by the Allies could not be negated by conflicting provisions in national law. Moreover, the post-war restitution scheme was extraordinary because it included neutral states, such as Switzerland and Sweden, who had not been party to the Declaration, but were also required to adopt similar legislation for the restitution of property taken in occupied territories during the war.[24]

At the end of 1945, the Paris Conference on Reparation reaffirmed the principle of restitution of all property, which is reflected in the post-war peace treaties. Under the Convention on the Settlement of Matters Arising out of the War and the Occupation, Germany accepted the duty to "search for, recover and restitute" cultural heritage taken from the occupied territories during the war.[25] The other two principal partners in the Axis alliance, Italy and Japan, were also required to return their looted cultural heritage to the states of origin. Italy was obliged to return "all works of art, religious objects, archives and objects of historical value belonging to Ethiopia or its nationals and removed from Ethiopia to Italy since October 3, 1935".[26] However, in enforcing the provision of the Treaty of Peace with Italy, actual restitution was extremely dilatory. For example, it was not until 1982 that the throne of Menelik II was returned to Ethiopia from Italy, some 78 years after it was initially taken.[27]

21 Third paragraph of the Declaration of London.

22 Prott, *History and Development for Recovery,* above n 19, 5.

23 Ibid, 5

24 See, e.g., the Swiss Decree of December 10 1945 concerning Actions for the Recovery of Goods taken in Occupied Territories. Ibid, 6–9.

25 Article 1, para. 1, of Chapter Five ("External Restitution") of the 1952 Convention on the Settlement of Matters Arising out of the War and the Occupation.

26 Article 37 of the 1947 Treaty of Peace between the Allied and Associated Powers and Italy.

27 Prott, *History and Development for Recovery,* above n 19, 9.

Although the recorded negotiations with Japan after WWII indicate a conscious decision to waive many claims for reparations, the San Francisco Peace Treaty with Japan of September 8 1951, ultimately provided that "Japan should pay reparations to the Allied Powers for the damage and suffering caused by it during the war".[28] On June 22 1965, South Korea and Japan concluded the settlement of the repatriation of cultural objects looted during the period beginning 1910, when Japan annexed Korea, to the end of WWII, when Japan surrendered to the Allied Forces. During this time, many sites were destroyed and plundered, and precious items were transported to Japan.[29] According to Article 2, Japan agreed to "within six months after the validation of this Treaty . . . deliver the cultural properties listed in the enclosed document". Eventually, Japanese authorities handed over about 1,400 cultural items to Korea, including celadon porcelain and old documents.[30] Thus, it can be concluded that state practice of all the Allies shows the general recognition of post-war restitution and also the recognition that cultural heritage wrongfully removed during wartime should be returned to states of origin.[31]

Furthermore, the international commitment to address looting and illegal export during wartime can be reflected by the continuous repatriation after the end of the Cold War, when many new incidences of Nazi-looted arts were revealed.[32] In 1998, 44 states participated in the Washington Conference on Holocaust-Era Assets, which concluded with the endorsement of the Washington Conference Principles on Nazi-confiscated Art (Washington Principles). Despite the principles being non-binding, the Washington Principles are significant in assisting governments to resolve issues relating to Jewish property confiscated by the Nazis.[33] However, various institutions that possess art with an ambiguous provenance are reluctant to facilitate the identification of artefacts, since clear evidence of ownership is often not provided.[34] Despite the slow movement, the response from the international community regarding Nazi-looted art nevertheless reflects the international consensus on the

28 ICRC, 'Practice Relating to Rule 150. Reparation' <www.icrc.org/customary-ihl/eng/docs/v2_cha_chapter42_rule150_sectionb>.

29 The Agreement between the Republic of Korea and Japan Concerning Cultural Property and Exchange, signed on June 22 1965.

30 Geoffrey R. Scott, 'Spoliation, Cultural property, and Japan' (2008) 29(4) *University of Pennsylvania Journal of International Law* 803, 857.

31 Sandholtz, *Plunder, Restitution, and International Law*, above n 3, 160.

32 It should be first clarified that Nazi spoliation of cultural objects cannot be viewed as "traditional" spoils of war, as the confiscation program was a systematic plunder perpetrated against European Jews, rather than a general destruction associated with more common military action. Christa Roodt, *Private International Law, Art and Cultural Heritage* (Edward Elgar Publishing, 2015), 121–122.

33 Patty Gerstenblith, '2010 Cultural Heritage Legal Summary' (2011) 36(3) *Journal of Field Archaeology* 257, 260.

34 Robert Peters, 'Remedying Historical Injustice: Ethical and Historical Considerations in Returning Cultural Materials' in Silvia Borelli and Federico Lenzerini (eds), *Cultural Heritage, Cultural Rights, Cultural Diversity* (Martinus Nijhoff Publishers, 2012) 141, 148.

condemnation of both the looting and illegal export of cultural items from conflict zones, and the return of such heritage.[35]

3.3. Early Efforts for the Recovery of Chinese Cultural Heritage

The Japanese Occupation saw the destruction and pillage of Chinese cultural relics on a wide scale. While the damage to China's cultural relics was so great, it was exceptionally important to investigate and determine the scale of the destruction and looting, which was indispensable for the return of cultural relics in the future. After the outbreak of WWII, the government of Shaan-Gan-Ning Border Region under the Communist Party published an order to investigate and record "ancient objects, documents, and historical sites".[36]

Soon after the surrender of Japan, on December 26 1945, the War Damage on Cultural Relics Commission under the Department of Education was established, whose main purpose was to investigate the damage and loss of cultural relics during the Japanese Occupation and to restore cultural relics and historical sites.[37] Members of the War Damage Commission came from the Ministry of National Defence, the Ministry of the Interior, the Department of Education, the Ministry of Foreign Affairs, research institutions and universities.[38] To investigate and record all Chinese cultural relics looted and destroyed during the Japanese Occupation, the War Damage Commission further set up five offices in Jinghu, Pingjing, Yuegang, Wuhan, and Dongbei Districts that would be responsible for investigating the scale of destruction and looting within its area. The Guidelines of the War Damage Commission were published in 1945, and provided that the scope of the investigation of war damage was "important buildings, art works, historical sites, ancient objects".[39] Also, the term "cultural relics" was first adopted in official legal documents, which indicated that the scope of protection was not limited to ancient objects from earlier times.[40] By the Guidelines, it was clearly shown that the War Damage Commission was intended to cover all damage occurring to all types of cultural relics during the Occupation. The final official Report on the Loss of Cultural Relics and the Values during the War, included categories of Books, Paintings, Stone Inscriptions, Ancient Objects, Historical Sites, Instruments, Samples, Maps, Art Works, and Groceries.[41] Further, the report

35 Ana Filipa Vrdoljak, *International Law, Museums and The Return of Cultural Objects* (Cambridge University Press, 2006), 141.
36 Li Xiaodong, *An Analysis on the Legal Documents regarding Cultural Relics in Republi of China* (Cultural Relics Press, 2013), 204.
37 Article 2 of the Guidelines of the War Damage Commission 1945.
38 Ibid.
39 Ibid.
40 Article 1 of the Guidelines of the War Damage Commission 1945.
41 China Second Historical Archives of China, *A Collective Documents about the Republic of China, Volume 5, Issue 3, Culture* (Jiangsu Phoenix House, 1999) 458–460.

of the war damage included the names of cultural relics, when and where they were destroyed or lost, who or which army was responsible, and estimated values. The damage to China's cultural relics during the Japanese Occupation was massive. In the City of Chongqing, for example, 741 historical sites, more than 15,000 paintings, and over 3,000,000 books were damaged or lost.[42]

Based on the nationwide investigation of war damage to Chinese cultural relics, official requests for the return of cultural relics and for compensation for war damage started to be sent to Japan soon after the end of the Japanese Occupation. On June 12 1946, the Department of Education requested that "cultural relics taken by Japan since 1894 should be returned and all cultural relics discovered by Japan under the name of scientific research without the permission of the Chinese Government should be returned".[43] While no special treaty was signed between China and Japan regarding damages, the Japanese peace treaty ultimately stated that "Japan should pay reparations to the Allied Powers for the damage and suffering caused by it during the war".[44]

Regarding those Chinese cultural relics that were already in Japan, the Chinese Government requested the Allies (countries opposed to the Axis powers, including the UK, the Soviet Union, the US, and China) to pass special orders to protect Chinese relics and prevent them from being smuggled out of Japan. The request included imposing bans on any transfers or sales of Chinese cultural relics in Japan, stopping Japan taxing Chinese cultural relics held by private art dealers, and requesting Japan to investigate and record all Chinese cultural relics taken by Japan since 1894 and to impose a total ban on any export of Chinese books that were published before the Republic of China.[45]

As official requests for the return of these relics were sent to Japan, some Chinese cultural relics were returned. For example, on December 25 1945, the Examination Commission requested the return of a sculpture from the Song Dynasty that was taken to Japan and restored in the Tokyo National Museum during the Occupation. On March 28 1946, another letter was sent by the Ministry of Foreign Affairs to the Department of Education, informing them that more than 25,000 ancient books found in a library located in Ueno, Tokyo, would be returned. However, the majority of Chinese heritage looted by the Japanese forces were still maintained in Japan, largely due to the fact that the Chinese Civil War between the Communist and National Parties restarted soon after the Japanese Occupation and China's contribution to WWII was overlooked. The consequence is that a separate peace treaty was

42 'War Damage on Cultural Relics Commission under the Department of Education', *China Cultural Relics* August 22, 2007 <www.xhgxt.com/html/View_9270.html>.

43 Second Historical Archives of China, *A Collective Documents, Volume 5, Issue 3,* above n 41, 449.

44 Dinah Shelton, 'The World of Atonement: Reparations for Historical Injustices' (2003) 50(3) *Netherlands International Law Review* 289, 292.

45 Second Historical Archives of China, *A Collective Documents, Volume 5, Issue 3,* above n 41, 449–450.

not signed between Japan and China until the normalisation of diplomatic relations in 1972.

3.4. Increasing Recognition, but Unsolved Issues Constituting a Powerful Deterrent

One of the major developments after WWII with regard to tangible cultural heritage was the reaffirmation of the corresponding obligation of restitution. The post-war settlements following WWI and WWII addressing the removal of cultural objects by one state from another, regularly included the return of those items. State practice of the involved parties shows recognition that cultural valuables seized during conflicts should be subject to specific restitution. While the number of instances is not large and, in some cases, the enforcement of the provisions of peace treaties has been dilatory, the state practice of wartime restitution has been consistent. The post-war settlements made it very clear that cultural heritage looted during armed conflicts should be returned to the states of origin. This is consistent with the basic ideas underpinning the proposed customary rule, which argues that wrongfully removed heritage should be returned to states of origin. Moreover, the principle of wartime restitution is further incorporated into the 1954 Hague Convention and its two protocols. In this regard, it can be argued that developments during and since WWII on the return of cultural heritage pave the way for formal legal recognition of restitution of heritage looted during wartime on a much more substantial scale than was the case after WWI.[46]

Despite the increasing recognition, it should be admitted that the unresolved issues of war repatriations during the two world wars have constituted a powerful deterrent to the creation of the proposed customary rule. For example, after Japan returned a small group of cultural objects to Korea in 1965, the contradictive opinions regarding the remaining Korean art closed further negotiations until the late 1980s.[47] For South Korea, that set of returned cultural objects constituted the first step in a broader restoration of lost cultural heritage. However, South Korean historians believe the number of repatriated objects was minuscule, estimating that tens of thousands of looted cultural items remain in Japan. Conversely, although Japan agreed to partial repatriation, it considered all the appropriations and removals made after 1910 lawful by virtue of its sovereign capacity.[48]

The return of Chinese cultural heritage removed during the Japanese Occupation is another deterrence to the creation of the customary law. Japan insists that the matter of war reparations for WWII had been settled pursuant to the 1972 Japan–China Joint Communique, according to which the Chinese Government

46 Prott, *History and Development for Recovery,* above n 19, 9.
47 Jakubowski, *State Succession,* above n 18, 293.
48 Discussed in Chapter 7, Section 7.2.

renounced its right for reparations.[49] The question then becomes whether individuals still have a means to vindicate their rights to request restitution, even though the state renounced its claims for war reparations against Japan in a peace treaty. Chinese Foreign Minister Qian Qichen stated that individual claims of war compensation to Japan were the right of the Chinese people and that the government would neither obstruct nor intervene in such situations.[50] However, Japan alleges that the Communique has concluded all war redress issues between the two countries and thus, no individual claims may be brought. The question as to whether Chinese individuals are entitled to claim for restitution is not entirely answered, given that an increasing number of claims have been filed by private individuals against Japan's actions during WWII.[51] In summary, the settlements following WWI and WWII reflect the uniformity of state practice regarding the repatriation of wrongfully removed heritage to states of origin, which signals the emergence of the proposed customary rule. However, inconsistencies regarding the unresolved recovery issues during WWII suggests the lack of concurrence of those particularly affected states with the proposed customary rule.

4. Legal Obligation to Return Cultural Heritage

4.1. International Treaties

The considerable destruction of cultural heritage that took place during WWII finally convinced the international community that a multilateral treaty universally dedicated to ensuring the protection of cultural heritage during armed conflict was necessary.[52] This was accomplished in the 1954 Hague Conven-

49 'Joint Communique of the Government of Japan and the Government of the People's Republic of China' (1972) *Ministry of Foreign Affairs of Japan* <www.mofa.go.jp/region/asia-paci/china/joint72.html>.

50 China and The World Program, 'The Bitter Legacies of the 1972 Sino-Japanese Normalization Talks' <https://cwp.princeton.edu/news/bitter-legacies-1972-sino-japanese-normalization-talks-article-cwp-alumni-yinan-he>.

51 In a Japanese case concerning Chinese victims of sexual violence, the judgment of the Tokyo District Court of April 24 2003 held that the 1972 Joint Communiqué does not necessarily contain the renouncement of individuals' claims for "compensation for damages", after distinguishing the terms "war reparations" from "compensation for damages" in its ruling:

> The Declaration is to be interpreted within the basic framework of international law; in this Declaration the counterpart, the People's Republic of China . . . only renounced the "war reparations" in relation to Japan, the offending State during the China-Japan War, and did not renounce the so-called "compensation for damages", which are claims by individual victims belonging to the counter-part State.

Shin Hae Bong, 'Compensation for Victims of Wartime Atrocities: Recent Developments in Japan's Case Law' (2005) 3(1) *Journal of International Criminal Justice* 187, 202.

52 After the Second World War, developments in the protection of cultural property during times of armed conflict were reflected in the Fourth Geneva Convention of August 12 1949 Relative to the Protection of Civilian Persons in Time of War. Article 53, however,

tion, whose obligations are now widely accepted by the specially affected states as customary international law.[53] Article 14 prohibits the seizure of cultural heritage as prizes or trophies of war, which was created in direct response to the German military's looting during WWII. Additionally, Article 4 places absolute obligation on the states to prevent others from looting or vandalising cultural heritage, which cannot be waived on the grounds of military necessity.[54] However, the Convention does not expressly contemplate an obligation of restitution. Despite the silence, some scholars argue that "the obligation to return illicitly taken cultural object[s] is customary because it is inherent in the obligation to respect cultural property and in the prohibition on the seizing and pillaging of cultural property".[55] Therefore, if cultural heritage must be respected and not seized or pillaged, then it should be returned.[56]

The clear obligation to return cultural heritage that has been illegally exported from occupied territory is set forth in the First Protocol to the 1954 Hague Convention, which has been ratified by 101 states. According to paragraphs 3 and 4, each contacting party is required "to prevent the exportation of cultural property from the territory occupied" and "to return, at the close of hostilities, to the competent authorities of the territory previously occupied, cultural property which is in its territory". In addition, it is clearly stated that such cultural heritage "shall never be retained as war reparations".[57] Hence, the return is unconditional and there is no time limit for initiating a claim for return.[58]

Although the 1970 UNESCO Convention primarily focuses on the movement of artworks during peacetime through the international market, the provisions can be applied to the removals that occurred during armed conflicts. Article 2(2) requires its party states to oppose the illicit import, export and

---

states only that any destruction of real or personal property, whether publicly or privately owned, is prohibited. As a result, it became necessary to adopt a convention specifically for the protection of cultural property during armed conflict.

53 David A. Meyer, 'The 1954 Hague Cultural Property Convention and its emergence into customary international law' (1993) 11(2) *Boston University International Law Journal* 349; Wayne Sandholtz, 'The Iraqi National Museum and International Law: A Duty to Protect' (2005) 44(1) *Columbia Journal Transnational Law* 185, 238.

54 James A.R. Nafziger and Robert Paterson, 'Cultural Heritage Law' in James A.R. Nafziger and Robert Paterson (eds), *Handbook on the Law of Cultural Heritage and International Trade* (Edward Elgar Publishing, 2014) 1, 4–5; Joshua E. Kastenberg, 'The Legal Regime for Protecting Cultural Property During Armed Conflict' (1997) 42 *Air Force Law Review* 277, 293.

55 Chechi, *Settlement of Cultural Disputes,* above n 5, 264.

56 Henckaerts and Doswald-Beck, *Customary Rule (Volume 1),* above n 4, 136–137; Silvio Ferrari and Andrea Benzo, *Between Cultural Diversity and Common Heritage: Legal and Religious Perspectives on the Sacred Places of the Mediterranean* (Ashgate, 2014), 307.

57 Talia Einhorn, 'Restitution of Archaeological Artifacts: The Arab-Israeli Aspects' (1996) 5(1) *International Journal of Cultural Property* 133, 139.

58 Jiri Toman, *The Protection of Cultural Property In the Event of Armed Conflict: Commentary on the 1954 Hague Convention and on Other Instruments of International Law Concerning Such Protection* (Dartmouth, 1996), 3.

transfer of ownership of cultural heritage "with the means at their disposal, and particularly by removing their causes, putting a stop to current practices, and by helping to make the necessary reparations". This provision is important for the return of cultural heritage, not only because an importing state acknowledges the problems with the unlawful removal of cultural heritage, but more importantly, that they oppose those practices subject to their control.[59] Further, Article 11 states that "the export and transfer of ownership of cultural property under compulsion arising directly or indirectly from the occupation of a country by a foreign power shall be regarded as illicit". In this regard, the UNESCO Convention goes further than the First Protocol because it not only outlaws the export of looted art, but also the transfer of ownership.

However, the evolving laws of war failed to prevent looting and destruction during the First Gulf War and the Yugoslav War. This in turn triggered further developments in international law, including the Second Protocol.[60] Article 9(1) requires an occupying party to prohibit and prevent certain activities in the territory concerned, such as "any illicit export, other removal or transfer of ownership of cultural property" and "any archaeological excavation". Furthermore, Article 21 of the Second Protocol explicitly obliges that each party shall adopt such legislative, administrative or disciplinary measures as may be necessary to suppress "any illicit export, other removal or transfer of ownership of cultural property from occupied territory". In other words, commanders of military forces have the obligation to prevent the looting of cultural assets and to adopt punitive measures against individuals who have violated or have ordered a violation to be committed, whether they are soldiers or civilians. This provision implies a positive obligation to prevent or stop the prohibited acts regardless of who is responsible.[61]

In summary, the overview of the relevant international legal instruments applicable to the return of heritage looted during wartime shows that international law is sufficient on both the prevention and the restitution sides.[62] However, what is missing is the efficient implementation at a national level. For example, before the looting of the National Museum in Baghdad in 2003, the US Government was warned that Iraq's National Museum would be a "prime target for looters" and it "merits securing as soon as possible to

59 Craig Forrest, *International Law and The Protection of Cultural Heritage* (Routledge, 2010), 176.

60 Jan Hladik, 'The Review Process of the 1954 Hague Convention for the Protection of Cultural Property in the Event of Armed Conflict and its Impact on International Humanitarian Law' (1998) 1 *Yearbook of International Humanitarian Law* 313, 313–314.

61 Article 53 of Protocol I and Article 16 of Protocol II; Ferrari and Benzo, *Cultural Diversity and Common Heritage,* above n 56, 308.

62 European Parliament Think Tank, 'Cross-Border Restitution Claims of Art Looted in Armed Conflicts and Wars and Alternatives to Court Litigations' <www.europarl.europa.eu/RegData/etudes/STUD/2016/556947/IPOL_STU(2016)556947_EN.pdf>, 13–14.

prevent further damage, destruction and or pilferage of records and assets".[63] However, the US Government ignored these warnings and did not post any soldiers outside the museum, which was subsequently ransacked, with more than 270,000 artefacts taken.[64] As shown above, the protection and return of looted cultural heritage in armed conflicts relies on individual states applying the principles applicable to their domestic systems. To argue for the proposed customary rule, the attention must focus on state practice in implementing the 1954 Hague Convention and its Protocols.

4.2. *National Law and Practice*

In discussing the proposed customary rule, specially affected states should be in favour of the proposed customary rule or, more precisely, the basic idea underpinned the proposed rule, which is that wrongfully removed heritage should be returned to states of origin. The following section examines the practice of Germany, the UK, the US, the Netherlands, and Switzerland to see whether the proposed customary rule is emerging.

4.2.1. Germany

The obligation to return exported cultural heritage is recognised in different forms of Germany's practice relating to the looting and plunder of cultural heritage during WWII. In 1991, the German Government declared that it "fully accepts the fact that cultural property has to be returned after the end of hostilities" and it has returned cultural heritage in all cases where the cultural goods were found and could be identified.[65] In 1997, the Government reiterated that "thefts and destruction of cultural property by the Nazi regime . . . during and after the WWII were breaches of international law".[66] More importantly, Germany's Law Implementing the 1954 Cultural Property Convention (2007) includes the obligation to return cultural heritage from occupied territory after the close of hostilities.[67]

63 Ed Vulliamy and Gaby Hinsliff Paul Martin, 'US Army Was Told to Protect Looted Museum', *The Guardian* April 21 2003 <www.theguardian.com/world/2003/apr/20/internationaleducationnews.iraq>.

64 It should be noted that prior to 1991, there was virtually no illicit trade in Iraqi antiquities before 1911. Iraqi national law has vested that all immovable and movable antiquities to be owned by the states and the Iraqi Government established severe criminal penalties for the looting of archaeological sites and illegal export. Marion Forsyth, 'Casualties of War: The Destruction of Iraq's Cultural Heritage as a Result of US Action During and After the 1991 Gulf War' 73 (2004) XIV *DePaul-LCA Journal of Art & Entertainment Law* 73, 76–77.

65 Jean-Marie Henckaerts and Louise Doswald-Beck, *Customary International Humanitarian Law, Volume 2* (Cambridge University Press, 2005), 809.

66 Ibid, 809.

67 Section 1 of Act implementing the Convention of May 14 1954 for the Protection of Cultural Property in the Event of Armed Conflict <www.kulturgutschutz-deutschland.

4.2.2. The US

As the US is the most significant military power, if its state practice shows the acceptance of the obligation to return looted cultural heritage, this is strong evidence regarding the recognition of states of origin's interests in their wrongfully removed cultural heritage, which is at the heart of the proposed customary rule. Although the US helped to draft the 1954 Hague Convention and signed it in the same year, the Executive Branch decided not to transmit the treaty to the Senate for ratification due to military concerns about how it might affect policy at the height of the Cold War.[68] At the end of the Cold War, the Department of Defense withdrew its objections. Subsequently, in 1999 President Bill Clinton transmitted the 1954 Hague Convention and a part of the First Protocol to the US Senate Committee on Foreign Relations with his support for ratification, stating that "I believe that ratification of the Convention and accession to the Protocol will underscore our long commitment, as well as our practice in combat, to protect the world's cultural resources."[69] President Clinton emphasised that "because the United States traditionally has held a leadership position in matters relating to the law of war, our ratification would help give Protocol II the visibility."[70]

However, the Senate Committee did not take any action until the looting of the Iraq Museum in Baghdad in April 2003 and of archaeological sites in southern Iraq.[71] The US Committee of the Blue Shield, the Lawyers' Committee for Cultural Heritage Preservation, and the Archaeological Institute of America formed a coalition of preservation organisations that submitted testimony to the Senate Committee in support of ratifying the 1954 Hague Convention and its Protocols. Eventually, the full Senate voted to give its consent to ratification on September 25 2008 and the US became a party to the Hague Convention on March 13 2009. By taking this significant step, the US has demonstrated its commitment to the preservation of the world's cultural, artistic, religious, and historic legacy.

4.2.3. The UK

At the time of writing, the UK has yet to ratify the Convention, but is one step closer to ratifying the 1954 Hague Convention and its two Protocols. On

de/SharedDocs/ExterneLinks/EN/Gesetze_en/KultgSchKonvAG_en.pdf;jsessionid=40024BC88161857C417ADAB4679C55D2.1_cid350?__blob=publicationFile>.

68 US Committee of the Blue Shield, 'The 1954 Hague Convention' <http://uscbs.org/1954-hague-convention.html>.

69 'The Hague Convention and the Hague Protocol (Message from the President of the United States)' <www.gpo.gov/fdsys/pkg/CDOC-106tdoc1/html/CDOC-106tdoc1.htm>.

70 Ibid.

71 It should be noted that prior to 1991, there was virtually no illicit trade in Iraqi antiquities before 1991 Iraqi national law has vested that all immovable and movable antiquities are owned by the state and the Iraqi Government established severe criminal penalties for the looting of archaeological sites and illegal export. Forsyth, *Destruction of Iraq's Cultural Heritage*, above n 64, 76–77.

February 20 2017, the Cultural Property (Armed Conflicts) Bill (the Bill) had its Third Reading in the House of Commons and was passed without amendment. The Bill will enable the UK to finally accede to the Convention—63 years after its enactment. This is strong evidence to create the proposed customary rule, not only because the UK, as an important military power, plays an indispensable role in wartime protection of cultural heritage, but also because its ratification efforts reflect the endorsement of ideas that underpinned the Hague Convention.

Before the Third Reading, there was an indicative change of policy in the UK in the willingness of the government to ratify the 1954 Hague Convention and, particularly, its two Protocols. In 2008, the Bill went before the Parliament. Section 18 of the Bill clearly states that "it is an offence to deal in unlawfully exported cultural objects, knowing or having reason to suspect they have been unlawfully exported".[72] Accordingly, a court can order the forfeiture of an unlawfully exported object and the Secretary of State must return the item to any authority to whom the return is obligated under the First Protocol.[73] If the Bill were passed, it would have been a step forward in the protection of the cultural heritage and return of illegally exported cultural heritage. As commented by Margaret Hodge, then Labour Minister of State for Culture, Media and Sport, the Bill "will send a signal to the international community that the UK takes seriously its obligations under international humanitarian law to respect and safeguard the cultural property of other nations".[74] However, the Bill was not approved by the Government in 2008.

Despite the rejection, it should be noted that there has been a continuous appeal for the UK government to ratify the Hague Convention.[75] In July 2014, a group of around 100 leading figures from the museum and antiquity world signed a letter to *The Daily Telegraph*, pointing out that Britain is the most significant worldwide military power not to have ratified the convention, with the US having done so in 2009.[76] It also emphasised that "ministers of successive governments have pledged their commitment to ratification as soon as parliamentary time can be found. This commitment is to

72 Draft Cultural Property (Armed Conflicts) Bill <www.gov.uk/government/uploads/system/uploads/attachment_data/file/243113/7298.pdf>.

73 Sophie Vigneron, 'Protecting Cultural Objects: Enforcing the Illicit Export of Foreign Cultural Objects' in Valentina Vadi and Hildegard Schneider (eds), *Art, Cultural Heritage and the Market: Ethical and Legal Issues* (Springer, 2014) 117, 134.

74 Ibid, 134.

75 UK Government, 'New Scheme to Protect Cultural Sites from Destruction' <www.gov.uk/government/news/new-scheme-to-protect-cultural-sites-from-destruction>; ICOM, 'UK to Adopt Hague Convention To Protect Artefacts In War Zones' <http://uk.icom.museum/uk-to-adopt-hague-convention-to-protect-artefacts-in-war-zones/>; Institute of Art and Law Blog, 'Call for UK Government to ratify Hague Convention' <www.ial.uk.com/news/call-for-uk-government-to-ratify-hague-convention/>.

76 'Britain Should Ratify Convention to Protect Cultural Objects in Time of War', *Telegraph* July 21 2014 <www.telegraph.co.uk/comment/letters/10979564/Britain-should-ratify-convention-to-protect-cultural-objects-in-time-of-war.html>.

be applauded. . . . It has all-party support." In June 2015, the Director of the British Museum, Neil MacGregor called on the UK Government to explain why it has not signed the 1954 Convention: "there is a significant international agreement, the Hague Convention about the protection of cultural property in war zones. Only one country in the security council hasn't ratified it, the UK."[77] MacGregor's assertion added further weight to previous calls for the UK Government to ratify the 1954 Convention. As a response, a spokesman for the Department for Culture, Media and Sport said that the Government would seek to legislate on the Convention "as soon as parliamentary time allows".[78] Eventually, on June 22 2015, John Whittingdale, the Culture Secretary, announced that the UK Government is to bring forward legislation to ratify the 1954 Hague Convention.[79] Furthermore, to coincide with plans to ratify the Convention, Whittingdale has confirmed that the UK Government will develop a new cultural protection fund to support the protection of cultural heritage and the recovery of artefacts from acts of cultural destruction.[80] The purpose of the fund is to help safeguard the heritage of countries affected by conflict or at risk of coming under attack for ideological reasons.[81] Thus, it can be said that the UK's ratification of the 1954 Hague Convention and its two Protocols will be the conclusion of growing endorsement of the need to protect cultural heritage during armed conflicts and the recent government's projects which is consistent with the principles underpinned the 1954 Hague Convention and its two Protocols.

4.2.4. The Netherlands

The Netherlands adopted a statute in March 2007, the Cultural Property Originating from Occupied Territory Return Act, to address the issue of restitution of art objects wrongfully removed in the context of armed conflicts.[82] This Act was created as a result of a specific case which was brought before the Dutch courts and related to works of ancient arts illicitly exported from Turkey-occupied

77 'British Museum 'Guarding' Object Looted from Syria', *BBC* June 5 2015 <www.bbc.co.uk/news/entertainment-arts-33020199>.

78 *Call for UK Government to ratify Hague Convention,* above n 75.

79 UK National Committee of the Blue Shield, 'British Government Announces Plans to Ratify the 1954 Hague Convention' <http://ukblueshield.org.uk/british-government-announces-plans-to-ratify-the-1954-hague-convention/>.

80 Ibid.

81 Historic England, 'Government Tackles International Cultural Destruction' <www.historicengland.org.uk/news-and-features/news/the-hague-ratify>.

82 Act of 8 March 2007 containing rules on the taking into custody of cultural property from an occupied territory during an armed conflict and for the initiation of proceedings for the return of such property <www.unesco.org/culture/natlaws/media/pdf/netherlands/netherlands_actmarch2007_engtof.pdf>; 'Explanatory Memorandum' <www.unesco.org/culture/natlaws/media/pdf/netherlands/netherlands_memo_returnoccupiedterritory_engtof.pdf>.

territory in Cyprus.[83] A Cyprus Orthodox church claimed for the return of ancient icons by invoking the First Protocol and its provisions on the return of looted cultural heritage. However, the Dutch did not support the recovery claim, as specific provisions of the Protocol were deemed to be non-self-executing. The court found that these provisions created obligations of purely intergovernmental character, which were not capable of trumping provisions of the Civil Code regarding the acquisition of property titles in good faith.[84]

After the trial, questions arose regarding the effectiveness of the Protocol to counter spoliation of cultural heritage in war and in occupied territories when national legislation is absent.[85] This led to the adoption of the 2007 Dutch Act, whose purpose is precisely to declare the Protocol directly applicable in the Netherlands.[86] The stated purpose of this new law is to make it possible to initiate proceedings for the return of cultural heritage taken from a territory occupied during an armed conflict. Section 2 laid down the foundation, stating that "it is prohibited to import cultural property from an occupied territory into the Netherlands or to have such property in one's possession in the Netherlands". Chapter 2 of the 2007 Act regulates the procedures for the custody of the object and Chapter 3 details the legal proceedings for return. The Act is an important example of returning cultural objects looted during war, not only because it shows that the non-self-executing character of the Protocol can be easily overcome via national legislation, but it also sets a good example for other countries to follow.[87]

4.2.5. Switzerland

On June 20 2014, Switzerland adopted the Federal Law on the Protection of Cultural Objects in the Event of Armed Conflict, Disaster and Emergency Situations (Federal Law).[88] The law aims to "protect cultural property in the

83 *Greek Orthodox Church of Cyprus v Lans*, Rotterdam Civil Court, 44053 HAZ 95/2403, February 4 1999.

84 Stephan Matyk, 'The Restitution of Cultural Objects and the Question of Giving Direct Effect to the Protocol to the Hague Convention for the Protection of Cultural Property in the Event of Armed Conflict 1954' (2000) 9(2) *International Journal of Cultural Property* 341, 341–346.

85 Francesco Francioni, 'The Evolving International Legal Framework for the Protection of Cultural Heritage' in Silvia Borelli and Federico Lenzerini (eds), *Cultural Heritage, Cultural Rights, Cultural Diversity* (Brill, 2012) 3, 14.

86 'Act of 8 March 2007 containing rules on the taking into custody of cultural property from an occupied territory during an armed conflict and for the initiation of proceedings for the return of such property (Cultural Property Originating from Occupied Territory (Return) Act)' <www.eui.eu/Projects/InternationalArtHeritageLaw/Documents/NationalLegislation/Netherlands/actof2007coveringoccupiedterritory.pdf>.

87 *Cross-Border Restitution Claim,* above n 62, 17.

88 This law replaced and repealed the Federal Law on the Protection of Cultural Property in the Event of Armed Conflict of 1966. 'Federal Law on the Protection of Cultural Objects in the Event of Armed Conflict, Disaster and Emergency Situations' <www.unesco.org/culture/natlaws/media/pdf/switzerland/suisse_fedactprotcltprop_entof>.

event of armed conflict, disaster or emergency situation", by taking all such civil measures, both practical and organisational, that may be appropriate to prevent or mitigate any damage to cultural heritage.[89] A very important provision included in this 2014 Swiss Law is Article 12, which regulates the granting of "safe havens" for foreign countries when cultural heritage is under threat due to armed conflicts, disasters or emergency situations. Article 2(c) defines "safe havens" as secure premises provided by the Federal Government for the temporary fiduciary custody of moveable cultural heritage which forms part of the cultural heritage of a given state, and that is under serious threat in the territory of the state possessing or holding such property. The law makes it clear that the fiduciary safekeeping of threatened artefacts is provided under the auspices of UNESCO.[90] The Swiss Federal Council may conclude international treaties with requesting states, which should govern the arrangements and conditions for the transport, the perfection and maintenance during custody, and the repatriation, of cultural heritage.

4.3. Return of Looted Cultural Heritage Being Recognised as Customary Law

In conclusion, both international and national laws clearly prohibit the looting of cultural heritage during wartime and enable its restitution. The ICRC Customary Law Study found the rule on export and return of cultural objects illicitly removed during wartime is customary and is therefore binding on all states, irrespective of their participation in the treaty. Rule 41 states that "the occupying power must prevent the illicit export of cultural property from occupied territory and must return illicitly exported property to the competent authorities of the occupied territory".[91] The clear obligation on the return of heritage looted during armed conflicts is important evidence of state practice. This state practice is significant in creating the proposed customary rule, not only because return is an indispensable part of seeking redress for unlawful acts committed wars, but also because it shows respect for the integrity of states of origin's cultural heritage. From this perspective, state practice regarding the return of looted cultural heritage shows the increasing recognition and respect of the interest states of origin have in their wrongfully removed cultural heritage, and, more importantly, supports the proposed customary rule in the return of cultural heritage to its original owner.

5. International Responses to the Looting of Cultural Heritage in Recent Conflicts

Despite the legal obligation, issues of looting and destruction continue to surface. After the Western incursion of 1991, Iraqi museums suffered serious loss

89 Article 6.
90 Article 12(1).
91 Henckaerts and Doswald-Beck, *Customary Rule (Volume 1),* above n 4, 135.

and destruction, as looters took advantage of the void created by the sudden collapse of national authorities and removed thousands of priceless items from the collections.[92] It is reported that the plunder of the National Museum in Baghdad in 2003 has resulted in at least 13,515 cultural objects being stolen or damaged.[93] Similar problems occurred during the conflicts in Afghanistan and Syria. Faced with massive losses, the international community, in particular the market states, have reacted timely to the looting and illicit trafficking of cultural heritage from the conflict zones.

5.1. Iraqi Heritage

In response to the massive loss of Iraqi heritage, the UN Security Council Resolution 1483 (2003) called on states to take appropriate steps to facilitate the safe return of Iraqi cultural heritage and other items of archaeological, historical, cultural, rare scientific, and religious importance, which had been illegally removed from Iraq.[94] The 2003 UN Resolution is strong evidence to reflect the international community's commitment to respect Iraq's interests in its cultural heritage in a number of ways. First, the Resolution does not distinguish between peace and wartime situations, which allows Iraq to recover the largest possible number of objects taken due to armed conflicts. Second, the Iraq Resolution has become one of the very few international instruments that are retroactive, as it applies not only to objects that were illegally removed from 2003 onwards, but also to all objects illegally removed since August 6 1990.[95] An exception to the statute of limitations defence regarding misappropriation related to war crimes is not only a form of respect for the morally compelling nature of these cases, but also a meaningful interpretation of national law in light of international law.[96]

To coincide with the 2003 UN Resolution, many market states have published regulations to prevent the possibility of those valuable properties being imported into their territories. For example, the Japanese Government issued the Public Notice of Deputy Commissioner of the Agency for Cultural Affair No. 37 in order to deter museums and similar institutions in Japan from acquiring these items.[97] In the UK, the Iraq (United Nations Sanctions) Order

92 It should be noted that prior to 1991, there was virtually no illicit trade in Iraqi antiquities before 1911. Iraqi national law has vested that all immovable and movable antiquities to be owned by the states and the Iraqi Government established severe criminal penalties for the looting of archaeological sites and illegal export. Forsyth, *Destruction of Iraq's Cultural Heritage,* above n 64, 76–77.

93 Neil Brodie and Colin Renfrew, 'Looting and the World's Archaeological Heritage: The Inadequate Response' (2005) 34 *Annual Review of Anthropology* 343, 346.

94 Paragraph 7.

95 Article 3(2)(a).

96 Robert Paterson, 'Resolving Material Culture Disputes: Human Rights, Property Rights, and Crimes against Humanity' in James A.R. Nafziger and Ann Nicgorski (eds), *Cultural Heritage Issues* (Martinus Nijhoff Publishers, 2009) 371, 379.

97 Shigeru Kozai and Toshiyuki Kono, 'Japan' in James A.R. Nafziger and Robert Paterson (eds), *Handbook on the Law of Cultural Heritage and International Trade* (2014) 257, 266.

2003 prohibits the import of any illegally removed Iraqi cultural heritage. It also states that handling illegally removed Iraqi materials is a criminal offence with a maximum penalty of seven years' imprisonment.[98] However, because of the uncertainty of provenance and time of export, many Iraqi cultural objects have still been sold at auction and scattered around the world. To address this problem, the UK Iraq Order is significant in reversing the burden of proof in legal proceedings, requiring the current possessor of an archaeological artefact to prove legitimate background. The change should be an effective measure in curbing the illicit trafficking of Iraqi heritage on the London market, as it requires a possessor to demonstrate that they have no reason to believe that the cultural material was illegally removed from Iraq. Although this has been done only in the UK to a limited extent, it will still curb the illegal trade of Iraqi arts as London is one of the world's most vibrant art markets.[99] Consequently, some of the stolen Iraqi objects have been returned. In 2013, 13 ancient artefacts were handed over to Iraq, among them at least one object stolen from the National Museum of Iraq in Baghdad in 2003.[100]

Apart from the special laws addressing the restitution of Iraqi arts, on October 28 2015, the British Government announced the launch of the £3 million Iraqi Emergency Heritage Management Project run by the British Museum. The government-backed project aims to help preserve and recover cultural objects and sites in Iraq that are under threat. According to the press release: "it will create a team of local experts to assess, document and stabilise afflicted sites in Iraq, and help begin the process of reconstruction and preservation of some of the world's most precious cultural artefacts".[101]

5.2. *Syrian Heritage*

With regard to the recent destruction of cultural heritage in Syrian due to Isis's systematic attack, state practice reaffirms that the international community is committed to fighting against the illicit trafficking of Syrian cultural objects. In 2015, the UN Security Council called on all states to "take appropriate steps to prevent the trade in Iraqi and Syrian cultural property, thereby allowing for their eventual safe return to the Iraqi and Syrian people".[102] In December 2013, the EU introduced a trade ban in view of the situation in

98 Section 20(1) Iraq (United Nations Sanctions) Order, Statutory Instrument 2003 No. 1519 <www.unesco.org/culture/natlaws/media/pdf/gb/gb_iraqunitednations-sanctions2003_engorof.pdf>.

99 Patty Gerstenblith, 'Increasing Effectiveness Of The Legal Regime For The Protection Of The International Archaeological Heritage' in James A.R. Nafziger and Ann Nicgorski (eds), *Cultural Heritage Issues* (Martinus Nijhoff Publishers, 2009) 305, 316.

100 UNESCO, 'Other Cases of Return or Restitution of Cultural Objects' <www.unesco.org/new/en/culture/themes/illicit-trafficking-of-cultural-property/other-cases-of-return-or-restitution-of-cultural-objects/>.

101 *New Scheme,* above n 75.

102 United Nations Security Council Resolution 2199 <http://unesdoc.unesco.org/images/0023/002321/232164e.pdf>.

Syria. According to Article 11c of the Council Regulation No. 1332/2013, trade in Syrian cultural heritage is prohibited "where there are reasonable grounds to suspect that the goods have been removed from Syria without the consent of their legitimate owner or have been removed in breach of Syrian law or international law".[103]

Prompted by the 2013 Council Regulation, the important market states have enacted national legislation to prevent becoming a hub for trade in illegally exported Syrian cultural heritage. In December 2014, the Swiss Federal Council extended the existing sanctions against Syria by introducing a trade ban on cultural objects stolen or illegally exported from Syria.[104] It should also be noted that while foreign export laws are only enforced in Switzerland in cases where a bilateral agreement with the foreign state exists, no such bilateral agreement is required to return Syrian cultural objects. The waiver of the bilateral agreement is important to allow the largest number of illegally removed Syrian arts to be returned. In the UK, the Export Control (Syria Sanctions) (Amendment) Order 2014 was enacted to prohibit any form of import, export, or transfer of Syrian cultural heritage, where there are reasonable grounds to suspect they have been removed illegally or without the consent of their owner. In the US, on May 9 2016, the President signed the Engel Bill to crack down on the sale of artefacts looted by Isis from cultural sites in Syria. The new law imposes tough import restrictions on antiquities that are trafficked out of Syria, bringing US policy in line with a UN Security Council Resolution that called on governments to deny funding to Isis by preventing trade in Iraqi and Syrian cultural heritage. As commented by Patty Gerstenblith, "with this legislation, the US has taken a significant step toward reducing the destruction of cultural heritage in the Syrian conflict and preventing the sale of looted antiquities from providing income to ISIL and others engaged in the conflict".[105] The law provides exceptions to allow artefacts to enter the US for temporary protection and restoration. Restrictions will remain in effect until the crisis in Syria is resolved and the US is able to work with a future Syrian government to protect cultural heritage from trafficking under a bilateral agreement.

Thus, it can be concluded that there is universal agreement among the specially affected states that cultural heritage illegally exported from conflict zones should not be traded. This agreement is significant in promoting respect and protection of states of origin's interests in their wrongfully removed heritage.

103 Article 11c Council Regulation (EU) No 1332/2013 of 13 December 2013 Amending Regulation (EU) No 36/2012 Concerning Restrictive Measures in View of the Situation in Syria <http://eur-lex.europa.eu/legal-content/EN/TXT/HTML/?uri=CELEX:32012R0036%20&from=EN>.

104 Institute of Art and Law Blog, 'Switzerland Limits Trade in Syrian Cultural Property' <www.ial.uk.com/news/switzerland-limits-trade-in-syrian-cultural-property/>.

105 'President Signs Engel Bill to Stop ISIS From Looting Antiquities', *US Committee of the Blue Shield* May 9 2016 <http://uscbs.org/news/president-signs-engel-bill-stop-isis-looting-antiquities/>.

The international recognition and commitment to protecting cultural heritage looted from conflict zones can be concluded by the words of the UK Minister for the Middle East and North Africa Tobias Ellwood:

> The humanitarian crisis in the Middle East takes priority and the UK is at the forefront of the international effort to support those affected by the conflicts in Syria and Iraq. But we cannot stand by and ignore this appalling, deliberate attempt to erase the rich cultural heritage and sense of belonging for all communities in Iraq and Syria.[106]

6. Conclusion

Armed conflicts have long been viewed as one of the causes for the violation of cultural heritage. Apart from direct attacks at heritage sites during armed conflicts, many cultural heritage objects have been looted, stolen, or illegally exported from the original states largely due to the chaos of war. Therefore, the return of looted cultural objects is significant, not only as a remedy for the destruction and looting of heritage belonging to states of origin, but also as a form of respecting the integrity of this cultural heritage.

As shown above, the evolving state practice has clearly reflected an increasing recognition that cultural heritage looted during armed conflicts should be returned to the countries from which they were taken. This state practice can be reflected in three dimensions: first international and national law clearly prohibits the looting of cultural heritage during wartime, and enables its restitution. Second, the post-war settlements following conflicts, in which one state removed cultural objects from another, have regularly included the return of those items. Cultural valuables seized during the Napoleonic Wars, the Franco-Prussian War, WWI, and WWII have been subject to specific return agreements. While the number of instances is not large, the practice of restitution across them has been consistent. Third, in response to the recent regional conflicts, the important market states not only condemn the looting of heritage, but have taken a step further and agreed that cultural heritage illegally exported from conflict zones should not be traded.

These three dimensions clearly respect and recognise the interests of states of origin in regards to their cultural heritage taken during armed conflicts. The fundamental idea running through the development of international law and state practice is that looting cultural heritage from occupied territories or conflict zones is not tolerated and such property should be returned. Both the laws and practice of returning looted cultural heritage is significant in suggesting the emergence of the proposed customary rule. However, the unresolved issues of the war repatriations during the two world wars, for example, the return of Korean and Chinese cultural heritage taken by Japan in the early

106 *New Scheme*, above n 75.

20th century, have constituted a powerful deterrent to the creation of the proposed customary rule. In summary, the state practice with regards to the return of cultural heritage looted during armed conflicts reflects an increasing recognition of states of origin's interest in their wrongfully taken heritage and signals the emerging of the proposed customary rule.

Bibliography

'The 1954 Hague Convention' US Committee of the Blue Shield <http://uscbs.org/1954-hague-convention.html>

'Act implementing the Convention of 14 May 1954 for the Protection of Cultural Property in the Event of Armed Conflict' <www.kulturgutschutz-deutschland.de/SharedDocs/ExterneLinks/EN/Gesetze_en/KultgSchKonvAG_en.pdf;jsessionid=40024BC88161857C417ADAB4679C55D2.1_cid350?__blob=publicationFile>

'Act of 8 March 2007 containing rules on the taking into custody of cultural property from an occupied territory during an armed conflict and for the initiation of proceedings for the return of such property' <www.unesco.org/culture/natlaws/media/pdf/netherlands/netherlands_actmarch2007_engtof.pdf>

'Act of 8 March 2007 containing rules on the taking into custody of cultural property from an occupied territory during an armed conflict and for the initiation of proceedings for the return of such property (Cultural Property Originating from Occupied Territory (Return) Act)' <www.eui.eu/Projects/InternationalArtHeritageLaw/Documents/NationalLegislation/Netherlands/actof2007coveringoccupiedterritory.pdf>

'Britain Should Ratify Convention to Protect Cultural Objects in Time of War', *Telegraph* July 21 2014 <www.telegraph.co.uk/comment/letters/10979564/Britain-should-ratify-convention-to-protect-cultural-objects-in-time-of-war.html>

'British Government Announces Plans to Ratify the 1954 Hague Convention' (UK National Committee of the Blue Shield, June 22 2015) <http://ukblueshield.org.uk/british-government-announces-plans-to-ratify-the-1954-hague-convention/>

'British Museum 'Guarding' Object Looted from Syria', *BBC* June 5 2015 <www.bbc.co.uk/news/entertainment-arts-33020199>

'Council Regulation (EU) No 1332/2013 of 13 December 2013 Amending Regulation (EU) No 36/2012 Concerning Restrictive Measures in View of the Situation in Syria' <http://eur-lex.europa.eu/legal-content/EN/TXT/HTML/?uri=CELEX:32012R0036%20&from=EN>

'Draft Cultural Property (Armed Conflicts) Bill' (January 2008) <www.gov.uk/government/uploads/system/uploads/attachment_data/file/243113/7298.pdf>

'Explanatory Memorandum' <www.unesco.org/culture/natlaws/media/pdf/netherlands/netherlands_memo_returnoccupiedterritory_engtof.pdf>

'Federal Law on the Protection of Cultural Objects in the Event of Armed Conflict, Disaster and Emergency Situations' <www.unesco.org/culture/natlaws/media/pdf/switzerland/suisse_fedactprotcltprop_entof>

'Government Tackles International Cultural Destruction' (Historic England, June 22 2015) <www.historicengland.org.uk/news-and-features/news/the-hague-ratify>

'The Hague Convention and the Hague Protocol (Message from the President of the United States)' <www.gpo.gov/fdsys/pkg/CDOC-106tdoc1/html/CDOC-106tdoc1.htm>

'Iraq (United Nations Sanctions) Order, Statutory Instrument 2003 No. 1519' (June 22 2003) <www.unesco.org/culture/natlaws/media/pdf/gb/gb_iraq unitednationssanctions2003_engorof.pdf>

'Joint Communique of the Government of Japan and the Government of the People's Republic of China' (1972) *Ministry of Foreign Affairs of Japan* <www.mofa.go.jp/region/asia-paci/china/joint72.html>

'New Scheme to Protect Cultural Sites from Destruction' (UK Government, October 28 2015) <www.gov.uk/government/news/new-scheme-to-protect-cultural-sites-from-destruction>

'Other Cases of Return or Restitution of Cultural Obejcts' (UNESCO <www.unesco.org/new/en/culture/themes/illicit-trafficking-of-cultural-property/other-cases-of-return-or-restitution-of-cultural-objects/>

'Practice Relating to Rule 150. Reparation' ICRC <www.icrc.org/customary-ihl/eng/docs/v2_cha_chapter42_rule150_sectionb>

'President Signs Engel Bill to Stop Isis From Looting Antiquities', US Committee of the Blue Shield May 9 2016 <http://uscbs.org/news/president-signs-engel-bill-stop-isis-looting-antiquities/>

'United Nations Security Council Resolution 2199' <http://unesdoc.unesco.org/images/0023/002321/232164e.pdf>

'War Damage on Cultural Relics Commission under the Department of Education', *China Cultural Relics* August 22 2007 <www.xhgxt.com/html/View_9270.html>

Bassiouni, M. Cherif, 'Reflections on Criminal Jurisdiction in International Protection of Cultural Property' (1983) 10(2) *Syracuse Journal of International Law and Commerce* 281

Bong, Shin Hae, 'Compensation for Victims of Wartime Atrocities: Recent Developments in Japan's Case Law' (2005) 3(1) *Journal of International Criminal Justice* 187

Brodie, Neil and Colin Renfrew, 'Looting and the World's Archaeological Heritage: The Inadequate Response' (2005) 34 *Annual Review of Anthropology* 343

Chechi, Alessandro, *The Settlement of International Cultural Heritage Disputes* (Oxford University Press, 2014)

Downey, William Gerald, 'Captured Enemy Property: Booty of War and Seized Enemy Property' (1950) 44(3) *The American Journal of International Law* 488

Einhorn, Talia, 'Restitution of Archaeological Artifacts: The Arab–Israeli Aspects' (1996) 5(1) *International Journal of Cultural Property* 133

Ferrari, Silvio and Andrea Benzo, *Between Cultural Diversity and Common Heritage: Legal and Religious Perspectives on the Sacred Places of the Mediterranean* (Ashgate, 2014)

Forrest, Craig, *International Law and The Protection of Cultural Heritage* (Routledge, 2010)

Forsyth, Marion, 'Casualties of War: The Destruction of Iraq's Cultural Heritage as a Result of US Action During and After the 1991 Gulf War' (2004) XIV *DePaul-LCA Journal of Art & Entertainment Law* 73

Francioni, Francesco, 'The Evolving International Legal Framework for the Protection of Cultural Heritage' in Silvia Borelli and Federico Lenzerini (eds), *Cultural Heritage, Cultural Rights, Cultural Diversity* (Brill, 2012) 3

Freeman, Alwyn V., 'General Note on the Law of War Booty' (1946) 40(4) *The American Journal of International Law* 795

Gerstenblith, Patty, '2010 Cultural Heritage Legal Summary' (2011) 36(3) *Journal of Field Archaeology* 257

Gerstenblith, Patty, 'Increasing Effectiveness of The Legal Regime for the Protection of the International Archaeological Heritage' in James A.R. Nafziger and Ann Nicgorski (eds), *Cultural Heritage Issues* (Martinus Nijhoff Publishers, 2009) 305

He, Yinan, 'The Bitter Legacies of the 1972 Sino-Japanese Normalization Talks' (China and The World Program, May 29 2017) <https://cwp.princeton.edu/news/bitter-legacies-1972-sino-japanese-normalization-talks-article-cwp-alumni-yinan-he>

Henckaerts, Jean-Marie and Louise Doswald-Beck, *Customary International Humanitarian Law, Volume 1* (Cambridge University Press, 2005)

Henckaerts, Jean-Marie and Louise Doswald-Beck, *Customary International Humanitarian Law, Volume 2* (Cambridge University Press, 2005)

Hladik, Jan, 'The Review Process of the 1954 Hague Convention for the Protection of Cultural Property in the Event of Armed Conflict and its Impact on International Humanitarian Law' (1998) 1 *Yearbook of International Humanitarian Law* 313

Jakubowski, Andrzej, *State Succession in Cultural Property* (Oxford University Press, 2015)

Jote, Kifle, *International Legal Protection of Cultural Heritage* (Juristforlaget, 1994)

Kastenberg, Joshua E., 'The Legal Regime for Protecting Cultural Property During Armed Conflict' (1997) 42 *Air Force Law Review* 277

Kowalski, Wojciech, *Art Treasures and War: A Study on the Restitution of Looted Cultural Property Pursuant to Public International Law* (Art, Antiquity and Law, 1998)

Kozai, Shigeru and Toshiyuki Kono, 'Japan' in James A.R. Nafziger and Robert Paterson (eds), *Handbook on the Law of Cultural Heritage and International Trade* (2014) 257

Matyk, Stephan, 'The Restitution of Cultural Objects and the Question of Giving Direct Effect to the Protocol to the Hague Convention for the Protection of Cultural Property in the Event of Armed Conflict 1954' (2000) 9(2) *International Journal of Cultural Property* 341

Meyer, David A., 'The 1954 Hague Cultural Property Convention and its emergence into customary international law' (1993) 11(2) *Boston University International Law Journal* 349

Nafziger, James A.R. and Robert Paterson, 'Cultural Heritage Law' in James A.R. Nafziger and Robert Paterson (eds), *Handbook on the Law of Cultural Heritage and International Trade* (Edward Elgar Publishing, 2014) 1

Neuhaus, Nina M., 'Switzerland Limits Trade in Syrian Cultural Property' (Institute of Art and Law Blog, January 14 2015) <www.ial.uk.com/news/switzerland-limits-trade-in-syrian-cultural-property/>

Nicholas, Lynn H., *The Rape of Europa: The Fate of Europe's Treasures in the Third Reich and the Second World War* (Vintage, 1995)

Paterson, Robert, 'Resolving Material Culture Disputes: Human Rights, Property Rights, and Crimes against Humanity' in James A.R. Nafziger and Ann Nicgorski (eds), *Cultural Heritage Issues* (Martinus Nijhoff Publishers, 2009) 371

Paul Martin, Ed Vulliamy and Gaby Hinsliff, 'US Army Was Told to Protect Looted Museum', *The Guardian* April 21 2003 <www.theguardian.com/world/2003/apr/20/internationaleducationnews.iraq>

Peters, Robert, 'Remedying Historical Injustice: Ethical and Historical Considerations in Returning Cultural Materials' in Silvia Borelli and Federico Lenzerini (eds), *Cultural Heritage, Cultural Rights, Cultural Diversity* (Martinus Nijhoff Publishers, 2012) 141

Prott, Lyndel, 'The History and Development of Processes for the Recovery of Cultural Heritage' in Lyndel Prott (ed), *Witnesses to History* (UNESCO, 2008) 2

Redmond-Cooper, Ruth, 'Call for UK Government to ratify Hague Convention' (Institute of Art and Law Blog, 2015) <www.ial.uk.com/news/call-for-uk-government-to-ratify-hague-convention/>

Renold, Marc-André, 'Cross-Border Restitution Claims of Art Looted in Armed Conflicts and Wars and Alternatives to Court Litigations' (European Parliament Think Tank <www.europarl.europa.eu/RegData/etudes/STUD/2016/556947/IPOL_STU(2016)556947_EN.pdf>

Roberts, Adam, *Documents on the Laws of War* (Oxford University Press, 2000)

Roodt, Christa, *Private International Law, Art and Cultural Heritage* (Edward Elgar Publishing, 2015)

Sandholtz, Wayne, 'The Iraqi National Museum and International Law: A Duty to Protect' (2005) 44(1) *Columbia Journal Transnational Law* 185

Sandholtz, Wayne, 'Plunder, Restitution, and International Law' (2010) 17(2) *International Journal of Cultural Property* 147

Sandholtz, Wayne, *Prohibiting Plunder: How Norms Change* (Oxford University Press, 2007)

Scott, Carol, 'UK to Adopt Hague Convention to Protect Artefacts in War Zones' (ICOM, June 22 2015) <http://uk.icom.museum/uk-to-adopt-hague-convention-to-protect-artefacts-in-war-zones/>

Scott, Geoffrey R., 'Spoliation, Cultural property, and Japan' (2008) 29(4) *University of Pennsylvania Journal of International Law* 803

Second Historical Archives of China, China, *A Collective Documents about the Republic of China, Volume 5, Issue 3, Culture* (Jiangsu Phoenix House, 1999)

Shelton, Dinah, 'The World of Atonement: Reparations for Historical Injustices' (2003) 50(3) *Netherlands International Law Review* 289

Toman, Jiri, 'The Hague Convention—A Decisive Step Taken by the International Community' (2005) 57(4) *Museum International* 7

Toman, Jiri, *The Protection of Cultural Property In the Event of Armed Conflict: Commentary on the 1954 Hague Convention and on Other Instruments of International Law Concerning Such Protection* (Dartmouth, 1996)

Vigneron, Sophie, 'Protecting Cultural Objects: Enforcing the Illicit Export of Foreign Cultural Objects' in Valentina Vadi and Hildegard Schneider (eds), *Art, Cultural Heritage and the Market: Ethical and Legal Issues* (Springer, 2014) 117

Vrdoljak, Ana Filipa, *International Law, Museums and The Return of Cultural Objects* (Cambridge University Press, 2006)

Xiaodong, Li, *An Analysis on the Legal Documents regarding Cultural Relics in Republic of China* (Cultural Relics Press, 2013)

6 Return of Cultural Heritage Stolen and Illegally Exported in Peacetime

1. Introduction

Aside from looting during armed conflicts, theft and smuggling across state borders in peacetime has been declared one of the main causes for the impoverishment of the states of origin of such property.[1] In order to protect their heritage, the states of origin often enact laws by placing their heritage under state control and restricting exports. Meanwhile, in order to bring their heritage home, states of origin have been active in taking legal action against museums and art dealers, arguing that the takings were in violation of their national laws. However, such laws can have little success unless they are recognised and enforced by another state. In this regard, there is a clear tendency for market states to be more willing to return stolen and illegally exported heritage to the states of origin.

Chapter 6 focuses on those state practices related to the return of cultural heritage illicitly trafficked during peacetime. First, this chapter outlines the problems in enforcing foreign state ownership laws and export laws. Following this is an examination of the relevant laws supporting the return of such objects at both the international and regional levels, which serve as a catalyst for individual market states to return stolen and illegally exported cultural objects. The chapter then continues to analyse the law and practices in the important market states, including the US, Germany, Switzerland, the Netherlands and the UK, to analyse whether their state practices reflect an increasing recognition that stolen and illegally exported heritage should be returned. The last section provides a brief outline of the emerging rules that are increasingly being used or suggested in the return of cultural heritage. As will be analysed, the practices of the specially affected states shows a recognition and respect of the states of origin's interests in their wrongfully removed heritage; however it is very limited. This lack of uniformity suggests that the proposed customary rule is at the very beginning of the process of its formation.

1 Article 2(1) of 1970 UNESCO Convention.

2. Difficulties in Enforcing State Ownership Laws and Export Laws

Faced with the destruction and illegal removal of heritage, many source states have responded to the problem with a two-pronged legal approach: enacting ownership law and export controls. Beginning in the mid-19th century, many countries rich in cultural heritage enacted national laws that vested ownership of all cultural heritage, whether known or unknown, in the state.[2] The aim of this so-called "blanket" legislation is to protect cultural heritage under an umbrella of state ownership before its discovery. That is to say, any object found in the state belongs to the state, and if any such object is removed from the country without the state's knowledge, such object can be classified as stolen property. This enables both the punishment of the looter and the recovery of possession of the antiquity from ether the thief or a subsequent purchaser.[3] In addition to ownership law, states of origin also place export controls that restrict the export of cultural objects, except in limited circumstances. Export controls usually take the form of licence requirements. Compared with ownership law, export laws are created to prevent the outflow of art objects without affecting the title and to give states an opportunity to prevent the export of lawfully, privately-owned cultural objects.

As many cultural relics have been in the possession of foreign museums or private dealers for many years, recovery claims are normally directed to the competent authorities in the place where the objects are found and, thus, disputes often involve more than one legal system.[4] The question then becomes whether a foreign state can use its state ownership laws or export laws as the legal basis for the return of the items.[5] While courts of all countries are open to actions for the recovery of property stolen from individuals, the main obstacle for states to recover illegally removed heritage is the principle of territory, under which only ownership law enjoys extraterritorial effect.[6] In other words,

2 Many countries who have many archaeological sites enacted such blanket legislations, and these laws have been examined in different cases. For example, in Turkey (e.g., *Republic of Turkey v OKS Partners* (1994 US Dist LEXIS 17032, D Mass 1994); Egypt (e.g., *R. v Tokeley-Parry*, [1999] Crim LR 578 (CA); Peru (e.g., *Government of Peru v Johnson* (720 F Supp 810, CD Cal 1989); Mexico (e.g., *United States v McClain* (545 F 2d 988, 5th Cir, reh'g denied, 551 F 2d 52, 5th Cir 1977); and Iran (e.g., *Government of the Islamic Republic of Iran v The Barakat Galleries Ltd* [2007] EWCA Civ 1374).

3 Alessandro Chechi, *The Settlement of International Cultural Heritage Disputes* (Oxford University Press, 2014), 66–67.

4 Christa Roodt, *Private International Law, Art and Cultural Heritage* (Edward Elgar Publishing, 2015), 40–41.

5 Lyndel Prott, 'Problems of Private International Law for the Protection of the Cultural Heritage' in Hague Academy of International Law (ed), *Collected Courses of the Hague Academy of International Law* (Nijhoff, 1989) 215, 223.

6 James Gordley, 'The Enforcement of Foreign Law: Reclaiming One Nation's Cultural Heritage in Another Nation's Courts' in Francesco Francioni and James Gordley (eds), *Enforcing International Cultural Heritage Law* (Oxford University Press, 2013) 110, 110–118.

a state is not obliged to recognise and enforce other states' export laws in the absence of a treaty or bilateral agreement. Thus, even though a cultural object is illegally exported, its illicit export does not necessarily constitute an illegal import.

In this situation, a legal alternative for a claiming state is to argue that it owns the object, not because its export laws have been violated. However, questions still remain. The first is whether the cultural heritage owned by a foreign state should be treated differently from other types of stolen property. Second, even though foreign ownership law can be used as a legal basis for recovery claims, questions still exist with regards to blanket legislation and their application to artefacts clandestinely excavated and then illegally exported overseas. Pursuant to blanket legislation, states have absolute ownership rights at all times after discovery, without performing any further act of appropriation or possession. However, this does not always work out in many lawsuits.[7] For example, in *Peru v Johnson*, concerning some 89 allegedly stolen pre-Columbaian gold, ceramic and fabric objects in the defendant Johnson's collection, the government of Peru sued to retrieve these cultural objects from Johnson on the basis that Peru's 1985 Supreme Decree claimed that all pre-Hispanic artistic objects belonged to the "nation's cultural wealth".[8] However, the court did not favour the recovery. Among the reasons was that "the laws of Peru concerning its artefacts could reasonably be considered to have no more effect than export restriction".[9] Thus, following the court decision in *Peru v Johnson*, to claim for stolen cultural objects or, more precisely, clandestinely excavated antiquities, a requesting state needs to prove that it has obtained possession associated with ownership.[10] But the question is the burden of proof, as a state will never have the opportunity to keep records of these clandestinely excavated antiquities, unless they are forfeited during the export attempt.

Apart from the difficulties in enforcing foreign ownership law and export law, when a state of origin sues for the return of cultural heritage objects, the lawsuit usually involves various complex issues. For example, in the auction case in 2009, a group of Chinese lawyers also launched a legal bid in a Paris court to stop the sale. However, the court ruled against stopping the auction, concluding that the plaintiff did not have a direct interest in the two statues and therefore no standing before the court. This case illustrates that in order to be able to be a party to a court action, it is necessary to be a juristic person recognised by the court and to have a legal standing. Another difficulty in the recovery comes from the *lex situs* rule, according to which it is the law of the place where the transfer is said to have taken effect. However, this rule is interpreted differently in different jurisdictions: in UK the law of the last

7 Janet Blake, *International Cultural Heritage Law* (Oxford University Press, 2015), 57.
8 *Government of Peru v Johnson* (720 F Supp 810, CD Cal 1989), paras 813–814.
9 Ibid.
10 Gordley, *Enforcement of Foreign Law*, above n 6, 119.

transaction is applied, while the US law favours the law of the place where the goods were at the time of the last transaction.[11] This general rule entails unpredictable outcomes, as thieves can easily take advantage of the differences among jurisdictions and launder the title of illicitly removed objects and profit from their wrongdoings. Additionally, the question as to whether a recovery claim is to be time-barred under the statute of limitations of the jurisdiction within which the case is raised is another complex issue concerning the return of illegally removed cultural heritage objects.[12] All these issues have made the return problematic and hard to be realised.

However, in the past two decades, an increasing number of stolen and illegally exported objects have been ordered to be returned. Looking at these cases, it can be noted that many market states are inclined to recognise a foreign state's entitlement to claim for cultural heritage illicitly trafficked during peacetime. The following sections examine the relevant laws at the international, regional and national levels that are applied to the return of stolen and illegally exported cultural heritage. In discussing the proposed customary rule, this chapter aims to explore whether the practices of the specially affected states shows an increasing recognition of states of origin's interests in their wrongfully removed heritage.

3. The International and European Frameworks

While cultural objects are traded in violation of national ownership and/or exports laws, traffickers can take advantage of the differences among jurisdictions to launder the title of illicitly removed objects and to profit from their wrongdoings. Thus, cooperation from the market states is urgently required. Unless an importing state recognises foreign laws or has import restrictions in place, a state of origin would have little opportunity to bring their illicitly trafficked heritage home.

3.1. 1936 Treaty of Washington

The earliest multilateral treaty providing for the application of foreign laws and the subsequent return of cultural objects is the Treaty on the Protection of Movable Property of Historic Value, which is generally known as the Treaty of Washington. According to this treaty, for the import of protected objects from member states, the importer was required to present a valid export licence from the state of origin. If attempts were made to import an object without a valid export licence, the object would be confiscated and returned to the respective state of origin.[13] Additionally, states of origin were allowed

11 Blake, *Cultural Heritage Law*, above n 7.

12 See, e.g., *Republic of Turkey v Metropolitan Museum of Art*, 762 F Supp 44 (SDNY 1990).

13 Articles 2 and 3 of the Treaty of Washington.

to seek for return by initiating proceedings in a civil court of the holding state, which at that time was an innovative approach to recover illicitly trafficked objects.[14] However, the Treaty of Washington is relatively limited as it only applies to states in North America and Latin America, and covers a very small group of objects, dating from pre-Columbian, colonial times or the period of emancipation and the republic.[15] Thus, an international instrument, accepted by the majority of the international community, was urgently needed.

3.2. 1970 UNESCO Convention

In the late 1960s and 1970s, newly independent countries were not only anxious to recover their cultural relics, many of which had been placed in the museums of former colonising states, but were also concerned at the continuing loss of cultural relics. The 1970 UNESCO Convention was the result of a concerted push by newly independent states to obtain international cooperation in the effective protection of their cultural objects from theft and illicit export.[16]

With regards to the proposed customary rule, the UNESCO Convention is significant, as it favours the interests of the states of origin over market states. Support for this view is first evident in the Preamble, which declares that it is "incumbent upon every State to protect cultural property existing within its territory against the dangers of theft, clandestine excavation, and illicit export".[17] Claims for national retention by states of origin find support in the Convention, in that the true value of cultural heritage "can be appreciated only in relation to the fullest possible information regarding its origin, history and traditional setting".[18] This suggests that the importance of cultural heritage is diminished when it is removed from its original setting. Second, the definition of cultural heritage under the UNESCO Convention gives further evidence for respecting the states of origin. In establishing what would be qualified as cultural heritage, the Convention does not provide a uniform definition, but rather leaves a good deal of freedom for individual states to designate property they consider to be important for their archaeology, prehistory, history, literature, art or science.[19] The language, "specifically designated by each state", gives individual states a broad power to determine what they would protect as cultural heritage. Third, the other key term of being "illicit" is also given meaning through the national laws of individual states. Article 3

14 Article 6 of the Treaty of Washington.
15 Article 1 of the Treaty of Washington.
16 James A.R. Nafziger and Robert Kirkwood Paterson, 'Cultural Heritage Law' in James A.R. Nafziger and Robert Kirkwood Paterson (eds), *Handbook on the Law of Cultural Heritage and International Trade* (Edward Elgar Publishing, 2014), 4–6.
17 Preamble of the 1970 UNESCO Convention.
18 Ibid.
19 Article 1 of the 1970 UNESCO Convention.

suggests that any transfer of cultural heritage in violation of the laws enacted by the country of origin to protect its cultural heritage is illicit and prohibited under the Convention.[20] Thus, the UNESCO Convention is significant in the creation of the proposed customary rule, not only because it favours the interests of the states of origin over market states, but also because it constitutes an acknowledgement of the special connection between states of origin and their cultural heritage.

In arguing for the proposed customary rule, the UNESCO Convention is also significant in justifying the return of illicitly removed heritage and calling for international cooperation.[21] Article 7(b) applies to stolen heritage and contains two complementary subparts: Article 7(b)(i) requires states to prohibit the import of cultural heritage stolen from a museum or other public institution, while Article 7(b)(ii) requires states "to take appropriate steps to recover and return" such property. However, the obligation to return is not concerned with every stolen item. To fall within the protection of Article 7(b), cultural heritage must have been: (1) stolen after the Convention entered into force, (2) removed from a museum or similar institution, and (3) documented as belonging to the inventory of that institution. Thus, cultural heritage not stolen from a public institution, such as archaeological objects illegally excavated or objects from private collections, could still be legally imported. However, the limitations in Article 7(b) are arguably justified because the Convention covers cultural objects most likely to fall within the "core" of a nation's heritage since they would be documented as forming part of a public museum or institution's collection.[22]

With regards to illicitly exported cultural objects, Article 9 does not impose direct obligations on states to adopt import restrictions, but encourages states to participate in a concerted international effort though two different approaches. First, a bilateral agreement, as the result of negotiation, is required to initiate the procedure of restitution. This bilateral agreement contains a list of the types of cultural heritage subject to a recovery claim and restricts imports to apply only to those objects noted in the designated list. Thus, it is not a blanket ban on all antiquities being imported into the market. This approach was chosen, for example, by the US and Switzerland. Alternatively, Australia uses the second approach, which requires bilateral agreements with other signatories of the UNESCO Convention. In other words, any object illegally exported from another UNESCO state and brought to Australia will be returned to that state. Thus, the UNESCO Convention is indispensable in the return of wrongfully removed heritage, not only because an importing

20 Kevin Jower, 'Comment: International and National Legal Efforts to Protect Cultural Property: The 1970 UNESCO Convention, the United States, and Mexico' (2003) 38 *Texas International Law Journal* 145, 151.

21 The UNESCO Convention contains both export control from countries of origin (Article 6) and import restrictions from market states (Article 7).

22 Jower, *International and National Legal Efforts*, above n 20, 153.

state acknowledges the problems of illicit trafficking of cultural heritage by placing import restrictions but, more importantly, it provides a mechanism to facilitate the return of such objects.[23]

In conclusion, the UNESCO Convention is significant in showing the recognition of the interests of the states of origin in wrongfully taken heritage and creating the proposed customary rule. First, it was the first legal instrument to give international effect to property interests on the grounds of foreign state ownership laws and export laws with regards to cultural heritage.[24] In particular, through the recognition of foreign export law, the Convention has significantly changed the long-lasting rule that foreign public laws are non-justiciable. Second, it constitutes an acknowledgement that the rights of the states of origin with regards to their illegally removed cultural heritage are justifiable and that the enforcement of foreign export laws do not violate the sovereignty of the forum.[25] For example, in the case of *Iran v Barak*, the Government of Iran sued the London-based Barakat Galleries seeking the restitution of a collection of 18 carved jars, bowls, and cups that had been illicitly excavated in South-East Iran, and subsequently exported abroad. The Court of Appeal, overruling the trial court decision, referred to the UNESCO Convention and held that there are positive reasons of policy that Iranian claim should not be shut out on the ground of the principle that domestic courts should not entertain legal actions brought by foreign sovereigns to enforce, directly or indirectly, its penal, revenue, or other public laws.[26] Third, starting from the UNESCO Convention, there is a growing recognition that states should assist one another to prevent the unlawful removal of cultural objects. To coincide with the UNESCO Convention, major market countries, such as the UK, the US, Germany, Switzerland and France, ratified the UNESCO Convention and adopted implementing legislation. The high level of ratification of the Convention by specially affected states evidences both the increasing awareness of the problem of trafficking of cultural relics and,

23 The UNESCO Convention is not free from criticism. For example, the UNESCO Convention is not self-executing and requires the state parties to amend their domestic laws in accordance with its provisions. Many provisions consist of the insertion of phrases such as 'as appropriate for each country' (Article 5), 'to the extent feasible' (Article 9) or 'as far as possible' (Article 14). These provisions give state parties great leeway as to how they implement the Convention. For example, Sweden ratified the Convention in 2002, but followed a minimalistic approach. The ratification did not lead to any changes in the Swedish law and it is still legal to import objects smuggled out of other countries. M. Bouchenaki, 'Return and Restitution of Cultural Property in the Wake of the 1970 Convention' (2009) 61(1–2) *Museum International* 139, 140.

24 Mara Wantuch-Thole, *Cultural Property in Cross-Border Litigation: Turning Rights into Claims* (De Gruyter, 2014), 189.

25 Sophie Vigneron, 'Protecting Cultural Objects: Enforcing the Illicit Export of Foreign Cultural Objects' in Valentina Vadi and Hildegard Schneider (eds), *Art, Cultural Heritage and the Market: Ethical and Legal Issues* (Springer, 2014) 117, 125.

26 *Government of the Islamic Republic of Iran v The Barakat Galleries Ltd* [2007] EWCA Civ 1374, paras 154–155.

arguably, of the principle of return embodied in the Convention.[27] Although the UNESCO Convention does not apply retroactively, it is important evidence to argue for the proposed customary rule that paves the way for the return of historically removed cultural heritage.

3.3. 1995 UNIDROIT Convention

The 1995 UNIDROIT Convention was drafted by the International Institute for the Unification of Private Law with the approval of UNESCO. This Convention is a uniform law that aims at addressing the shortcomings of the UNESCO Convention, with the expectation that the two instruments could work together.[28] The UNIDROIT Convention deals with both the theft and illicit exportation of cultural objects.

Chapter II of the UNIDROIT Convention places an outright obligation on the return of stolen cultural heritage, even if the stolen cultural objects are recovered in those systems of law that protect the good faith possessor.[29] It should be noted that the obligations laid down in the UNIDROIT Convention concerning stolen cultural objects expand the protection provided by the UNESCO Convention, as the latter only applies to stolen objects inventoried by a museum or other public institution.[30] In addition, while illegal excavated property is excluded by the UNESCO Convention, the UNIDROIT Convention explicitly protects such property. Article 3(2) states that "a cultural object which has been unlawfully excavated or lawfully excavated but unlawfully retained shall be considered stolen", when consistent with the law of the state where the excavation took place.[31] This characterisation as theft is a significant recognition of foreign ownership law, because previous recovery cases suggested that blanket state ownership claims for clandestinely excavated cultural objects have not always been upheld. However, according to Article 3(2), recovery claims should not be barred on the basis that blanket legislation vesting the state with ownership is ineffective, or that the state must reduce an object to possession or exercise its right of appropriation in the first place.

27 Vigneron, *Enforcing the Illicit Export of Foreign Cultural Objects*, above n 27, 127.
28 For example, the protected scope of cultural property in the UNESCO and UNIDROIT Conventions are exactly the same. This was done on purpose so that states could become party to both and these two instruments could work together. But unlike the UNESCO Convention, the UNIDROIT Convention is self-executing and allows for no reservations (Article 18). If a treaty is self-executing, it only requires a signature and ratification in order to gain effect. Additionally, the UNIDROIT Convention pertains to private international law and implementing legislation creates private rights of action for recovery of stolen and illegally exported cultural objects, whereas the 1970 Convention operates on a state-to-state basis. Lyndel Prott, 'UNESCO and UNIDROIT: a Partnership against Trafficking in Cultural Objects' (1996) 1 *Uniform Law Review* 59, 64.
29 Article 3 of the 1995 UNIDROIT Convention.
30 Prott, *UNESCO and UNIDROIT*, above n 28, 64.
31 Article 3(2) of the UNIDROIT Convention.

The purpose of Article 3(2) is to provide uniform protection of the cultural heritage of those states of origin with rich archaeological resources and avoid various interoperations of their laws by foreign countries.[32]

Chapter III of the UNIDROIT Convention focuses on the return of illegally exported cultural heritage. The Convention establishes that a contracting state may request the court or other competent authority of another contracting state to order the return, provided two conditions are fulfilled.[33] First, the requesting state must act within the prescribed time limits.[34] Second, the requesting state must demonstrate that the removal of the object from its territory significantly impairs the physical preservation of the object or of its context, the preservation of information of a scientific or historical character, the traditional or ritual use of the object by a tribal or indigenous community, or establishes that the object is of "significant cultural importance" for the requesting state.[35] In this regard, the language "significant cultural importance" for a nation can be seen as a sweeping provision, which ensures the interests of the states of origin in a broad way.[36]

Despite the good intentions of the Convention, there are questions about its implementation. Many important market states have not shown their support for the UNIDROIT Convention, given the issues with the limitation period,[37] the reverse burden of proof,[38] the wide definition of stolen property by including archaeological artefacts,[39] and the underlying compromise

32 Sibel Ozel, 'Case note. The Basel Decisions: Recognition of the Blanket Legislation Vesting State Ownership Over the Cultural Property Found Within the Country of Origin' (2000) 9(2) *International Journal of Cultural Property* 315, 337.

33 Article 5(1) of the UNIDROIT Convention.

34 Article 5(5) of the UNIDROIT Convention.

35 Article 5(3) of the UNIDROIT Convention. This article has been criticised for "giving blank check enforcement of any form of export law a foreign government may enact". Monique Olivier, 'The UNIDROIT Convention: attempting to regulate the international trade and traffic of cultural property' (1996) 26(1–3) *Golden Gate University Law Review* 627, 661.

36 Janet Ulph and Ian Smith, *The Illicit Trade in Art and Antiquities: International Recovery and Criminal and Civil Liability* (Hart Publishing, 2012), 59.

37 For example, the state can claim for the repatriation of an illegally exported cultural object within a fixed period of three years from the time of its location and the identity of its possessor and within a maximum of 50 years from the date of export (Article 3). The initial purpose is to prevent thieves from taking advantage of the differences among jurisdictions and launder the title of the illicitly removed objects to profit from their wrongdoings. Patrick O'Keefe, 'Using UNIDROIT to Avoid Cultural Heritage Disputes: Limitation Periods' (2009) 14 *Willamette Journal of Internatioanl Law and Dispute Resolution* 227.

38 In most civil law countries, the good faith of the acquirer is presumed until the claimant can prove bad faith. However, under the UNIDROIT Convention, the possessor has to prove that he/she exercised due diligence when acquiring the object. Otherwise, the possessor will not be entitled to payment of a 'fair and reasonable compensation' (Article 4).

39 Article 3(2) is another major reason for countries' unwillingness to ratify UNIDROIT Convention, as market states could not be expected to enter into such far-reaching

it strikes.[40] For example, while the ratification of the UNIDROIT Convention was initially supported by the British Select Committee of the House of Commons, the Ministerial Advisory panel on illicit trade did not support the ratification because of the conflicts with English law, particularly the short time limitation for stolen objects.[41] The lack of wide ratification constitutes a powerful deterrent to the acceptance of the principles underpinned by the UNIDROIT Convention.

Despite the poor ratification, it should be noted that some principles of the UNIDROIT Convention have been transposed into national and European legal systems. For example, the higher standards of due diligence set forth by the UNIDROIT Convention have been endorsed by the UK through the enactment of Dealing in Cultural Objects (Offences) Act 2003. Another example is that the 1995 UNIDROIT Convention adopted the idea that the law of the state of origin is the controlling law in cases of cultural objects being stolen or illicitly excavated from a foreign state.[42] Similar ideas can be found in the EC Directive, as Article 12 reads that "ownership of the cultural object after return shall be governed by that law of the requesting Member State".[43] Applying the law of the requesting state is important in respecting the interests of the states of origin with regards to illegally removed cultural objects, not only because it will allow states of origin's own policies to be applied to govern the dispute and achieve the best outcomes, but it will also increase the transparency of the art market.

In summary, the UNIDROIT Convention is significant in contributing to the acknowledgement that states of origin should have sufficient interests to claim for both stolen and illegally exported objects, which is consistent with the proposed customary rule. However, due to the lack of extensive ratification, the impact of the UNIDROIT Convention is rather limited.

3.4. European Initiatives

The guiding principle of the European Union is the idea of free trade of all goods within the internal market. As such, there was wide concern that the

---

commitments with regard to such an array of categories of cultural objects, especially when reservations are not allowed.

40 Article 18 states that 'no reservations are permitted'.

41 In the UK, the basic rule is that title expires six years following a good faith conversion. 'Seventh Report of the Select Committee on Culture, Media and Sport' <www.parliament.the-stationery-office.co.uk/pa/cm199900/cmselect/cmcumeds/371/37106.htm>.

42 Article 3(2) reads that "a cultural object which has been unlawfully excavated or lawfully excavated but unlawfully retained shall be considered stolen, when consistent with the law of the State where the excavation took place".

43 Article 12 of the Council Directive 93/7/EEC of March 15 1993 on the return of cultural objects unlawfully removed from the territory of a Member State (1993 Council Directive).

opening of the single market would encourage the illegal removal of cultural relics.[44] At this point, Article 36 of the Treaty on the Functioning of the European Union (TFEU) provides an exception from free trade, allowing member states to include prohibitions or restrictions on the protection of those national treasures possessing artistic, historic or archaeological value.[45] Hence, if there is an illegal removal, the object must be returned to the member state of origin. The respect for the member states of origin cultural property is further reflected in two texts: Council Regulation No. 3911/1992 on the export of cultural goods (the 1992 Council Regulation) and Council Directive 93/7/EEC of 15 March 1993 on the return of cultural objects unlawfully removed from the territory of a Member State (the 1993 Council Directive).

The 1992 Council Regulation holds that cultural heritage defined as national treasures within the meaning of Article 36 TEFU and belonging to one of the categories listed in the Annex can be exported outside the EU only if accompanied by an export certificate by the member state of origin.[46] This regulation is important in preventing the export out of the EU of cultural objects unlawfully removed from the original state through the exploitation of the less stringent export rules of other member states.[47] Together with the Council Regulation, the 1993 Council Directive regulates that all member states are obliged to return cultural relics that were "unlawfully removed from another member state".[48] Therefore, the 1993 Council Directive introduces the extraterritorial enforcement of national protection policies and allows the return of illegally exported arts.[49] The 1993 Council Directive affirms the duty to return cultural heritage that has been illegally exported from a member state,[50] grants the right to a requesting member state to initiate proceedings against the possessor or holder before a competent court in the requested member state,[51] and encourages member states to cooperate in order to prevent "any

44 Norman Palmer, 'Statutory, Forensic and Ethical Initiatives in the Recovery of Stolen art and Antiquities' in Norman Palmer (ed), *The Recovery of Stolen Art: A Collection of Essays* (Kluwer Law International, 1998), 13; John O'Hagan and Clare McAndrew, 'Export Restrictions, Tax Incentives and the National Artistic Patrimony' (2000) 10(37) *Cultural Trends* 41, 53.

45 In order to facilitate uniform controls, the Regulation introduces an EU-wide system of export licences for the export of cultural goods outside the customs territory of the Community.

46 Kurt Siehr, 'Germany' in James A.R. Nafziger and Robert Paterson (eds), *Handbook on the Law of Cultural Heritage and International Trade* (Edward Elgar Publishing, 2014) 160, 167–168.

47 Wantuch-Thole, *Cultural Property in Cross-Border Litigation,* above n 24, 164.

48 Article 1(2) of the 1993 Council Directive.

49 Kurt Siehr, 'The Protection of Cultural Heritage and International Commerce' (1997) 6(2) *International Journal of Cultural Property* 304, 313–314.

50 Article 2 of the 1993 Council Directive.

51 Article 5 of the 1993 Council Directive.

action to evade the return procedure".[52] Thus, it can be said that the basic idea running through the evolving state practice within the EU legal regime is that the interests of the states of origin in their unlawfully removed heritage should be respected and such property should be returned. However, despite good intentions, there has not been one reported case ordering for the return of cultural objects on the grounds of the 1993 Council Directive and many member states supported proposals that it be revised in a more effective way.[53]

As a result, the 2014 Council Directive was published to make the recovery of illegally removed cultural objects easier and less costly.[54] The new legislation is a significant improvement for the facilitation of recovery claims by states of origin, and includes numerous new and simplified provisions.[55] First, all age and financial value limits have been removed from the new text.[56] The previous law covered only a limited scope of national treasures listed in the Annex or belonging to public collections or ecclesiastical lists. The 2014 Council Directive, however, supports a recovery claim if an object is classified as a "national treasure" under the relevant state's national laws and is unlawfully removed from its state of origin after 1993. Second, under the predecessor instrument, a recovery request was subject to two different limitation periods: the member state loses its right of action if it either fails to commence proceedings within a year of becoming aware of the whereabouts of the object, or if it fails to commence proceedings within 30 years of the unlawful removal. However, after the revision, states of origin will have more time to identify objects and apply for their restitution. Specifically, a requesting state has: (1) six months, up from the current two months, to establish whether an object found in another member state constitutes a classified cultural object, illegally removed from its territory, and (2) three years, instead of the current one year, to file a claim for restitution.[57] Third, the new 2014 Council Directive also aims to reduce the costs for claiming restitution, by increasing the level of "due diligence" when current possessors claim for compensation. A person who possesses a cultural object claimed by a member state would have to prove that, when acquiring the object, he or she took all of the necessary steps to ascertain that

52 Article 4(5) of the 1993 Council Directive.

53 European Commission, 'Fourth Report on the Application of Council Directive 93/7/EEC on the Return of Cultural Objects Unlawfully Removed From the Territory of a Member State' <http://eur-lex.europa.eu/legal-content/EN/TXT/PDF/?uri=CELEX:52013DC0310&from=EN>.

54 Directive 2014/60/EU of the European Parliament and of the Council of May 15 2014 on the return of cultural objects unlawfully removed from the territory of a Member State and amending Regulation (EU) No 1024/2012 (Recast) <http://eur-lex.europa.eu/legal-content/EN/TXT/PDF/?uri=CELEX:32014L0060&from=EN>. (the 2014 Council Directive).

55 European Parliament 'Return of Illegally Exported Cultural Objects: Simpler Rules' <www.europarl.europa.eu/news/en/news-room/content/20140120IPR33131/html/Return-of-illegally-exported-cultural-objects-simpler-rules>.

56 Article 2 of the 2014 Council Directive.

57 Article 5 of the 2014 Council Directive.

it came from a legal source, in particular the documentation on the object's provenance, the authorisations for removal, the character of the parties, the price paid, whether the possessor consulted any accessible register of stolen cultural objects, and any relevant information that they could have reasonably obtained.[58] Thus, it can be concluded that the evolving EU legal regime clearly reflects an increasing willingness for wrongfully removed cultural relics to be returned to states of origin.

In conclusion, the evolving international and European legal instruments reflect the recognition that illegally removed cultural heritage should be returned. In particular, the recognition of foreign export law at both the international and European levels has changed the long-lasting position that foreign public law cannot be used as a basis for recovery claims. This change is significant in arguing for the proposed customary rule, not only because it constitutes an acknowledgement of the interests of the states of origin in their wrongfully removed cultural heritage, but also provides an important impetus for the wider acceptance by market states in returning stolen, clandestinely excavated or illegally exported cultural objects.

4. Law in the Market States

While international instruments generally support the restitution of illegally removed objects, their actual recovery largely depends on the legal system of each market state. As the practices in each specially affected state are the crucial factors in creating a new customary rule, the following section examines the law and returning practices in the important market states, including the US, the UK, Switzerland, the Netherlands and Germany. To argue for the proposed customary rule, this section aims to illustrate how likely it is that a market state would recognise foreign ownership and export laws in such a way as to favour recovery claims by the states of origin.

4.1. The US

In the past two decades, the US has become an important forum in which to resolve recovery disputes. As a principal art market, the state practices in the US are important evidence in suggesting whether the proposed customary rule is emerging. In this regard, recent returning cases have shown clear indications that the US has a growing willingness to return those cultural objects that can be proved to have been illegally taken in contravention of foreign ownership or export laws.[59]

58 Article 10 of the 2014 Council Directive.

59 Blake, *Cultural Heritage Law*, above n 7, 54; Judith Church, 'Evolving US Case Law on Cultural Property' (1993) 2(1) *International Journal of Cultural Property* 47, 47–48.

4.1.1. Recognising Foreign Ownership Law

At this point, it is worth mentioning three pieces of legislation that would applied to the restitution of stolen cultural objects. The first legal instrument is the Archaeological Resources Protection Act (ARPA), which was initially designed to protect archaeological resources on federal and Indian lands that are at least 100 years old.[60] Despite the proclaimed purpose, the ARPA also prohibits the trafficking in interstate and foreign commerce of any archaeological resource taken or held in violation of federal, state, or local law.[61] The second instrument is the National Stolen Property Act (NSPA), which regards as a crime the receiving, concealing, storing, selling or disposing of US goods (with a minimum value of $5,000) from interstate or foreign trade, which are known by the holder to have been stolen. Although the NSPA is not specifically designed for stolen cultural heritage, it has been shown to be an effective tool to deter the illicit trade of cultural relics.[62] A breach of the NSPA permits the US Government to impose heavy criminal penalties on the violator and to bring an *in rem* forfeiture action against the stolen property. The third piece of legislation is the Cultural Property Implementation Act (CPIA), which is a US legislation implementing the UNESCO Convention, and is designed to exercise import controls over cultural heritage and to assist other parties to the UNESCO Convention in the recovery of cultural heritage. When the US Senate considered the draft CPIA testimony given at hearings, it addressed two issues. First, the demand for cultural objects had resulted in the destruction of archaeological sites and the resulting loss of the context and associations in which so much information about them resides. Such information is essential in understanding the development of cultures.[63] Second, because the US is a principal market for archaeological and ethnological objects, the discovery of

60 Sarah Marous and J. Michael Marous, 'ARPA in the International Context: Protecting the Articles of Faith' in Sherry Hutt, Marion Forsyth and David Tarler (eds), *Presenting Archaeology in Court: Legal Strategies for Protecting Cultural Resources* (AltaMira Press, 2006) 39, 39–45; Larry A. Mackey, 'ARPA on Private Lands: The GE Mound Case' in Sherry Hutt, Marion Forsyth and David Tarler (eds), *Presenting Archaeology in Court: Legal Strategies for Protecting Cultural Resources* (AltaMira Press, 2006) 47, 47–56.

61 In *United States v An Archaic Etruscan Pottery Ceremonial Vase c* concerning a set of Etruscan pottery which Italy claimed that that was stolen property, the US Attorney's Office filed a forfeiture complain under the section 470ee(c) of the APRA which prohibits knowingly holding stolen property. A. Slayman, 'Recent Cases of Repatriation of Antiquities to Italy from the United States' (1998) 7(2) *International Journal of Cultural Property* 456, 458.

62 Jessica Eve Morrow, 'The National Stolen Property Act and the Return of Stolen Cultural Property to Its Rightful Foreign Owners' (2007) 30(1) *Boston College International and Comparative Law Review* 249, 256–258.

63 'US Senate Report, 97–564 Implementing Legislation for the Convention on the Means of Prohibiting and Preventing the Illicit Import, Export and Transfer of Ownership of Cultural Property' <https://eca.state.gov/files/bureau/97-564.pdf>.

stolen or illegally exported artefacts there, in some cases, severely strains relations with the states of origin. As the Department of State noted in commenting on the bill, "the US considers that on grounds of principle, good foreign relations, and concern for the preservation of the cultural heritage of mankind, it should render assistance in these situations".[64] Therefore, the CPIA substantively implements only two sections of the UNESCO Convention: Article 7(b), which addresses the return of stolen cultural heritage that has been inventoried in the collection of a public secular or religious institution, and Article 9, which provides a mechanism by which state parties may call upon each other for assistance in cases of jeopardy to cultural heritage through the looting of archaeological and ethnological materials. The CPIA enables the US Government to apply civil forfeiture to claim for returns.[65] With restrictions on imports, the CPIA is intended to reduce the incentive to pillage by discouraging trade in undocumented cultural materials, and encouraging a legal trade in documented materials.

However, despite the mechanisms for the return of stolen property, the question arises as to whether stolen cultural heritage owned by a foreign state should be treated differently from other types of stolen property, such as property stolen from a private home.[66] This question was illustrated in the landmark case of *US v Schultz*, where prominent art dealer, Frederick Schultz, was convicted of importing and selling looted Egyptian antiquities.[67] Schultz had sought to dismiss the indictment, asking the court to rule that antiquities could not be considered "stolen" merely because an Egyptian law declares them to be state property. However, after evidentiary hearing, the court ruled that Egyptian law unequivocally asserts state ownership and that this law is vigorously enforced within Egypt, not just upon illegal exports. By upholding Egypt's ownership laws, the *Schultz* decision is significant in the return of stolen cultural objects and the recognition of the interests of the states of origin in their wrongfully removed heritage. Before Schultz's conviction at trial, a newspaper commentator remarked that "the Schultz trial will quite likely define how far the American judiciary is willing to let the US government go in regulating the antiquities trade and what legal weapons federal prosecutors can use".[68] The reason for this is that if the court recognised Egypt's state

64 Section III Reasons for the US Implementing Legislation US Bureau of Educatoinal and Cultural Affairs, 'Cultural Property Protection' <https://eca.state.gov/cultural-heritage-center/cultural-property-protection/process-and-purpose/background>.

65 Cultural objects forfeited under the CPIA must first be offered for return to the relevant state party. 19 USC § 2609(b) (1), (c)(2)(A).

66 Patty Gerstenblith, 'Schultz and Barakat: Universal Recognition of National Ownership of Antiquities' (2009) (1) *Art Antiquity and Law* 21, 21.

67 *United States v Schultz*, 178 F Supp 2d 445 (SDNY 2002), aff'd, 333 F 3d 393 (2d Cir 2003).

68 Kelly Elizabeth Yasaitis, 'National Ownership Laws as Cultural Property Protection Policy: The Emerging Trend in United States v Schultz' (2005) 12(1) *International Journal of Cultural Property* 95, 108.

ownership rights, cultural objects removed in violation of a nation's ownership law retain their characterisation as stolen property, even after they are brought to the US. This would thus clear the way for US law to be used to enforce other foreign ownership laws and further enhance the ability of states of origin to seek for the return of their stolen arts from the US.

Additionally, the *Schultz* decision cleared the argument that the enactment of the CPIA precluded the application of the NSPA, as Schultz argued that the CPIA is intended to be the sole congressional statement on international cultural heritage policy. However, this argument was rejected by the court, which concluded that the potential overlap of the two legal instruments is not a reason to limit the reach of the NSPA. The court decided that the CPIA was intended to exist concurrently with other criminal laws, for example, the NSPA. In addition, the court alleged that the NSPA's purpose of deterring theft was found to be more fitting in the case:

> We see no reason that property stolen from a foreign sovereign should be treated any differently from property stolen from a foreign museum or private home. The *mens rea* requirement of the NSPA will protect innocent art dealers who unwittingly receive stolen goods, while our appropriately broad reading of the NSPA will protect the property of sovereign nations.[69]

The significance in applying the NSPA to a dispute regarding foreign stolen objects is that the possibility of criminal conviction would usually have a deterrent effect on the illegal art trade.[70] The likelihood of criminal prosecution and punishment would cool the demand on the US market for objects stolen from foreign states. The *Schultz* trial was viewed as a test of the application of the NSPA in cases where the theft of the antiquities had taken place overseas. The indictment was seen as a sign that the federal government intended to follow through with aggressive enforcement: "the looting of artefacts deprives nations of their heritage and humankind of valuable archaeological knowledge", stated US Attorney James Comey. "This conviction sends the message that the United States will aggressively pursue such crimes and those who traffic in looted artefacts."[71]

Giving judicial recognition to a foreign country's claim of national ownership is a major victory for supporters of the return of cultural objects and, more importantly, crucial evidence in supporting the proposed customary rule. Given that many culturally rich states, including Egypt, Greece, Turkey, and Cambodia, also enacted similar national ownership laws beginning

69 *United States v Schultz*, 333F 3D 393, paras 410–411.
70 Simon Mackenzie, *Going, Going, Gone: Regulating the Market in Illicit Antiquities* (Institute of Art and Law, 2005), 149–156.
71 Martha Lufkin, 'Egyptian Antiquities Dealer Found Guilty', *Forbes* February 20 2002 <www.forbes.com/2002/02/20/0220hot.html>.

in the mid-19th century, these states should be entitled to recover their stolen objects when facing a similar situation.[72] In fact, this judicial recognition has been a backdrop for numerous recent restitutions of antiquities from US museums to the states of origin. Over the past three years, for example, Italy has successfully recovered a large number of works of ancient art and antiquities from the Met Museum,[73] the Boston Museum of Fine Art,[74] the Princeton Art Museum,[75] the J. Paul Getty Trust[76] and the Cleveland Art Museum.[77] Although these cases were settled with private museums, which do not constitute state practice, it should be noted that without the US law in favour of foreign ownership rights, the museums would not have been so cooperative in relinquishing their collections.

4.1.2. Blanket Legislation and Archaeological Resources

Despite the enactment of state ownership law, securing the return of stolen arts is not always guaranteed, particularly with regards to clandestinely excavated antiquities. For example, in *Peru v Johnson*, Peru claimed for the return of 89 pre-Columbian artefacts seized by US customs from Johnson. One important legal issue in this case was to prove that Peru was the owner of the artefacts at the time of their removal. Peruvian law provided that the government owned all pre-Columbian cultural objects, whether they had been excavated or not, but could not exercise any of the rights usually connected with ownership. However, the court found that Peru had made no real effort to enforce these laws and its claim of ownership amounted to a form of export control. It is clear in this case that the court refused to recognise that a country owns an object unless it has the rights of exclusive use and possession associated with ownership. However, the decision has been criticised by some scholars, as the concept of ownership taken by the court is too narrow where items of cultural importance to a state or people are concerned.[78] It should be noted that when the US considered implementing the UNESCO Convention in 1982, the US

72 Lawrence M. Kaye, 'Recovery of Stolen Cultural Property: A Practitioner's View—War Stories and Morality Tales' (1998) (5) *Villanova Sports & Entertainment Law Journal* 5, 7–17.

73 Elisabetta Povoledo, 'Met to Sign Accord in Italy to Return Vase and Artifacts', *New York Times* February 21 2006 <www.nytimes.com/2006/02/21/arts/design/21anti.html?pagewanted=print>.

74 Elisabetta Povoledo, 'Boston Museum Returns 13 Ancient Works to Italy', *New York Times* September 29 2006 <www.nytimes.com/2006/09/29/arts/design/29mfa.html?_r=0>.

75 Krystal Knapp, 'Princeton University Returns Art to Italy', *Planet Princeton* January 26 2012 <http://planetprinceton.com/2012/01/26/princeton-university-returns-art-to-italy/>.

76 Elisabetta Povoledo, 'Italy and Getty Sign Pact on Artifacts', *New York Times* September 26 2007 <www.nytimes.com/2007/09/26/arts/design/26gett.html?_r=0&pagewanted=print>.

77 Steven Litt, 'Cleveland Museum of Art Strikes Deal With Italy to Return 14 Ancient Artworks', *Cleveland* November 19 2008 <www.cleveland.com/arts/index.ssf/2008/11/cleveland_museum_of_art_1.html>.

78 Blake, *Cultural Heritage Law*, above n 7, 57.

Senate report recognised that archaeological and historical sites in the US were equally subject to pillage and looting:

> The destruction of such sites and the disappearance of the historic records evidenced by the articles found in them has given rise to a profound national interest in joining other countries to control the trafficking of such articles in international commerce.[79]

However, recent recovery cases indicate a change of view with regards to the blanket legislation and its application to excavated antiquities.[80] In the case of *Turkey v Met*, the subject was a 6th century BC collection of gold and silver objects of the Lydian culture, which the Turkish Government claimed to have been clandestinely excavated and illegally smuggled out of Turkey in the 1960s and then purchased by the Met Museum.[81] A formal demand for its return was made by Turkey in 1988, but the request was rejected. Turkey then commenced legal proceedings against the Met Museum and the case was settled out of court in 1993 with the Met agreeing to return the Lydian Hoard. It should be noted that had this case gone to trial, a decision in favour of Turkey was a likely outcome.[82] *Turkey v Met* is significant in strengthening the argument that states of origin' interests in their clandestinely excavated antiquities should be protected. In this case, Turkey claimed the return referring to the Turkish legislation in force in 1966, under which both the unauthorised excavation of the antiquities and their exportation were in a violation of Turkish law. The law also provided for the blanket legislation by the Turkish Government of all antiquities found within Turkey. But the question is that the Lydian Hoard collection had been stolen after illegal excavation without the items ever having been reduced to possession by the Turkish Government before their illegal export from Turkey. If following the court decision in *Peru v Johnson*, Turkey would not have been able to obtain the return of Lydian Hoard. However, the decisions in *Turkey v Met* provide an alternative for states of origin in recovering such antiquities, especially when the defendant in this case was a prestigious US museum. As commented by Janet Blake:

> a decision against the Met in this case could have created potentially dangerous precedent for all museums in the US (and, possibly, beyond) with important collections of antiquities that would encourage other state to

79 *US Senate Report on Implementing UNESCO Convention*, above n 63, 3.

80 Patty Gerstenblith, 'Enforcement by Domestic Courts: Criminal Law and Forfeiture in the Recovery of Cultural Objects' in Francesco Francioni and James Gordley (eds), *Enforcing International Cultural Heritage Law* (Oxford University Press, 2013) 150, 167–170.

81 *Republic of Turkey v The Metropolitan Museum of Art*, 762 F Supp 44, 1990 US Dist LEXIS 18771 (SDNY 1990).

82 Lawrence Kaye and Carla Main, 'The Saga of the Lydian Hoard Antiquities: From Usak to New York and Back and Some Related Observations on the Law of Cultural Repatriation' in Kathryn Tubb (ed), *Antiquities Trade or Betrayed: Legal, Ethical & Conservation Issues* (Archetype, 1995), 154.

attempt to sue for the return of items in museum collections they believed to have been stolen.[83]

In another case, *Turkey v Oks Partners*, concerning the Elmali Hoard of 1,750 rare ancient coins, Turkey sued for the recovery of the Elmali antiquities from the OKS Partners.[84] Turkey argued that the disputed antiquities were illegally excavated and smuggled out of Turkey in 1984, relying on its national law, which regulates that undiscovered cultural objects, such as archaeological artefacts, belong to the state. In response, OKS argued that Turkish law was not clear on this issue, arguing that the 1983 Antiquities Act had changed the meaning of the phrase "state ownership" as used in the 1906 and 1973 versions to a lesser interest of "having the property of state ownership". In addition, OKS argued that Turkey's property interests were contingent upon the acceptance of the cultural relics and the payment of the reward and, thus, Turkey did not have sufficient proprietary interest in the coins to give it standing to sue. The reason for this is that under Turkish law, after learning of the existence of any undiscovered cultural items, for example the coins in dispute in this case, the person must report the discovery to the government within a certain period and must deliver them to the Ministry of Culture or an appropriate state museum for the purpose of classification and evaluation.[85] If the government determines the items have value to be protected by the state, the state keeps the objects and pays a reward to the finder and the owner of the land where the cultural items were found. However, after expert testimonies, the court decided that Turkey "has an immediate and unconditional right of possession which accrues immediately upon the discovery of the antiquities".[86] This recognition was essential since, in the absence of such an interest, Turkey would not have standing to bring the claim. The case was settled out of court in 1999 with the result that the disputed antiquities were returned. It can be argued that the settlement was prompted by the prospect of Turkey's likely success at trial.[87] While this successful recovery required a decade of litigation, it has clearly been a catalyst for the subsequent restitution of other illicit Turkish antiquities from the US, without the need for litigation.[88]

The recognition of blanket legislation is significant in allowing states of origin to recover antiquities that were clandestinely excavated and smuggled to another country even though they did not have possession in the first place. Without such recognition, art traffickers do not need to worry about recovery claims as long as the antiquities were taken out of the state.

83 Blake, *Cultural Heritage Law*, above n 7, 60.

84 *Republic of Turkey v OKS Partners*, 1994 US Dist LEXIS 17032 (D Mass 1994).

85 Janet Blake, 'Turkey' in James A.R. Nafziger and Robert Paterson (eds), *Handbook on the Law of Cultural Heritage and International Trade* (Edward Elgar Publishing, 2014), 455–456.

86 Kaye, *Recovery of Stolen Cultural Property*, above n 72, 8–9.

87 Kaye and Main, *The Saga of the Lydian Hoard Antiquities*, above n 82, 151.

88 Blake, *Cultural Heritage Law*, above n 7, 61.

4.1.3. Return of Illegally Exported Cultural Heritage

Shortly after the enactment of the UNESCO Convention, the US took its first action to return illegally exported objects by enacting the Regulation of Importation of Pre-Columbian Monumental or Architectural Sculpture or Mural (Pre-Columbian Regulation).[89] In this regulation, any object covered by the Pre-Columbian Regulation not accompanied by a certificate from the country of origin certifying that the export was not in violation of the laws of that country must be seized and returned. Consequently, the export control laws for pre-Columbian artefacts will be enforced in the US. However, the effect of the Pre-Columbian Regulation is limited, as it only applies to Latin American countries.

In 1982, the US Congress passed the CPIA as the special legislation to implement the UNESCO Convention. This legislation enables the US President to impose import restrictions, following a request by another state party, upon designated categories of archaeological and ethnological materials pursuant to either an emergency action or a bilateral agreement between the US and the requesting state. For example, China and the US entered into a bilateral agreement in 2009, which is intended to "reduce the incentive for pillage of irreplaceable archaeological material representing the rich cultural heritage of China".[90] The agreement stipulated that the US would ban the import of antiquities dating from the Paleolithic period, starting in 75,000 BC, through to the end of the Tang dynasty, in AD 907, and all monumental sculpture and wall art at least 250 years old.[91] Such a programme of cooperation has proven to be effective, as the US–China bilateral agreement was renewed in 2014.[92] However, questions arise regarding the effectiveness of the US model, as only 15 foreign countries have such cooperation with the US and so, in that respect, it remains somewhat of a limited remedy.[93] Despite the small number of bilateral agreements, it should be noted that all of the culturally rich states active in restitution, including Peru, Greece, Italy, and Cambodia, have signed

89 Jower, *International and National Legal Efforts,* above n 20, 166–167.

90 Bureau of Educational and Cultural Affairs, 'Memorandum of Understanding (MOU), to Protect Categories of Archaeological Material from the Paleolithic Period through the Tang Dynasty, and Monumental Sculpture and Wall art at least 250 Years Old' <http://eca.state.gov/cultural-heritage-center/international-cultural-property-protection/bilateral-agreements/china>.

91 Rhonda Schechter, 'Preventing Pillage and Promoting Politics: The Dual Goals of the 2009 US-China Bilateral Agreement to Restrict Imports of Chinese Cultural Property' (2009) 4 *Art Antiquity and Law* 317, 323.

92 For a detailed evaluation of the US–China bilateral agreement, see Mia J. Logan, 'Limiting Access to Art in Hopes of Decreased Cultural Property Destruction: An Assessment of the United States and China's Memorandum of Understanding for 2014' (2014) 1 *Art Antiquity and Law* 1.

93 Matthew R. Hoffman, 'Cultural Pragmatism: A New Approach to the International Movement of Antiquities' (2010) 95(2) *Iowa Law Review* 665, 680–682.

with the US.[94] A growing number of cultural objects have been returned worldwide under the terms of these bilateral agreements and the mechanism provided by the UNESCO Convention.[95]

4.1.4. *Shifts in Recovery Methods: From Civil Replevin and Criminal Prosecution to Civil Forfeiture*

When states of origin initially took legal actions for the return of artefacts, many of the cases involving restitution were civil replevin[96] or criminal prosecution actions.[97] Civil replevin applies when a cultural object is stolen from its true owner, regardless of whether the object is stolen in the traditional sense or it is an archaeological object whose ownership is vested in the state.[98] Thus, a country of origin can bring a suit for the return of stolen cultural heritage, pursuant to its national ownership law. However, to apply civil replevin actions, a requesting party must establish that the antiquities were found within the modern territory of the state, and the act of theft must have taken place after the effective date of the vesting legislation. This is particularly difficult in the case of clandestinely excavated antiquities, because a state will never have the opportunity to keep records of these antiquities, unless they are forfeited during the export attempt. When coming to a criminal conviction, it further requires the establishment that the defendant knew that his or her conduct was illegal beyond a reasonable doubt. The high standard of proof means that it is extremely difficult for a state of origin to recover its stolen heritage through either civil replevin actions or criminal prosecutions.

However, the picture has changed substantially in the past decade, as fewer actions of civil replevin or criminal prosecution have been filed by foreign nations to recover stolen antiquities. This occurred after the US Government became involved in assisting original states to recover illegally removed cultural relics through civil forfeiture.[99] Many cultural objects were returned after the US Government filed a forfeiture action against the possessors. Civil

94 For the list of emergency actions, agreements, and Designated Lists of objects subject to import restrictions, see 'Bilateral Agreements' <http://eca.state.gov/cultural-heritage-center/cultural-property-protection/bilateral-agreements>.

95 UNESCO, 'Recent Examples of Successful Operations of Cultural Property Restitutions in the World' <www.unesco.org/new/en/culture/themes/restitution-of-cultural-property/successful-restitutions-in-the-world/>.

96 See, e.g., *Republic of Turkey v OKS Partners* (1994 US Dist LEXIS 17032, D Mass 1994); and *Republic of Turkey v Metropolitan Museum of Art*, 762 F Supp 44 (SDNY 1990).

97 See, e.g., *United States v McClain* (545 F 2d 988, 5th Cir, reh'g denied, 551 F 2d 52, 5th Cir 1977); and *United States v Schultz* (178 F Supp 2d445, SDNY, January 3 2002, aff'd, 333 F 3d 393, 2nd Cir NY, June 10 2003).

98 Gerstenblith, *Enforcement by Domestic Courts*, above n 80, 160–161.

99 Ibid, 165; Aaron Kyle Briggs, 'Consequences of the Met–Italy Accord for the International Restitution of Cultural Property' (2007) 7(2) *Chicago Journal of International Law* 623, 639.

forfeiture of cultural heritage originating in a foreign country most frequently occurs when an object has been imported illegally into the US. The result of a forfeiture action is to transfer the title to the US Government, after which the Government typically returns the object to the country of origin.

The shift towards civil forfeiture is significant in the return of illegally removed heritage to states of origin and also strong evidence in arguing for the proposed customary rule, primarily owing to its special features. For example, civil forfeiture can be applied in a broad way when an object is imported illegally in violation of the CPIA[100] or the Customs law, for example, presenting a false statement concerning the object as to the country of origin.[101] Additionally, civil forfeiture means that the US Government bears much of the cost of litigation, including the expenses of litigation, hiring of attorneys, investigation of the theft circumstances, procuring of evidence and witnesses and learning the legal system of another nation.[102] Further, the statute of limitations for a claim based on a violation of the customs laws is five years from the time the US Government learns of the illegal importation or the transfer of stolen property across international or state lines, rather than from the time of the original theft.[103] This will substantially reduce the likelihood that a claim will be barred by the statute of limitations. Lastly, when disputed goods are imported in violation of a customs statute, the government's burden of proof is one of probable cause, a relatively low standard.[104]

All of these advantages have made civil forfeiture a powerful method for the recovery of cultural relics to states of origin. As is reflected in some cases, the current possessor or importer may simply "walk away" from the property without contest. For example, in 2011, when Sotheby's in New York offered at auction a 10th-century sandstone statue, Cambodia claimed that it was illegally removed from the site Koh Ker during the 1970s and should be returned to them.[105] Sotheby's neither agreed to its return, nor agreed to sell it to a private collector willing to donate it to Cambodia. Instead, it awaited a court

100 Articles of cultural property and archaeological and ethnological materials forfeited under the Section of Stolen Cultural Property (§ 2607) must first be offered for return to the relevant State Party. 19 USC § 2609(b) (1), (c)(2)(A).

101 The relevant section of the Customs statute states: "Merchandise which is introduced or attempted to be introduced into the United States contrary to law shall be treated as follows: (1) The merchandise shall be seized and forfeited if it—(A) is stolen, smuggled, or clandestinely imported or introduced." 19 USC § 1595a(c).

102 Stefan D. Cassella, 'Using the Forfeiture Laws to Protect Archaeological Resources' (2006) 41 *Idaho Law Review* 129, 132.

103 19 USC § 1621 (stating that no action for forfeiture of property can be commenced more than "five years after the time when the alleged offense was discovered, or in the case of forfeiture, within two years after the time when the involvement of the property in the alleged offense was discovered, whichever was later").

104 Gerstenblith, *Enforcement by Domestic Courts,* above n 80, 166.

105 *United States of America v A 10th Century Cambodian Sandstone Sculpture, Currently Located at Sotheby's in New York, New York*, Verified Complaint, 12 Civ 2600 (GBD), April 2 2012, 6–7.

decision on the matter of ownership. However, the statue was quickly settled when it became the subject of a federal US lawsuit, with prosecutors seeking its forfeiture on the grounds that it had been looted from Cambodia and illegally imported into the US.[106] In December 2013, Sotheby's voluntarily returned the statue to Cambodia in exchange for the US Government dropping a lawsuit brought on behalf of the Cambodian government.

In conclusion, the evolving US laws and judicial practices have proven to be generally conducive to the return of illegally removed cultural objects to states of origin and the courts are, in general, willing to condemn reckless professionals or art dealers.[107] In particular, civil forfeiture filed by the US Government not only releases original states from costly and complicated litigation, but also serves as an effective tool to obtain the return. In summary, it is clear that the US is committed to reducing the incentive for pillage by discouraging trade in wrongfully removed cultural objects and returning such objects to their states of origin.

4.2. Switzerland

As a major transit point, Switzerland has been criticised for its free ports, where titles to illicitly removed cultural heritage are able to be laundered. In 2003, Swiss Customs discovered 200 stolen ancient Egyptian treasures, including two mummies, at Geneva's free port.[108] In discussing the proposed customary rule, it is necessary for Swiss state practices to show a commitment to changing this situation and to combatting the illicit trade of foreign cultural objects.

4.2.1. The Basel *Decisions: Swiss Courts Reluctant to Recognise Blanket Legislation*

While it is possible under Swiss law to recover stolen cultural heritage, this has not always been the case when foreign states have claimed for the return of

106 *United States of America v A 10th Century Cambodian Sandstone Sculpture, Currently Located at Sotheby's in New York, New York*, No. 12-cv-2600-GBD (SDNY March 28 2013), 11.

107 Patty Gerstenblith, 'For Better and For Worse: Evolving United States Policy on Cultural Property Litigation and Restitution' (2015) 22(2–3) *International Journal of Cultural Property* 357, 369; Lawrence M. Kaye, 'Art Wars: The Repatriation Battle' (1998) 31 *New York University Journal of International Law and Politics* 79, 92–93; Sue J. Park, 'The Cultural Property Regime in Italy: An Industrialized Source Nation's Difficulties in Retaining and Recovering its Antiquities' (2002) 23(4) *University of Pennsylvania Journal of International Economic Law* 931, 946; Blake, *Cultural Heritage Law,* above n 7, 54.

108 Michèle Laird, 'Closing in on the Archaeological Underworld', *Swissinfo* July 18 2012 <www.swissinfo.ch/eng/free-port-problem_closing-in-on-the-archaeological-underworld/33088854>.

excavated antiquities on the basis of blanket legislations. In *Turkey v The City of Basel*, Turkey sued for the return of five gravestones, which were displayed at the Antiquities Museum in the City of Basel.[109] Turkey claimed that under Article 697 of the Turkish Civil Code all antiquities found in Turkey are state property and, consequently, the gravestones were stolen property and should be returned to Turkey. The issue in this case was whether the Swiss courts should recognise and apply the Turkish law on the disputed cultural heritage. Although the same ownership law helped Turkey recover its stolen cultural objects from the US, Turkey's claim was rejected by the Swiss courts (including the Swiss Trial Court, the Court of Appeals and the Federal Court). The decisions all concluded that, although Turkish ownership law should be recognised by the Swiss courts, Turkey had lost all rights to the stones in dispute through inactivity. For example, the trial court held that Turkey had failed to exercise its power of acquisition over two of the gravestones and that Turkey's power of acquisition was not proven for the other three stones. Therefore, Article 697 did not apply.

The three *Basel* decisions reflected the Swiss courts' reluctance to recognise blanket legislation providing state ownership as a means of claiming for recovery. After the trial, the court decisions received bitter criticism that the approach in interpreting blanket legislation was too restrictive.[110] The approach in *Basel* was the traditional method in interpreting blanket legislation regarding clandestinely excavated heritage, which has been rejected by many courts in the US and the UK in recent cases. State ownership by blanket legislation has also been recognised in other art-importing countries. In this regard, Switzerland is expected to take responsibility for decreasing illegal traffic in cultural heritage and recognise blanket legislation of states of origin. Additionally, the *Basel* approach is contrary to the protection of cultural heritage from illicit trafficking. If one were to adopt the Swiss interpretation, the country of origin would never be able to recover antiquities that were clandestinely excavated and smuggled to another country if they failed to have possession in the first place. In this case, art traffickers do not need to worry about recovery claims as long as the antiquities were taken out of the state.[111]

4.2.2. Return of Illegally Exported Objects

Under the former Swiss legal regime, foreign states were unable to claim for the return of illegally exported cultural objects from Switzerland, because of the

109 Unpublished decisions, reported by Ozel, *Basel Decisions,* above n 32, 324–336; Wantuch-Thole, *Cultural Property in Cross-Border Litigation,* above n 24, 48–49.

110 For a critical analysis of the *Basel* decisions, see Ozel, *Basel Decisions,* above n 32, 324–336.

111 Sibel Ozel, 'Under the Turkish Blanket Legislation: The Recovery of Cultural Property Removed from Turkey' (2010) 38(2) *International Journal of Legal Information* 177, 183–184.

traditional obstacle that foreign export law was not enforceable.[112] However, this situation has changed after Switzerland became a party to the 1970 UNESCO Convention in 2001 and enacted its domestic legislation, the Federal Act on the International Transfer of Cultural Property (CPTA), in June 2003. Section 9 of the CPTA now recognises restitution claims for cultural objects illicitly imported into Switzerland. Claims for the return of smuggled cultural objects require a supplementary legal basis in the form of a bilateral treaty with the country of origin.[113] An import is illicit when it is made in violation of a bilateral agreement between Switzerland and another state party and in violation of the other party's export rules.[114] Switzerland has agreements in force with Italy (2008), Greece (2011), Colombia (2011), Egypt (2011), China (2014), Cyprus (2014), and Peru (2016). Pursuant to the bilateral agreements, an increasing number of illegally exported objects have been handed over to the states of origin.[115]

Despite good intentions, the precondition of a bilateral agreement means that without such agreements there is no need to consider foreign rules prohibiting the export of cultural objects. This has significantly restricted the application of foreign laws being applied to the return of illegally exported heritage. For example, in 2005, when India brought a case for the return of gold coins before the Swiss Federal Supreme Court, the Indian Government argued that the export was in violation of the Antiquities and Art Treasures Act in 1972, according to which antiquities, such as the gold coins in question, could not have been exported without authorisation by the Indian Government. However, the court rejected India's claim for recovery on the basis that there was no bilateral agreement between the two countries that would allow a Swiss court to apply the Indian export law. Despite the precondition of a bilateral agreement set out in the CPTA, it is questionable whether the court should unhesitantly state that Indian public law "cannot be applied outside the territory of Indian", by neglecting the recent changes in the Swiss legal system.[116] Article 13(1) of the Swiss Private International Law Act (PIL-Act) specifically provides that "the application of foreign law should not be excluded on the sole ground that the rule to be applied has a public law character".[117] The Swiss Government's report that was issued when the PIL-Act was adopted states that the goal of the PIL-Act was to overcome the Supreme Court's reservation regarding the non-applicability of foreign public law. Further, pursuant to Article 19 of the PIL-Act, a contract that violates

112 Marc-André Renold and Beat Schönenberger, 'Switzerland' in James A.R. Nafziger and Robert Paterson (eds), *Handbook on the Law of Cultural Heritage and International Trade* (Edward Elgar Publishing, 2014) 408, 410.

113 Article 7 of the CPTA.

114 Renold and Schönenberger, *Switzerland,* above n 112, 417.

115 Institute of Art and Law Blog, 'Switzerland Returns 32 Antiquities to Egypt' <www.ial.uk.com/news/switzerland-returns-32-antiquities-to-egypt/>.

116 Marc-André Renold, 'An Important Swiss Decision Relating to the International Transfer of Cultural Goods: The Swiss Supreme Court's Decision on the Giant Antique Mogul Gold Coins' (2006) 13(3) *International Journal of Cultural Property* 361, 367.

117 Article 13(1) of the Swiss PIL Act.

foreign rules prohibiting the export of national treasures could be considered null and void independently of its validity on the basis of the Swiss substantive law applicable to the contract. The PIL-Act provides for the application of foreign public law and a Swiss judge may theoretically enforce foreign law even in the form of export prohibitions.[118] As commented by Marc-André Renold, "the CPTA is not the exclusive means by which Switzerland wishes to fight against the illicit traffic of cultural property, and it seems the legislator did not intend to proscribe any other means to deal with it".[119]

However, a recent case concerning a Chinese cultural statue provides a much easier approach for states of origin to recover illegally exported objects, not through the recognition of foreign export laws, but through the misdeclaration of importing documents presented to Customs. In 2014, Swiss Customs Authorities at Basel Airport discovered the 47 cm tall statue in an inconspicuous parcel sent from the UK to a private individual in Switzerland.[120] This statue was later revealed to be over 2,200 years old, dating from the Chinese Han dynasty, which qualified it as a cultural object within the scope of the CPTA and UNESCO Convention. According to the CPTA, a person importing cultural heritage is obliged to declare to Customs the type of item and its country of origin.[121] However, the importing party failed to do so in this case, meaning the Chinese statue was brought into Switzerland illegally. As a result, Swiss Customs Authorities filed a report with the competent Cantonal Criminal Prosecution Authorities, which allowed the Chinese statue eventually to be repatriated to China.[122] This case provides an alternative for curbing illicit trafficking, bypassing the pre-condition of a bilateral agreement to initiate the return of illegally exported objects. Additionally, the return of the Chinese statue sent a clear warning that investigations against illegal importing may become more widespread and, when they occur, the consequences can be severe. According to the CPTA, failing to declare cultural heritage constitutes a criminal offence, and acting negligently and intentionally may lead to a fine of up to Swiss Francs 20,000 and one year's imprisonment respectively.[123] If the offender acts on a professional basis, the sanction is jail for up to two years or a fine of up to 200,000 Swiss Francs.[124]

4.2.3. Government's Participation to Combat the Illicit Traffic of Cultural Objects

A wide range of illicitly removed arts have been returned from Switzerland without the need for litigation, in particular with cooperation from the Swiss

118 Wantuch-Thole, *Cultural Property in Cross-Border Litigation,* above n 24, 348.
119 Renold, *Swiss Court's Decision on the Mogul Gold Coins,* above n 116, 367.
120 'Switzerland Returns Illegally Imported Terracotta Statue To China' <www.ial.uk.com/news/switzerland-returns-illegally-imported-terracotta-statue-to-china/>.
121 Articles 19 and 25(1) of the CPTA.
122 Article 19(2) of the CPTA.
123 Article 24(1) and (2) the CPTA.
124 Article 24(3) of the CPTA.

Federal Office for Cultural Property for the International Transfer of Cultural Property (Swiss Federal Office for Cultural Property). The main responsibility of the Swiss Federal Office for Cultural Property is to assume tasks such as investigating compliance with the duty of due diligence of those persons active in the art trade and providing information about illegal transfers to contracting states. With the involvement of the Swiss authorities, many illegally removed foreign objects have been returned to the states of origin. In 2007, some 1,400 Afghan ethnographic and archaeological objects were returned, which had been preserved in Switzerland since 1999 under the aegis of UNESCO.[125] In 2015, over 5,000 stolen ancient objects were returned to Italy following a complex 14-year criminal investigation, constituting the single, greatest recovery of cultural relics for the country.[126] Additionally, Switzerland has revised the Federal Custom Act by requesting stricter supervision of the storage of cultural relics in the free port in response to the wide criticism against the abusive use of the free port in the illicit trafficking of cultural relics. All of these changes have made Switzerland less desirable as an intermediate market country.

In conclusion, the state practices of Switzerland arguing for the proposed customary rule are two-fold: on the one hand, Swiss laws have incorporated many new changes that significantly improve the ability to fight against the illicit trafficking of foreign arts and enable the return of such objects to states of origin. On the other hand, the *Basel* decisions constitute a powerful deterrent for the return of stolen antiquities from Switzerland, especially when international jurisprudence commonly recognises blanket legislation vesting state ownership over cultural heritage.

4.3. *Germany*

As Germany is another significant market country for cultural goods, its state practices are indispensable in combatting the illicit trade in heritage and facilitating the return of such objects. In particular, Germany is particularly involved in the disputes with Egypt and Turkey over ancient antiquities. Egypt has demanded the return of the 3,400-year-old bust of Queen Nefertiti, the star attraction of the Egyptian collection at the Neues Museum in Berlin. Egypt has persistently requested the return of Nefertiti to Egypt since 1930, but Germany has insisted the piece was bought legally and that there are documents to prove it.[127] Turkey requested Germany to return the sculpture the

125 *Recent Examples of Cultural Property Restitutions,* above n 95.

126 Michael Day, 'Italy Celebrates as 5,000 Plundered Artefacts Worth €50m are Returned following 14-year Inquiry', *Independent* January 22 2015 <www.independent.co.uk/news/science/archaeology/news/italy-celebrates-as-5000-plundered-artefacts-worth-50m-are-returned-following-14year-inquiry-9996427.html>.

127 Sonia Phalnikar, 'Germany Acquired Nefertiti Illegally, Egyptian Official Says', *DW* December 22 2009 <www.dw.com/en/germany-acquired-nefertiti-illegally-egyptian-official-says/a-5046115>.

sphinx, warning that if the sphinx were not returned, German archaeologists would not be permitted to carry out excavations in Turkey.[128] Hence, as a specially affected state, the state practice of Germany is significant in signalling whether the proposed customary rule is emerging or not.

4.3.1. Nigeria Bronzes *Case: Return of Illicitly Exported Objects*

In 1972, a Nigerian company entered into an insurance contract with a German company covering the transport by sea of three African masks and six statues from Nigeria to Hamburg.[129] However, the contract was in breach of a Nigerian prohibition on the export of cultural objects. During the transport, six valuable bronze figures were lost. After the insurance company refused to pay compensation, the Nigerian company filed a lawsuit in Germany, but failed in all instances. The German court held that the contract was null and void, as the transaction was immoral under section 138 of the German Civil Code, which stated that "a legal transaction which is contrary to public policy is void".[130] Usually, public policy defined under the Civil Code occur when the conduct in question contradicts "common business practices, integrity requirement, rationality, and principles of fairness in Germany".[131] However, in the *Nigeria* case, the court found that the term "public policy" also included "international public policy", which is based on internationally accepted common values and rules of fairness and may include interests of foreign states.[132] The court reasoned that foreign public law should be applied if the policy of the law has been recognised by the international community, as for example in an international convention, which represents the emerging international public policy on the issue of restitution:

> In the interest of the safeguarding of the morality of the international trade in cultural goods, the export of cultural objects in violation of an export prohibition of the State of origin does not deserve the protection by private law including the protection by the insurance of the transportation of cultural goods from the territory of a foreign State in violation of that State's export control laws.[133]

Through the argument for public policy, the German court made an exception for the return of illegally removed heritage. The court emphasised that "in the interest of decency in the international trade in cultural objects, the export

128 Further discussed in Chapter 8.
129 'The Nigerian Bronzes Case' in Lyndel Prott (ed), *Witnesses to history. Documents and Writings on the Return of Cultural Objects* (UNESCO, 2009) 33, 33.
130 Section 138 of the German Civil Code.
131 Section 138 of the German Civil Code.
132 Wantuch-Thole, *Cultural Property in Cross-Border Litigation,* above n 24, 342.
133 Ibid, 342.

of heritage items in violation of export prohibitions of the state of its origin does not deserve the protection through private law, including the insurance contract".[134] This case is important evidence to reflect the public attitudes to the UNESCO Convention and the return of cultural objects.[135] It should be noted that the court based its reasoning on the 1970 UNESCO Convention, which, at that time, had been in force for only two years, and to which Germany was not even a party.

Despite the important precedent in *Nigeria Bronzes*, a recent case did not conclude in the same manner.[136] In 2010, Turkey claimed for the return of three Phrygian offering cups and two Byzantine incense burner cases, which were bought by a German couple at an Istanbul antiquities market in the 1980s. In this case, Turkey made one of its arguments, referring to the *Nigeria* case, that the transaction should be considered void as it was in breach of foreign export prohibitions.[137] However, the court did not consider enforcing Turkey's export law on the grounds of public policy, following in *Nigeria Bronzes* footsteps. After comparing the case to *Nigeria Bronzes*, the court came to the conclusion that it was not applicable as the transaction took place within the territory of Germany and after the objects had been exported. In the *Nigeria Bronzes* case, however, it was the actual contract governing the transport of the Nigerian artefacts that violated the Nigerian export laws. The court thus stated that transactions within Germany were not to be considered void "just because they were in breach of a foreign country's export prohibition".[138] Comparing these two cases, it can be seen that while Germany recognised the necessity of combatting the illicit trade of cultural objects by applying foreign export laws rather early, the latter case related to Turkey's claim reflects the uncertainty with respect to the return of unlawfully exported cultural heritage.

4.3.2. The 2007 German Implementation Act

With the ratification of the UNESCO Convention by Germany in 2007, Germany adopted the Act on the Return of Cultural Property of 2007 to implement the UNESCO 1970 Convention.[139] Unlike in the US and Switzerland, in Germany, no bilateral agreement with another state party is needed; Germany returns those objects designated by other state parties as having national importance and, as such, are registered in a list that must also be accessible in

134 Ibid, 342.

135 *Nigerian Bronzes Case,* above n 129, 33.

136 Wantuch-Thole, *Cultural Property in Cross-Border Litigation,* above n 24, 343–347.

137 Ibid, 346.

138 Ibid, 345.

139 Act Implementing the UNESCO Convention of November 14 1970 on the Means of Prohibiting and Preventing the Illicit Import, Export and Transfer of Ownership of Cultural Property and Implementing Council Directive 93/7/EEC of March 15 1993 on the Return of Cultural Objects Unlawfully Removed from the Territory of a Member State.

Germany.[140] The claim for return must be commenced within a year from the time the country of origin gains knowledge of the excavation to place archaeological objects in the inventory.[141]

However, this approach has been criticised for not being effective in confronting the growing problems of clandestine excavation and cross-border trafficking in illegally excavated cultural heritage.[142] Many cultural sites are recklessly looted and are generally not known about until they appear in a market country. The requirement for being registered has already created a major problem for states of origin in claiming their secretly excavated archaeological objects. For example, when Turkey claimed for the return of three Phrygian offering cups and two Byzantine incense burners case in 2010, Turkey claimed that the objects in question were illegally excavated and later exported from Turkey in breach of the Turkish Cultural Property Statute, by which Turkey argued it was the rightful owner. However, the court held that Turkey could not be the owner of the excavated antiquities as it had never obtained possession of the objects. In this reasoning, the judge still applied the principle of territoriality, similar to the ration in the *Ortiz* case and the first instance of the *Barakat* case, which were later overturned.[143]

4.3.3. The 2016 New German Law

Recognising the limits of the 2007 Act, Germany carried out two evaluations between 2008 and 2013 and, in 2013, the Federal German Government published a report stating the importance of amending Germany's cultural heritage protection law. On August 6 2016, the new Act on the Protection of Cultural Property entered into force after it had been adopted by German parliament without any dissenting votes and with the broad support of the Federal Assembly early in July 2016.[144] As stated by the Federal Government Commissioner for Culture and the Media, with the reform of the cultural heritage protection Act, Germany aimed to take its responsibility to "protect the cultural heritage of mankind—both on national and international level" and "to combat illicit trafficking in cultural property".[145] This new Act has been applauded by countries seeking to recover their illegally removed heritage, as

140 Section 1(3).

141 Section 6 Conditions for an obligation to return.

142 Patty Gerstenblith, 'Implementation of the 1970 UNESCO Convention by the United States and Other Market Nations' <www.law.upenn.edu/live/files/6423-gerstenblith-patty-2017-implementation-of-the-1970>, 17.

143 Wantuch-Thole, *Cultural Property in Cross-Border Litigation,* above n 24, 346.

144 'The New Act on the Protection of Cultural Property in Germany: implementing the UNESCO 1970 Convention and new EU law' <www.unesco.org/fileadmin/MULTIMEDIA/HQ/CLT/pdf/presentation_UNESCO_Germany.pdf>.

145 Germany's Federal Government Commissioner for Culture and the Media, 'Key Aspects of the New Act on the Protection of Cultural Property in Germany' <www.congreso.es/docu/docum/ddocum/dosieres/sleg/legislatura_12/spl_3/pdfs/22.pdf>, 4.

it contains rules that make recovery more effective. Of greater relevance to this discussion are the new provisions for the import of unlawfully removed cultural objects and the corresponding return of such objects. The new law relies on the simple equation that cultural heritage illegally exported from a state party to the UNESCO Convention is considered illegally imported into Germany. Under the new law, an importer must present documentation that the cultural heritage was legally exported if it left another state party to the 1970 UNESCO Convention after 2007, the date of Germany's ratification of the Convention. Such a provision takes into account the fact that most states require a licence to export cultural heritage. This requirement particularly helps protect archaeological cultural heritage, which in many states is subject to export bans. More importantly, this new Act significantly shifts the burden to the importer to present such documentation; in the absence of such documentation, the cultural heritage is considered unlawfully removed.[146] As stated by Germany's Federal Government, this shows that "Germany recognizes foreign export and protection provisions for national cultural property in its own legislation".[147]

Germany's cooperation in returning illicitly removed heritage is further reflected by the fact that if the possessor of the cultural heritage in Germany does not present evidence proving that he or she already possessed the disputed cultural heritage prior to April 26 2007, that cultural heritage is presumed to have been unlawfully exported from the respective state after that date. This provision includes stronger return mechanisms for unlawfully exported cultural heritage. Under the previous 2007 Act, Germany was not obliged to return any object unlawfully exported from a relevant state party before 2007, due to the fact that the UNESCO Convention does not apply retroactively and the provisions of the UNESCO Convention became binding for Germany in 2007. However, finding proof is always difficult, especially when clandestine excavations are generally unknown until undocumented artefacts appear in an art market. Considering the problem that a requesting state is often unable to provide information as to when the cultural heritage was unlawfully exported from its territory, the 2016 Act introduces a new rule, providing that "cultural property is presumed to have been unlawfully exported from the respective state party after 26 April 2007, if the possessor of the cultural property in Germany does not present evidence proving that he or she already possessed the cultural property prior to this date".[148] Accordingly, the burden is further shifted onto the importer because the legislation creates a presumption that, in the absence of documentation that establishes otherwise, cultural objects were unlawfully exported from the relevant state party after 2007.

In conclusion, the state practices of Germany reflect an increasing recognition that illegally removed cultural heritage should be returned to states of

146 Gerstenblith, *Implementation of the UNESCO Convention,* above n 142, 18.
147 *Key Aspects,* above n 145, 7.
148 Ibid, 9.

origin. These practices should also be considered positive evidence in creating the proposed customary rule. German case law stands out in that Germany recognised the necessity for combating illicit trade by applying foreign export law rather early. However, the judgement in a later case concerning Turkish antiquities and 2007 German Act reflect the inconsistency in judicial practice. As a response, the new 2016 Act harmonises the previous provisions and brings them together in a single piece of legislation, thereby making the law easier to apply. This new law reflects an increasing recognition that states of origin in their illegally removed heritage should be respected and such heritage should be returned.

4.4. The UK

The UK is widely acknowledged to be a significant market for looted antiquities in global terms. Antiquities looted from source countries routinely travel to London to be sold by international dealers and auction houses to other dealers, private collectors and museums. The state practices of the UK have played an indispensable role in combating the illicit trade of cultural objects and influencing the development of the proposed customary rule.

4.4.1. Dealing in Cultural Objects (Offences) Act 2003

When the UK ratified the 1970 UNESCO Convention, it originally took the position that it did not need to enact implementing legislation. However, in July 2000, the Culture, Media and Sport Committee of the House of Commons recommended that "the criminal law be changed to include a criminal offence of trading in cultural property in designated categories from designated countries which had been stolen, illegally excavated or illegally exported from foreign countries".[149] Although the offence of handling stolen goods contrary to the Theft Act 1968 extends to goods stolen abroad, there are a number of significant instances not covered by the handling offence. For example, the offence does not apply to cases where an item has been illegally excavated. In such cases a prosecution for the new offence may be possible.

Considering that the UK can play its part in preventing and prohibiting the illicit trade, in 2003 the UK enacted new criminal legislation, the Dealing in Cultural Objects (Offences) Act 2003 (2003 UK Act). Although this was not characterised as a direct means of implementing the 1970 UNESCO Convention, it would nevertheless help to complement the UK's treaty obligations and reinforce the Convention's implementation in the UK. This 2003 UK Act created a new offence for dealing in "tainted" cultural objects: a person is guilty of an offence to "dishonestly deal in a cultural object that is tainted,

149 UK Parliament, 'Exlanatory Notes on Dealing In Cultural Objects (Offences) Bill' <www.publications.parliament.uk/pa/ld200203/ldbills/090/en/03090x—.htm>.

knowing or believing that the object is tainted".[150] The 2003 UK Act defines a tainted object as one that after December 30 2003, (1) was "excavated", or "removed from a building or structure of historical, architectural or archaeological interest", or "removed form a monument of such interest", and (2) such excavation or removal constituted a criminal offence.[151] Given that the legislation of each country will differ as to which offences are capable of rendering an object tainted, the Act does not identify particular provisions where the removal or excavation would constitute an offence. For the purposes of the statute, it does not matter whether the excavation or removal took place within the UK or in another country or whether the law being violated is a domestic or foreign law.[152] It is sufficient that the excavation or removal constitutes an offence (however defined) under the law of the UK or of some other country. In this respect, then, source country controls are an important element in constituting a theft charge against a buyer of looted property overseas, if not instrumental in preventing the practice of looting in the first place.[153]

To be convicted of an offence a person also needs to know or believe that an object is tainted. This means that a mere failure by the accused to carry out adequate checks on the provenance of an object will not constitute knowledge or belief. However, the 2003 UK Act took the degree of expertise of the accused and the knowledge of the art trade into consideration to determine whether the accused knew or believed that an object was tainted. For example, a dealer specialising in the buying and selling of objects of the same kind as the object in question could be expected to have a greater knowledge as to whether an object might be tainted. The 2003 UK Act is significant in combatting the traffic of unlawfully removed cultural objects and will assist in maintaining the integrity of buildings, structures and monuments worldwide by reducing the commercial incentive to those involved in the looting of such sites. As reflected by the Government's Guidance, the 2003 Act "will send a strong signal that the Government is determined to put a stop to such practices".[154]

4.4.2. Iran v Barakat*: Recognising Foreign Ownership Laws*

In 2007, Iran sued the London-based Barakat Galleries for the return of a collection of 18 carved jars, bowls, and cups based on the fact that these objects

150 Article 1 Offence of dealing in tainted cultural objects.
151 Article 2 Meaning of "tainted cultural object".
152 Gerstenblith, *Implementation of the UNESCO Convention*, above n 142, 24.
153 Simon Mackenzie and Penny Green, 'Introduction: A Context for the Engagement of Criminology and Archaeology' in Simon Mackenzie and Penny Green (eds), *Criminology and Archaeology: Studies in Looted Antiquities* (Hart Publishing, 2009) 1, 1.
154 'Guidance on the Dealing in Cultural Objects (Offences) Act 2003' <http://old.culture.gov.uk/images/publications/Dealincultural.pdf>.

had been recently unlawfully excavated in violation of its national ownership law.[155] The claim was first dismissed by the High Court of London as Iran had not established its state ownership and, consequently, did not have title to claim for their theft. However, the decision was overruled by the Court of Appeal, which stated that Iran sought to assert a patrimonial claim (that is, it relates to the property interests of the state), and not to enforce a public law or to assert sovereign rights.[156] In other words, the Court distinguished between the recognition of a nation's ownership rights and the enforcement of a foreign nation's laws. To do so, the Court recalled that, under English conflict of laws principles, the transfer of title for tangible, movable property depends on *lex situs*, that is, the law of the country where the movable was situated at the time of the transfer.[157] Therefore, if a foreign state has acquired title to property situated within its jurisdiction, there is no reason why an English court should not recognise it.[158] The same would apply where domestic laws provide that ownership of cultural objects is vested in the state without the need to have taken actual possession. With respect to the issue of ownership, the Court found that the relevant laws of Iran (such as the Civil Code of 1928, the National Heritage Protection Act of 1930 and the Regulations of 1932) were sufficiently clear to vest ownership and an immediate right of possession of the relics in the Iranian state. The fact that Iran never had possession of the antiquities was not an issue, since ownership was conferred by legislation and not transferred as a sanction of an unlawful export. The Court even highlighted that there were positive reasons of policy not to bar a claim for the restitution of an unlawfully exported cultural object. Following the decisions in *Barakat*, the English courts now give effect to any foreign law that is patrimonial in nature and the fact that a law may be a "public law" does not per se make it unenforceable in the English courts, unless giving effect to it would be contrary to public policy.

After the judgement, the owner of the Barakat gallery complained that "that means the Iranian Government could claim every Persian item at a British museum, and that does not make any sense".[159] While such words are not true, it clearly illustrates that a state with legislation under which all antiquities form part of its cultural heritage and are deemed the property of the state and that also makes exports without a licence illegal, may pursue a claim for the recovery of any such object that has been illegally exported on the basis

155 *Government of the Islamic Republic of Iran v The Barakat Galleries Ltd* [2007] EWHC 705 QB.

156 *Government of the Islamic Republic of Iran v The Barakat Galleries Ltd* [2007] EWCA Civ 1374, para 154.

157 Ibid, para. 131.

158 Ibid, para. 148.

159 Derek Fincham, 'Iran v Barakat: Iran Wins Barakat Appeal' in Lyndel Prott (ed), *Witnesses to History: A Compendium of Documents 2009and Writings on the Return of Cultural Objects* (United Nations Educational, Scientific and Cultural Organization, 2009) 388, 390.

that the state owns the object in question.[160] Therefore, the *Barakat* decisions bring the English courts in line with the US courts, which recognise the ownership title of foreign states to clandestinely excavated cultural materials, even when states never had possession of such objects.

4.4.3. Recover Illegally Exported Cultural Objects from the UK

Despite the good intentions of combatting the traffic of unlawfully removed cultural objects, UK law is still conservative in that offences wholly unrelated to the process of excavation or removal, such as a breach of foreign export laws, would not taint the object. The government's guideline clearly states that the 2003 Act was not enacted as a means for returning any cultural objects unlawfully exported from a foreign country. However, the return of illicitly removed heritage from the UK is still possible in two situations where it is likely that a person who contravenes a foreign state's export laws will also contravene UK laws. First, section 24 of the Theft Act 1968 made it clear that the offence of handling stolen goods included goods stolen overseas. In the prominent *Schultz* case, Frederick Schultz was convicted of conspiring to receive stolen Egyptian antiquities. His co-conspirator, the British conservator Jonathan Tokeley-Parry, who had illegally obtained and removed the antiquities from Egypt, including a sculpture of the head of Pharaon Amenhotep III, was also convicted in Britain in 1997 on the basis that his offences reflected "dishonesty on a large, elaborate and sophisticated scale".[161] In 2008, the head was returned to Egypt, more than ten years after Tokeley-Parry was charged for these activities. Thus, in some situations, illegally exported objects will be returned to the original states when the criminal prosecution has come to an end.

The second situation allowing for the repatriation of illegally exported foreign arts is when the object was imported using false statements on the import forms, which might entitle HM Revenue & Customs (HMRC) to seize the object and apply for forfeiture. According to the Customs and Excise Management Act 1979 (CEMA), an object can be forfeited if there is a misdeclaration, particularly one that has been made knowingly.[162] In a recent case, a statue from Libya that was mis-declared upon import as to both the value and country of origin, was ordered forfeited under the CEMA.[163] The return

160 Kevin Chamberlain and Kristin Hausler, 'United Kingdom' in James A.R. Nafziger and Robert Paterson (eds), *Handbook on the Law of Cultural Heritage and International Trade* (Edward Elgar Publishing, 2014) 460, 488.

161 James Mellor, 'Egyptian Treasures Smuggler is Jailed', *Independent* June 18 1997 <www.independent.co.uk/news/egyptian-treasures-smuggler-is-jailed-1256685.html>.

162 Goods improperly imported in breach of revenue laws are liable to forfeiture under Section 49 of the CEMA 1979. Ulph and Smith, *Illicit Trade in Art and Antiquities*, above n 36, 126.

163 Institute of Art and Law Blog, 'UK Customs seizure of looted Libyan statue' <www.ial.uk.com/news/uk-customs-seizure-of-looted-libyan-statue/>.

of the Libyan statue illustrates that an importer making a false declaration to the effect that an object has been exported legally commits a customs offence, rendering the importer subject to penalties and the object being imported liable to forfeiture.[164] In summary, the UK laws are adequate to deal with the illicit trafficking of foreign arts, resulting in the repatriation of certain illegally exported arts to original states.

However, it should be noted that such return is the result of contravening UK law rather than foreign export law. The landmark case of *Ortiz* created the foundation for the view that property rights in heritage arising from foreign export laws were incapable of being enforced in foreign courts.[165] Given the recent changes, it is doubtful whether this position is still sustainable, and whether it is possible for UK courts to recognise foreign export laws for recovery claims. In this regard, there is increasing recognition that a foreign state should be entitled to sue the possessor/owner of a cultural object in an English court whenever such an object is brought to England in violation of the foreign state's export regulations. Such recognition is reflected in the following aspects. First, in *Iran v Barakat*, the court noted that "if we are wrong in the view that this is not a claim to enforce foreign public law, then we do not consider that it should be precluded by any general principle that this country will not entertain an action whose object is to enforce the public law of another state".[166] In addition, the court continued by arguing that there were positive reasons of policy to ensure that a claim by a state to recover antiquities forming part of their national heritage should not be shut out. In supporting this, reference was made to international and national instruments, such as the UNESCO Convention, the UNIDROIT Convention, the Commonwealth Scheme and the relevant EU Directives, which all have the purpose of preventing unlawful dealing in cultural relics that form part of a state's cultural heritage. The court concluded that the variety of instruments enacted by the international community to combat the illicit trade indicated a certain common public policy:

> None of these instruments directly affects the outcome of this appeal, but they do illustrate the international acceptance of desirability of protection of the national heritage. A refusal to recognize the title of a foreign State, conferred by its law, to antiquities unless they had come into the possession of such State, would in most cases render it impossible for this country to recognize any claim by such a State to recover antiquities unlawfully exported to this country.[167]

Support for a new Act to sanction the return of cultural objects exported in violation of those rules can also be found in the 2003 Act. A person is guilty of

164 Chamberlain and Hausler, *UK,* above n 160, 489.
165 Wantuch-Thole, *Cultural Property in Cross-Border Litigation,* above n 24, 13.
166 *Government of the Islamic Republic of Iran v The Barakat Galleries Ltd* [2007] EWCA Civ 1374, para 151.
167 Ibid, para. 163.

an offence if he or she dishonestly deals with a tainted cultural object from an unlawful excavation or unlawful removal. Although well intentioned, the official guideline clearly states that offences wholly unrelated to the process of excavation or removal, such as a breach of foreign export laws, would not taint the object. However, this position is questionable as to whether it is effective in regulating the trade of arts. As commented by Simon Mackenzie, when objects that have been exported in breach of a foreign export restriction are not included in the definition of "tainted" under the 2003 Act, a considerable proportion of illicit antiquities are excluded from its scope.[168] Thus, there is a need for a new Act to sanction the violation of a foreign country's export controls and to facilitate the return of cultural objects exported in violation of those rules.

In conclusion, in arguing for the proposed customary rule, the UK legal system is complex: on the one hand, the UK laws are adequate to deal with the illicit trafficking of foreign arts, resulting in the repatriation of stolen and certain illegally exported arts to original states. Such repatriation largely allows the reunion of illegally taken cultural relics with their states of origin. On the other hand, it must be noted that the repatriation ordered by the UK laws is not a direct result of the UK's recognition of states of origin's interests in their illegally taken heritage. Particularly in the area of returning illegally exported objects, the prerequisite for repatriation is a contravention of UK laws. Such precondition places certain restrictions on the return of illegally removed heritage to states of origin.

4.5. The Netherlands

The Netherlands ratified the UNESCO Convention via the 1970 UNESCO Convention on the Illicit Import, Export and Transfer of Ownership of Cultural Property (Implementation) Act (the Dutch Act) on June 12 2009.[169] The Dutch Government also amended its Civil Procedure Code and the Civil Code to make sure that the provisions were in keeping with existing provisions of a similar nature introduced by the Dutch Act.[170] The Dutch Act is indispensable in evidencing a rule of customary law on the grounds that it has shown the maximum respect for the interests of the states of origin in their illegally taken heritage. Unlike other market states, the Dutch approach does

168 Simon Mackenzie and Penny Green, 'Criminalising the Market in Illicit Antiquities: an Evaluation of the Dealing in Cultural Objects (Offences) Act 2003 in England and Wales' in Simon Mackenzie and Penny Green (eds), *Criminology and Archaeology: Studies in Looted Antiquities* (Hart Publishing, 2009) 145, 154.

169 Netherland's Implementation of the Convention on the Means of Prohibiting and Preventing the Illicit Import, Export and Transfer of Ownership of Cultural Property adopted in Paris on November 14 1970 (1970 UNESCO Convention on the Illicit Import, Export and Transfer of Ownership of Cultural Property (Implementation) Act.

170 Section 4 Legal proceedings for return of Netherlands' Explanatory Memorandum to 1970 UNESCO Convention on the Illicit Import, Export and Transfer of Ownership of Cultural Property (Implementation) Act.

not distinguish whether the disputed object was illegally removed in violation of ownership law or export regulation.[171] The Dutch Act stands out in that Article 3(b) also prohibits the import of cultural relics that have "been unlawfully appropriated in State Party".[172] As the term "unlawfully appropriated" includes not only theft, but also offences such as obtaining objects under unlawful excavation or false documentation, original states have more opportunity to claim the largest possible objects.[173]

The recovery process for unlawfully taken heritage in the Netherlands is subject to a more flexible return procedure. For example, states of origin can initiate a claim for the recovery without the need of a bilateral agreement, thereby meaning the Dutch Act is not limited to a small group of contracting states.[174] Additionally, a state of origin concerned may apply directly to the Minister of Education, Culture and Science for the return of a cultural object unlawfully appropriated from a museum or similar institution.[175] The Dutch Minister of Education, Culture and Science is granted more power to take measures at the request of a state party, including provisional attachment, taking into custody, appointment of an administrator or application for an interim injunction, which make the return a much easier and more accessible procedure. The request need not be made through diplomatic offices as stipulated in the UNESCO Convention.[176]

More importantly, it should be noted that the Dutch law served as the inspiration for particular provisions now contained in the Directive 2014. For example, the Dutch Act does not impose any restriction on the designation scope and allows the requesting states a great deal of freedom in determining what objects fall within the scope of protection, as cultural relics are defined as being of importance for "archaeology, prehistory, history, literature, art or science and hence of essential importance to its cultural heritage".[177] In this regard, the EC Directive 2014 removes all age and financial value requirements and only requires disputed objects to be classified as a "national treasure" by a member state. In conclusion, the state practice of the Netherlands is important evidence in arguing for the proposed customary rule, as the Dutch

171 Section 3 reads that: It is prohibited to import into the Netherlands cultural property which:

a) has been removed from the territory of a State Party in breach of the provisions adopted by that State Party in accordance with the objectives of the Convention in respect of the export of cultural property from that State Party or the transfer of ownership of cultural property; or
b) has been unlawfully appropriated in a State Party.

172 Article 3(b) of the Dutch Act.
173 Wantuch-Thole, *Cultural Property in Cross-Border Litigation*, above n 24, 204.
174 Section 6 Illicit trade of the Dutch Explanatory Memorandum.
175 Section 7 Unlawful appropriation from a museum or similar institution of the Dutch Explanatory Memorandum.
176 Article 7 of the UNESCO Convention.
177 Section 2 Scope of the Bill of the Dutch Explanatory Memorandum.

law is inclined to recognise that a foreign state should be entitled to claim for any cultural heritage that has been illicitly trafficked.

5. Better Environment for Litigation

The previous sections have examined the relevant laws supporting the return of such objects at all international, regional, and national levels and, in particular, the state practices of each significant market state regarding the return of stolen and illicitly exported objects. The following section focuses on some rules that are increasingly used, or suggested to be applied, to facilitate the return of wrongfully removed cultural heritage to states of origin. These trends should be understood as a means of assisting states of origin in recovering lost arts and protecting their interests in their wrongfully removed heritage.

5.1. From Lex Situs *Rule to* Lex Originis *Rule*

According to the *lex situs* rule, the transfer of title to a chattel is determined by the law of the law of the country where the property is located at the time of the last transaction. However, thieves can easily take advantage of the differences among jurisdictions and launder the title of illicitly removed objects and profit from their wrongdoings.[178] A stolen object can thus be moved across borders and sold in a country that allows a good faith purchaser of stolen objects.[179] Owing to the consequences for the art trade, the application of *lex situs* is not sufficient in dealing with the ownership issues arising out of cultural heritage and a special choice of legal rule should be introduced to govern the title of cultural relics.[180] At this point, the principle of *lex originis*, with its great advantages of simplicity and legal certainty, has become the most commonly recognised connecting factor in determining the applicable law.

The *lex originis* rule is an important alternative for dealing with stolen or illicitly excavated cultural relics, which original states could apply when governing the dispute.[181] The application of *lex originis* was first introduced by the Resolution on the International Sales of Works of Art from the Angle of Cultural Heritage by the Institute of International Law.[182] Following the idea

178 See, e.g., *Winkworth v Christie Manson & Woods Ltd* [1980] Ch 496, [1980] 1 All ER 1121.
179 In civil law jurisdictions, a good faith purchaser of stolen property can obtain title with the passage of time, usually a very short period and sometimes immediately, as is the case in Italy. Karen Theresa Burke, 'International Transfers of Stolen Cultural Property: Should Thieves Continue to Benefit From Domestic Laws Favoring Bona Fide Purchasers?' (1990) 13(2) *Loyola of Los Angeles International and Comparative Law Journal* 427, 458.
180 'Choice of Law in Litigation to Recover National Cultural Property: Efforts at Harmonization in Private International Law' (1990) 31 *Virginia Journal of International Law* 1, 11.
181 Derek Fincham, 'How Adopting the *lex originis* rule can Impede the Flow of Illicit Cultural Property' (2008) 32(1) *The Columbia Journal of Law & the Arts* 111, 111.
182 Wantuch-Thole, *Cultural Property in Cross-Border Litigation*, above n 24, 246.

that every country has the right and duty to take measures to preserve its cultural heritage, Article 2 reads that "the transfer of ownership of works of art belonging to the cultural heritage of the country of origin shall be governed by the law of that country".[183] By implementing *lex originis*, buyers and sellers have an incentive to know where an object came from and who the past owners have been, thereby increasing the transparency of the art and antiquities market. It will ensure original states' own policies govern disputes in order to achieve the greatest interests for original states and increase the transparency of the art and antiquities market. In favouring the *lex originis* rule, Symeon Symenoides agrees that "the most logical choice [when laws conflict] is the state in which the thing was situated at the time of the critical event, typically the theft or other unauthorized removal".[184] Thus, if *lex originis* can be accepted by individual jurisdictions, it would be a powerful tool to assist original states with recovering their heritage.

It should be noted that the *lex originis* rule has received growing endorsement, reflected in the various instruments with the intention to harmonise conflicts of law. Both the 1995 UNIDROIT Convention[185] and the EC Directive[186] contain provisions allowing for the application of the law of the original states if it offers more advantages to prospective claimants seeking restitution of cultural objects. However, the available judicial practice in individual jurisdictions indicates that the rule of *lex originis* has not been widely accepted. In *Nigeria Bronzes*, the German court confirmed that *lex situs* was the only law applicable to transactions regarding cultural heritage items and an application of *lex originis* would not be considered.[187] However, Belgium is more advanced in introducing *lex originis* to the settlement of disputes concerning cultural relics. Section 90 of Belgium's' revised Private International Law specifically applies to cultural heritage and identifies that the recovery of an object illegally removed from the country in whose cultural patrimony the object belongs is governed by the law of that country.

However, thus far, no cultural disputes have been settled on the grounds of the application of *lex originis* and the traditional *lex situs* rule is still the predominant governing law in the international movable cultural heritage law. With regards to the absent practice, Fincham argues that it is possible to apply the rule of *lex originis* in practice. The application would not even necessarily

183 Institute of International Law, 'The International Sale of Works of Art from the Angle of the Protection of the Cultural Heritage' <www.idi-iil.org/idiE/resolutionsE/1991_bal_04_en.PDF>.

184 Symeon C. Symeonides, 'A Choice-of-Law Rule for Conflicts Involving Stolen Cultural Property' (2005) 38(4) *Vanderbilt Journal of Transnational Law* 1177, 1183.

185 Article 3(2) reads "a cultural object which has been unlawfully excavated or lawfully excavated but unlawfully retained shall be considered stolen, when consistent with the law of the State where the excavation took place".

186 Article 12 reads that "ownership of the cultural object after return shall be governed by that law of the requesting Member State".

187 Wantuch-Thole, *Cultural Property in Cross-Border Litigation,* above n 24, 344–345.

require legislative action, as an individual judge could adopt the rule of *lex originis* unilaterally when confronted with a cultural heritage dispute.[188] This crucial step, the real test of the rule, could be applied in a forum that enjoys a vibrant cultural heritage trade, such as New York or London. Rather than trying to harmonise private law everywhere in the world, if even one key forum endorses the *lex originis* rule, it will have an immediate impact. On the other hand, it should be noted that a device that relies on discretion will result in unpredictable, ad hoc outcomes, whereas law reform in individual private law systems is likely to have a more stable impact on application. Although the *lex originis* rule has not been widely accepted by the specially affected states, the endorsement from Belgium and academics may serve as an important catalyst for a wider acceptance. If this rule is accepted in a broad way, it will be extremely helpful in the protection of the interests of states of origin with regards to their illegally taken heritage.

5.2. Increase in the Level of Due Diligence

With respect to stolen cultural heritage, the issues involved in their return almost always involve two equally legitimate interests: that of the person who has lost a cultural object through theft and wants it back, and that of a good faith purchaser of such an object who wishes to keep it. The protection of good faith purchasers, particularly through compensation, has constituted a deterrent to the recovery of stolen arts. As a response, it should be observed that laws have been introduced to avoid the strong protection of a good faith purchaser by adopting higher levels of due diligence.

At the international law level, the UNIDROIT Convention and the EC Directive[189] contained provisions for compensation, but only when the acquirer satisfies the relatively higher standards of due diligence in the acquisition. According to the 2014 revised version of the EC Directive, proof of "due diligence" is mandatory before compensating people in possession of recovered objects.[190] In determining this due diligence, the UNIDROIT Convention contains a wide range of factors that should be taken into consideration, including:

> The character of the parties, the price paid, whether the possessor consulted any reasonably accessible register of stolen cultural objects, and any other relevant information and documentation which it could reasonably have obtained, and whether the possessor consulted accessible agencies or took any other step that a reasonable person would have taken in the circumstances.[191]

188 Fincham, *Adopting the lex originis rule,* above n 181, 149.
189 For more discussion, see Section European Initiatives.
190 Article 10 of the 2014 Council Directive.
191 Article 4(4) of the 1995 UNIDROIT Convention.

Many of the above elements are those that one would commonly expect a serious purchaser of cultural relics to undertake. The purpose of the higher level of due diligence is to act as a deterrent to purchasers acting without obtaining the necessary information, such as checking the provenance history, and accepting cultural objects with questionable origins.[192] Additionally, the increased requirement of due diligence will release original states from the financial burden of recovering stolen objects.

In terms of national laws, it can be noted that both the US courts, a common host to international art disputes, have sought to avoid the strong protection of good faith purchasers by tightening the obligation to enquire and research on the part of purchasers.[193] In the case of *Porter v Wertz* to recover stolen arts, the US court criticised the failure of a New York City dealer to investigate the source of a painting, while admitting that such indifference was typical of the trade.[194] In an appeal to the Court of Appeals, the New York State Attorney General urged the court to impose the duty of inquiry on the art dealers, not the owners. The court noted that "commercial indifference to ownership or the right to sell facilitates traffic in stolen works of art", and that it "diminishes the integrity and increases the culpability of the apathetic merchant".[195] It thus held that a merchant or art dealer who failed to investigate the provenance of an object in acceptance or acquisition cannot be viewed as a bona fide purchaser, a position that has been confirmed in subsequent court decisions.[196] In another case, *Bakalar v Vavra*, which involved dealing with an ownership claim, the appellate court emphasised that there was

> the significantly greater interest of New York . . . in convincing that New York purchasers of artwork should take greater care in assuring themselves of the legitimate provenance of their purchase in order to prevent the state from becoming a marketplace for stolen goods.[197]

The above cases clearly reflect that a purchaser is expected to comply with an increased level of diligence.[198]

Furthermore, some precedents made in the civil law jurisdictions, which had traditionally protected the bona fide purchaser, indicate that they are prepared

192 Wantuch-Thole, *Cultural Property in Cross-Border Litigation,* above n 24, 218.

193 Burke, *International Transfers of Stolen Cultural Property,* above n 179, 463–464.

194 *Porter v Wertz,* 416 NYS 2d 254 (App Div 1979).

195 Sydney M. Drum, 'Deweerth v Baldinger: Making New York a haven for stolen art?' (1989) 64(4) *New York University Law Review* 909, 918.

196 Maritza F. Bolano, 'International Art Theft Disputes: Harmonizing Common Law Principles with Article 7 of the UNESCO Convention' (1991) 15(1) *Fordham International Law Journal* 129, 152.

197 Laurie Frey, 'Bakalar v Vavra and the Art of Conflicts Analysis in New York: Framing a Choice of Law Approach for Moveable Property' (2012) 112(5) *Columbia Law Review* 1055.

198 Chechi, *Settlement of Cultural Disputes,* above n 3, 289–290.

to change the law, in particular by requiring a higher level of due diligence. For example, the Swiss CPTA stated that an art dealer or auctioneer cannot enter into any transaction involving cultural relics if there are circumstances that give cause for reasonable doubt as to the provenance of the object.[199] In this regard, the CPTA goes further than the UNESCO Convention, as the CPTA affects the art trade as a whole: the CPTA places the burden of the provenance check on both the purchasers and the dealer, while the UNESCO Convention only regulates "a museum or a religious or secular public monument or similar institution".[200]

In conclusion, it can be noted that there is a clear tendency towards an increased level of diligence, which expects the purchaser to investigate suspicious circumstances. The tightening of the obligation to research on the part of purchasers is significant in the protection of the original states' interests in their illegally removed arts, not only because it renders the repatriation of stolen arts less costly, but also sends a clear warning to the art market that the acquisition of stolen arts may face severe consequences, for example, heavy financial losses. Both direct and indirect influences from the increase in the level of due diligence is significant in the protection of original states' illegally removed arts, and thereby strengthens the foundation for creating the proposed customary rule.

5.3. Extend the Time Limitations or Delay the Accrual

Time limitations have always been an important issue in recovery, as there is often a considerable delay between the offence and the discovery of the whereabouts of an item by the plaintiff. However, in some jurisdictions, time limitations begin to run from the date of the theft or loss, meaning that if the original owner failed to bring action to recover his object within the period

199 According to Article 16 para. 2, art dealers are obliged to:

(1) to establish the identity of the supplier or seller and require a written declaration from the same of his or her right to dispose of the cultural property;
(2) to inform their customers about existing import and export regulations of the contracting states;
(3) to maintain written records on the acquisition of cultural property by specifically recording the origin of the cultural property, to the extent known, and the name and address of the supplier or seller, a description as well as the sales price of the cultural property; and
(4) to provide to the specialized body all necessary information on fulfilling this duty of diligence.

200 The legal duties that must be followed by art dealers are endorsed by the codes of ethics in the Swiss museums' world. The Swiss Association of Dealers in Antiques and Art requires members of professional associations to check the identity of the seller and clarify whether the object has been stolen or illegally exported. Marc Weber, 'New Swiss Law on Cultural Property' (2006) 13(1) *International Journal of Cultural Property* 99, 107.

specified in the statute of limitations, the action may be barred.[201] This has made time limitations a tool that art traffickers can use to escape recovery actions, as cultural relics can be easily hidden in their basements until the required time lapses. To avoid the use of time in the prevention of claims for return, two approaches have been adopted: extending the time limitations and delaying the accrual.

The intention of extending the time limitations is simple: it allows original states more time to search for illegally taken heritage.[202] Pursuant to the UNIDROIT Convention, a state may still declare that an overall period of 75 years applies to stolen objects that form an integral part of an identified monument or archaeological site, or that belong to a public collection or "such longer period as is provided in its law".[203] The possibility of applying an overall 75-year period, or even longer, is an important remedy to ensure the integrity of cultural heritage and to respect the original states' interests over their cultural relics.[204] Under the former Japanese law, the original owner's right to claim for stolen property lapsed two years from the time of the loss or the theft of the property, which has been criticised for contributing in part to Japan's reputation as a "safe haven" for illegally transferred cultural heritage.[205] As a legal response, in the case of stolen specified foreign cultural heritage, a victim of theft may now claim for the recovery of the property from the possessor after two years have elapsed and within a total period of ten years from the time of the theft.[206]

Despite the extension of the time limitations, many jurisdictions apply the due diligence rule, according to which the owner can sue only within a certain number of years from the date that he could have been expected to discover the location of the property or the identity of the possessor with reasonable diligence.[207] The application of the due diligence rule unfairly prejudices owners, by effectively encouraging illicit trafficking in stolen art. As a response, the UK Culture, Media, and Sport Committee of the House of Commons suggested that "special limitation periods should apply to cultural heritage to reflect the cultural personal importance of its ownership and the possibilities of unique identification".[208]

201 Chechi, *Settlement of Cultural Disputes,* above n 3, 338–389.

202 Leah E. Eisen, 'Commentary, The Missing Piece: A Discussion of Theft, Statutes of Limitations, and Title Disputes in the Art World' (1991) 81(4) *Journal of Criminal Law and Criminology* 1067; Stephanos Bibas, 'The Case Against Statutes of Limitations for Stolen Art' (1996) 5(1) *International Journal of Cultural Property* 73.

203 Article 3(5).

204 O'Keefe, *Using UNIDROIT to Avoid Disputes,* above n 37, 235.

205 Shigeru Kozai and Toshiyuki Kono, 'Japan' in James A.R. Nafziger and Robert Paterson (eds), *Handbook on the Law of Cultural Heritage and International Trade* (2014) 257, 267.

206 Ibid, 267–268.

207 Andrea E. Hayworth, 'Stolen Artwork: Deciding Ownership Is No Pretty Picture' (1993) 43(2) *Duke Law Journal* 337, 341–346.

208 Section IV International Initiatives and Legislative Change of the Seventh Report of the Select Committee on Culture, Media and Sport.

Additionally, it should be noted that the courts have been reluctant to hold that the applicable statute of limitations bars a victim's right to recover stolen property.[209] In particular, the New York courts, a common host to international art disputes, took a step forward by introducing the "demand and refusal" rule, according to which the cause of action does not accrue against a good faith purchaser of stolen property until the true owner has made a demand for its return and the possessor has refused the demand.[210] The owner then has three years to commence a suit. Although the demand and refusal rule was criticised for allowing owners to postpone making a demand indefinitely and, thus, causing harm to innocent buyers, it has still been increasingly accepted by the New York courts on the grounds that the original owners prevail over good faith purchasers of stolen arts.[211] In the *Guggenheim* case, the New York Court of Appeals held that the New York's statute of limitations does not require the victim to search diligently for stolen property, even though the disputed art had been displayed openly in a prominent New York art gallery between 1967 and 1981.[212] Similarly, in the case of *Turkey v Metropolitan Museum of Art*, the Met moved to dismiss on the grounds that the three-year statute of limitations had expired because the artefacts had been acquired in the 1960s. The court, however, applied the "demand and refusal" rule, and decided that the legal action of the Turkey was not barred because it began in 1987, within the three-year limitation period from the accrual of the cause of action. Moreover, the court affirmed that the Turkish claim had been made within the appropriate time period also in the light of the fact that the MET concealed the collection in its storerooms until 1984. As a result, the court dismissed the motion filed by the MET. By this interpretation, the accrual of the cause of action will be delayed until the victim of the art theft has had a realistic opportunity to learn of the location of the stolen cultural object.[213] Thus, original states that eventually discover the location of stolen objects will not be time-barred from bringing an action to recover.

209 For example, the US courts have employed several distinct doctrines to aid their determinations of whether an original owner can bring a suit for stolen property: *Menzel v List*, 267 NYS2d 804, 809 (Sup Ct NY 1966), rev'd, 246 NE 2d 742 (NY 1969). (demand and refusal rule); *O'Keeffe* v *Snyder*, 83 NJ 478, 416 A 2d 862 (discovery rule). Eisen, *Theft, Limitations, and Title Disputes,* above n 202, 1070; Bibas, *Case Against Statutes of Limitations,* above n 202, 81.

210 See, e.g., *Republic of Turkey v The Metropolitan Museum of Art*, 762 F Supp 44, 1990 US Dist LEXIS 18771 (SDNY 1990) (artefacts stolen from Turkish burial mounds); *Guggenheim*. 569 N E 2d at 429 (stolen Chagall watercolor); *Duryea v Andrews*, 12 NYS 42, 43 (Sup Ct 1890) (holding that statute of limitations began to run upon demand for the return of the stolen horse, but not mentioning refusal).

211 Drum, *Deweerth v Baldinger*, above n 195, 930–931.

212 Lisa Borodkin, 'The Economics of Antiquities Looting and a Proposed Legal Alternative' (1995) 95(2) *Columbia Law Review* 377, 401.

213 Patty Gerstenblith, 'Increasing Effectiveness Of The Legal Regime For The Protection Of The International Archaeological Heritage' in James A.R. Nafziger and Ann

In discussing the proposed customary rule, extending the time limitations or delaying the accrual is significant in enhancing the ability of the states of origin to bring their heritage home. Avoidance of the use of a time bar will improve the transparency of the art trade, as art dealers or collectors will be more careful about their purchases and endeavour to exercise more diligence in ensuring they receive a good title.[214] More importantly, the demand and refusal rule provides a solution to allow original states to bring back illegally removed cultural relics as long as the original owner searches diligently for the stolen object, even many decades after the wrongdoing.[215]

6. Conclusion: Signs of Change

Theft and smuggling is the second cause violating the interests of original states with regards to their cultural relics. To obtain repatriation through litigation, although original states need to deal with a wide range of issues arising out of law and fact, the first hurdle preventing them from claiming for repatriation is the recognition and enforcement of foreign laws. However, there is an increasing recognition that foreign states should have sufficient interests to argue for the return of their illegally removed heritage.

With regards to stolen heritage, particularly clandestinely excavated antiquities, important market states have been inclined to support recovery claims. This recognition is significant in protecting the states of origins' interests in their wrongfully removed heritage and provides strong evidence for the creation of the proposed customary rule. With respect to illicitly exported heritage, through the ratification of the 1970 UNESCO Convention, the major market states, including the US, Germany, Switzerland and the Netherlands, have adopted special laws to allow original states to recover illicitly exported objects in their forums. Additionally, a growing body of national case law demonstrates that the principles underpinning the Conventions are beginning to influence judicial approaches to restitution claims.[216]

However, the uniformity among specially affected states is still lacking. For example, while the US has proven to be a forum favourable for original states in restitution after the US Government filed civil forfeiture for disputed objects, the UK still holds the position that foreign public law cannot be

---

Nicgorski (eds), *Cultural Heritage Issues* (Martinus Nijhoff Publishers, 2009) 305, 310; Drum, *Deweerth v Baldinger*, above n 195, 919–920.

214 Bibas, *Case Against Statutes of Limitations*, above n 202, 88–92.

215 Weil Stephen E, 'The American Legal Response to the Problem of Holocaust Art' (1999) IV(4) *Art Antiquity and Law* 285, 291.

216 Howard N. Spiegler, 'The UNESCO Convention's Role in American Cultural Property Law: The Journey to US v Frederick Schultz' in *Museum International: Protection and Restitution* (2005) 103, 103–108; Francesca Fiorentini, 'A Legal Pluralist Approach to International Trade in Cultural Objects' in James A.R. Nafziger and Robert Paterson (eds), *Handbook on the Law of Cultural Heritage and International Trade* (Edward Elgar Publishing, 2014) 589, 596.

enforced in British courts, rendering most national laws ineffective for dealing with the illegal export of cultural objects. In conclusion, the state practices of specially affected states clearly reflect that there is an increasing recognition of the interests of states of origin in their wrongfully removed heritage, which paves the way for the creation of the proposed customary rule. However, the lack of uniformity of state practices means the proposed rule is still emerging.

Bibliography

'Bilateral Agreements' <http://eca.state.gov/cultural-heritage-center/cultural-property-protection/bilateral-agreements>

'Choice of Law in Litigation to Recover National Cultural Property: Efforts at Harmonization in Private International Law' (1990) 31 *Virginia Journal of International Law* 1

'Cultural Property Protection' (US Bureau of Educational and Cultural Affairs <https://eca.state.gov/cultural-heritage-center/cultural-property-protection/process-and-purpose/background>

'Directive 2014/60/EU of the European Parliament and of the Council of 15 May 2014 on the return of cultural objects unlawfully removed from the territory of a Member State and amending Regulation (EU) No 1024/2012 (Recast).' <http://eur-lex.europa.eu/legal-content/EN/TXT/PDF/?uri=CELEX:32014L0060&from=EN>

'Exlanatory Notes on Dealing In Cultural Objects (Offences) Bill', UK Parliament <www.publications.parliament.uk/pa/ld200203/ldbills/090/en/03090x--.htm>

'Fourth Report on the Application of Council Directive 93/7/EEC on the Return of Cultural Objects Unlawfully Removed From the Territory of a Member State', European Commission, 2013 <http://eur-lex.europa.eu/legal-content/EN/TXT/PDF/?uri=CELEX:52013DC0310&from=EN>

'Guidance on the Dealing in Cultural Objects (Offences) Act 2003' <http://old.culture.gov.uk/images/publications/Dealincultural.pdf>

'The International Sale of Works of Art from the Angle of the Protection of the Cultural Heritage', Institute of International Law <www.idi-iil.org/idiE/resolutionsE/1991_bal_04_en.PDF>

'Key Aspects of the New Act on the Protection of Cultural Property in Germany', Germany's Federal Government Commissioner for Culture and the Media, September 2016 <www.congreso.es/docu/docum/ddocum/dosieres/sleg/legislatura_12/spl_3/pdfs/22.pdf>

'Memorandum of Understanding (MOU), to Protect Categories of Archaeological Material from the Paleolithic Period through the Tang Dynasty, and Monumental Sculpture and Wall art at least 250 Years Old', Bureau of Educational and Cultural Affairs <http://eca.state.gov/cultural-heritage-center/international-cultural-property-protection/bilateral-agreements/china>

'The New Act on the Protection of Cultural Property in Germany: implementing the UNESCO 1970 Convention and new EU law' <www.unesco.org/fileadmin/MULTIMEDIA/HQ/CLT/pdf/presentation_UNESCO_Germany.pdf>

'The Nigerian Bronzes Case' in Lyndel Prott (ed), *Witnesses to history. Documents and Writings on the Return of Cultural Objects* (UNESCO, 2009) 33

'Recent Examples of Successful Operations of Cultural Property Restitutions in the World' UNESCO <www.unesco.org/new/en/culture/themes/restitution-of-cultural-property/successful-restitutions-in-the-world/>

'Return of Illegally Exported Cultural Objects: Simpler Rules', European Parliament January 21 2014 <www.europarl.europa.eu/news/en/news-room/content/20140120IPR33131/html/Return-of-illegally-exported-cultural-objects-simpler-rules>

'Seventh Report of the Select Committee on Culture, Media and Sport' <www.parliament.the-stationery-office.co.uk/pa/cm199900/cmselect/cmcumeds/371/37106.htm>

'US Senate Report, 97–564 Implementing Legislation for the Convention on the Means of Prohibiting and Preventing the Illicit Import, Export and Transfer of Ownership of Cultural Property' <https://eca.state.gov/files/bureau/97-564.pdf>

Bibas, Stephanos, 'The Case Against Statutes of Limitations for Stolen Art' (1996) 5(1) *International Journal of Cultural Property* 73

Blake, Janet, *International Cultural Heritage Law* (Oxford University Press, 2015)

Blake, Janet, 'Turkey' in James A.R. Nafziger and Robert Paterson (eds), *Handbook on the Law of Cultural Heritage and International Trade* (Edward Elgar Publishing, 2014)

Bolano, Maritza F., 'International Art Theft Disputes: Harmonizing Common Law Principles with Article 7 of the UNESCO Convention' (1991) 15(1) *Fordham International Law Journal* 129

Borodkin, Lisa, 'The Economics of Antiquities Looting and a Proposed Legal Alternative' (1995) 95(2) *Columbia Law Review* 377

Bouchenaki, M., 'Return and Restitution of Cultural Property in the Wake of the 1970 Convention' (2009) 61(1–2) *Museum International* 139

Briggs, Aaron Kyle, 'Consequences of the Met–Italy Accord for the International Restitution of Cultural Property' (2007) 7(2) *Chicago Journal of International Law* 623

Burke, Karen Theresa, 'International Transfers of Stolen Cultural Property: Should Thieves Continue to Benefit From Domestic Laws Favoring Bona Fide Purchasers?' (1990) 13(2) *Loyola of Los Angeles International and Comparative Law Journal* 427

Cassella, Stefan D., 'Using the Forfeiture Laws to Protect Archaeological Resources' (2006) 41 *Idaho Law Review* 129

Chamberlain, Kevin and Kristin Hausler, 'United Kingdom' in James A.R. Nafziger and Robert Paterson (eds), *Handbook on the Law of Cultural Heritage and International Trade* (Edward Elgar Publishing, 2014) 460

Chechi, Alessandro, *The Settlement of International Cultural Heritage Disputes* (Oxford University Press, 2014)

Church, Judith, 'Evolving US Case Law on Cultural Property' (1993) 2(1) *International Journal of Cultural Property* 47

Day, Michael, 'Italy Celebrates as 5,000 Plundered Artefacts Worth €50m are Returned following 14-year Inquiry', *Independent* January 22 2015 <www.independent.co.uk/news/science/archaeology/news/italy-celebrates-as-5000-plundered-artefacts-worth-50m-are-returned-following-14year-inquiry-9996427.html>

Drum, Sydney M., 'Deweerth v Baldinger: Making New York a haven for stolen art?' (1989) 64(4) *New York University Law Review* 909
Eisen, Leah E., 'Commentary, The Missing Piece: A Discussion of Theft, Statutes of Limitations, and Title Disputes in the Art World' (1991) 81(4) *Journal of Criminal Law and Criminology* 1067
Fincham, Derek, 'How Adopting the *lex originis* rule can Impede the Flow of Illicit Cultural Property' (2008) 32(1) *The Columbia Journal of Law & the Arts* 111
Fincham, Derek, 'Iran v Barakat: Iran Wins Barakat Appeal' in Lyndel Prott (ed), *Witnesses to History: A Compendium of Documents 2009and Writings on the Return of Cultural Objects* (United Nations Educational, Scientific and Cultural Organization, 2009) 388
Fiorentini, Francesca, 'A Legal Pluralist Approach to International Trade in Cultural Objects' in James A.R. Nafziger and Robert Paterson (eds), *Handbook on the Law of Cultural Heritage and International Trade* (Edward Elgar Pub, 2014) 589
Frey, Laurie, 'Bakalar v Vavra and the Art of Conflicts Analysis in New York: Framing a Choice of Law Approach for Moveable Property' (2012) 112(5) *Columbia Law Review* 1055
Gerstenblith, Patty, 'Enforcement by Domestic Courts: Criminal Law and Forfeiture in the Recovery of Cultural Objects' in Francesco Francioni and James Gordley (eds), *Enforcing International Cultural Heritage Law* (Oxford University Press, 2013) 150
Gerstenblith, Patty, 'For Better and For Worse: Evolving United States Policy on Cultural Property Litigation and Restitution' (2015) 22(2–3) *International Journal of Cultural Property* 357
Gerstenblith, Patty, 'Implementation of the 1970 UNESCO Convention by the United States and Other Market Nations' <www.law.upenn.edu/live/files/6423-gerstenblith-patty-2017-implementation-of-the-1970>
Gerstenblith, Patty, 'Increasing Effectiveness Of The Legal Regime For The Protection Of The International Archaeological Heritage' in James A.R. Nafziger and Ann Nicgorski (eds), *Cultural Heritage Issues* (Martinus Nijhoff Publishers, 2009) 305
Gerstenblith, Patty, 'Schultz and Barakat: Universal Recognition of National Ownership of Antiquities' (2009) (1) *Art Antiquity and Law* 21
Gordley, James, 'The Enforcement of Foreign Law: Reclaiming One Nation's Cultural Heritage in Another Nation's Courts' in Francesco Francioni and James Gordley (eds), *Enforcing International Cultural Heritage Law* (Oxford University Press, 2013) 110
Green, Simon Mackenzie and Penny, 'Introduction: A Context for the Engagement of Criminology and Archaeology' in Simon Mackenzie and Penny Green (ed), *Criminology and Archaeology: Studies in Looted Antiquities* (Hart Publishing, 2009) 1
Hayworth, Andrea E., 'Stolen Artwork: Deciding Ownership Is No Pretty Picture' (1993) 43(2) *Duke Law Journal* 337
Hoffman, Matthew R., 'Cultural Pragmatism: A New Approach to the International Movement of Antiquities' (2010) 95(2) *Iowa Law Review* 665
Jower, Kevin, 'Comment: International and National Legal Efforts to Protect Cultural Property: The 1970 UNESCO Convention, the United States, and Mexico' (2003) 38 *Texas International Law Journal* 145

Kaye, Lawrence M., 'Art Wars: The Repatriation Battle' (1998) 31 *New York University Journal of International Law and Politics* 79

Kaye, Lawrence M., 'Recovery of Stolen Cultural Property: A Practitioner's View—War Stories and Morality Tales' (1998) (5) *Villanova Sports & Entertainment Law Journal* 5

Kaye, Lawrence and Carla Main, 'The Saga of the Lydian Hoard Antiquities: From Usak to New York and Back and Some Related Observations on the Law of Cultural Repatriation' in Kathryn Tubb (ed), *Antiquities Trade or Betrayed: Legal, Ethical & Conservation Issues* (Archetype, 1995)

Knapp, Krystal, 'Princeton University Returns Art to Italy', *Planet Princeton* January 26 2012 <http://planetprinceton.com/2012/01/26/princeton-university-returns-art-to-italy/>

Kozai, Shigeru and Toshiyuki Kono, 'Japan' in James A.R. Nafziger and Robert Paterson (eds), *Handbook on the Law of Cultural Heritage and International Trade* (2014) 257

Laird, Michèle, 'Closing in on the Archaeological Underworld', *Swissinfo* July 18 2012 <www.swissinfo.ch/eng/free-port-problem_closing-in-on-the-archaeological-underworld/33088854>

Litt, Steven, 'Cleveland Museum of Art Strikes Deal With Italy to Return 14 Ancient Artworks', *Cleveland* November 19 2008 <www.cleveland.com/arts/index.ssf/2008/11/cleveland_museum_of_art_1.html>

Logan, Mia J., 'Limiting Access to Art in Hopes of Decreased Cultural Property Destruction: An Assessment of the United States and China's Memorandum of Understanding for 2014' (2014) 1 *Art Antiquity and Law* 1

Lufkin, Martha, 'Egyptian Antiquities Dealer Found Guilty', *Forbes* February 20 2002 <www.forbes.com/2002/02/20/0220hot.html>

Mackenzie, Simon, *Going, Going, Gone: Regulating the Market in Illicit Antiquities* (Institute of Art and Law, 2005)

Mackenzie, Simon and Penny Green, 'Criminalising the Market in Illicit Antiquities: an Evaluation of the Dealing in Cultural Objects (Offences) Act 2003 in England and Wales' in Simon Mackenzie and Penny Green (eds), *Criminology and Archaeology: Studies in Looted Antiquities* (Hart Publishing, 2009) 145

Mackey, Larry A., 'ARPA on Private Lands: The GE Mound Case' in Sherry Hutt, Marion Forsyth and David Tarler (eds), *Presenting Archaeology in Court: Legal Strategies for Protecting Cultural Resources* (AltaMira Press, 2006) 47

Marous, Sarah and J. Michael Marous, 'ARPA in the International Context: Protecting the Articles of Faith' in Sherry Hutt, Marion Forsyth and David Tarler (eds), *Presenting Archaeology in Court: Legal Strategies for Protecting Cultural Resources* (AltaMira Press, 2006) 39

Mellor, James, 'Egyptian Treasures Smuggler is Jailed', *Independent* June 18 1997 <www.independent.co.uk/news/egyptian-treasures-smuggler-is-jailed-1256685.html>

Morrow, Jessica Eve, 'The National Stolen Property Act and the Return of Stolen Cultural Property to Its Rightful Foreign Owners' (2007) 30(1) *Boston College International and Comparative Law Review* 249

Nafziger, James A.R. and Robert Kirkwood Paterson, 'Cultural Heritage Law' in James A.R. Nafziger and Robert Kirkwood Paterson (eds), *Handbook on the Law of Cultural Heritage and International Trade* (Edward Elgar Publishing, 2014)

Neuhaus, Nina M., 'Switzerland Returns 32 Antiquities to Egypt', Institute of Art and Law Blog, June 10 2015 <www.ial.uk.com/news/switzerland-returns-32-antiquities-to-egypt/>

Neuhaus, Nina M., 'Switzerland Returns Illegally Imported Terracotta Statue To China', December 24 2014 <www.ial.uk.com/news/switzerland-returns-illegally-imported-terracotta-statue-to-china/>

O'Hagan, John and Clare McAndrew, 'Export Restrictions, Tax Incentives and the National Artistic Patrimony' (2000) 10(37) *Cultural Trends* 41

O'Keefe, Patrick, 'Using UNIDROIT to Avoid Cultural Heritage Disputes: Limitation Periods' (2009) 14 *Willamette Journal of International Law and Dispute Resolution* 227

Olivier, Monique, 'The UNIDROIT Convention: Attempting to Regulate the International Trade and Traffic of Cultural Property' (1996) 26(1–3) *Golden Gate University Law Review* 627

Ozel, Sibel, 'Case note. The Basel Decisions: Recognition of the Blanket Legislation Vesting State Ownership Over the Cultural Property Found Within the Country of Origin' (2000) 9(2) *International Journal of Cultural Property* 315

Ozel, Sibel, 'Under the Turkish Blanket Legislation: The Recovery of Cultural Property Removed from Turkey' (2010) 38(2) *International Journal of Legal Information* 177

Palmer, Norman, 'Statutory, Forensic and Ethical Initiatives in the Recovery of Stolen Art and Antiquities' in Norman Palmer (ed), *The Recovery of Stolen Art: A Collection of Essays* (Kluwer Law International, 1998)

Park, Sue J., 'The Cultural Property Regime in Italy: An Industrialized Source Nation's Difficulties in Retaining and Recovering its Antiquities' (2002) 23(4) *University of Pennsylvania Journal of International Economic Law* 931

Phalnikar, Sonia, 'Germany Acquired Nefertiti Illegally, Egyptian Official Says', *DW* December 22 2009 <www.dw.com/en/germany-acquired-nefertiti-illegally-egyptian-official-says/a-5046115>

Povoledo, Elisabetta, 'Boston Museum Returns 13 Ancient Works to Italy', *New York Times* September 29 2006 <www.nytimes.com/2006/09/29/arts/design/29mfa.html?_r=0>

Povoledo, Elisabetta, 'Italy and Getty Sign Pact on Artifacts', *New York Times* September 26 2007 <www.nytimes.com/2007/09/26/arts/design/26gett.html?_r=0&pagewanted=print>

Povoledo, Elisabetta, 'Met to Sign Accord in Italy to Return Vase and Artifacts', *New York Times* February 21 2006 <www.nytimes.com/2006/02/21/arts/design/21anti.html?pagewanted=print>

Prott, Lyndel, 'Problems of Private International Law for the Protection of the Cultural Heirtage' in Hague Academy of International Law (ed), *Collected Courses of the Hague Academy of International Law* (Nijhoff, 1989) 215

Prott, Lyndel, 'UNESCO and UNIDROIT: a Partnership against Trafficking in Cultural Objects" (1996) 1 *Uniform Law Review* 59

Renold, Marc-André, 'An Important Swiss Decision Relating to the International Transfer of Cultural Goods: The Swiss Supreme Court's Decision on the Giant Antique Mogul Gold Coins' (2006) 13(3) *International Journal of Cultural Property* 361

Renold, Marc-André and Beat Schönenberger, 'Switzerland' in James A.R. Nafziger and Robert Paterson (eds), *Handbook on the Law of Cultural Heritage and International Trade* (Edward Elgar Publishing, 2014) 408

Roodt, Christa, *Private international law, Art and Cultural heritage* (Edward Elgar Publishing, 2015)

Schechter, Rhonda, 'Preventing Pillage and Promoting Politics: The Dual Goals of the 2009 US–China Bilateral Agreement to Restrict Imports of Chinese Cultural Property' (2009) 4 *Art Antiquity and Law* 317

Siehr, Kurt, 'Germany' in James A.R. Nafziger and Robert Paterson (eds), *Handbook on the Law of Cultural Heritage and International Trade* (Edward Elgar Publishing, 2014) 160

Siehr, Kurt, 'The Protection of Cultural Heritage and International Commerce' (1997) 6(2) *International Journal of Cultural Property* 304

Slayman, A., 'Recent Cases of Repatriation of Antiquities to Italy from the United States' (1998) 7(2) *International Journal of Cultural Property* 456

Spiegler, Howard N., 'The UNESCO Convention's Role in American Cultural Property Law: The Journey to US v Frederick Schultz' in *Museum International: Protection and Restitution* (2005) 103

Stephen E, Weil, 'The American Legal Response to the Problem of Holocaust Art' (1999) IV(4) *Art Antiquity and Law* 285

Symeonides, Symeon C., 'A Choice-of-Law Rule for Conflicts Involving Stolen Cultural Property' (2005) 38(4) *Vanderbilt Journal of Transnational Law* 1177

Ulph, Janet, 'UK Customs seizure of looted Libyan statue', Institute of Art and Law Blog, October 22 2015 <www.ial.uk.com/news/uk-customs-seizure-of-looted-libyan-statue/>

Ulph, Janet and Ian Smith, *The Illicit Trade in Art and Antiquities: International Recovery and Criminal and Civil Liability* (Hart Publishing, 2012)

Vigneron, Sophie, 'Protecting Cultural Objects: Enforcing the Illicit Export of Foreign Cultural Objects' in Valentina Vadi and Hildegard Schneider (eds), *Art, Cultural Heritage and the Market: Ethical and Legal Issues* (Springer, 2014) 117

Wantuch-Thole, Mara, *Cultural Property in Cross-Border Litigation: Turning Rights into Claims* (De Gruyter, 2014)

Weber, Marc, 'New Swiss Law on Cultural Property' (2006) 13(1) *International Journal of Cultural Property* 99

Yasaitis, Kelly Elizabeth, 'National Ownership Laws as Cultural Property Protection Policy: The Emerging Trend in United States v Schultz' (2005) 12(1) *International Journal of Cultural Property* 95

7 Evolving Social and Ethical Norms

Practice of Individuals, Private Museums, and Auction Houses

1. Introduction

As analysed in the previous chapters, while evidence of state practice supporting the formation of the proposed customary rule exists, it is weak, suggesting that the proposed rule is still at the very beginning of formation. However, apart from the limited state practice, an increasing number of cultural objects have been returned to states of origin by private museums, non-governmental institutions, auction houses, and individuals throughout the world. All these examples constitute the acknowledgement that states of origin's interests in their wrongfully removed heritage should be respected and such heritage should be returned. The idea that there is a moral duty to return highly valuable or significant cultural heritage items is strongly gaining ground.[1]

However, complications arise because actions by individuals and institutions do not constitute state behaviour and can therefore not directly create customary international law. Despite not being recognised as state practice, they are important evidence in reflecting the public attitudes, and ethical and moral considerations, which generally precede the development of legal rules. In other words, they are important in signalling the future development of the law and suggesting whether the proposed customary rule is likely to come into existence.[2] Additionally, the return of cultural heritage is not a theme that can be treated convincingly without a fully grounded engagement with ethics. Recent developments have shown that ethical and historical considerations have played a significant role in facilitating return outcomes that are more results-oriented in practical terms than the mere application of any national or

1 Marie Cornu and Marc-André Renold, 'New Developments in the Restitution of Cultural Property: Alternative Means of Dispute Resolution' (2010) 17(1) *International Journal of Cultural Property* 1, 3.

2 Lyndel Prott, *Witnesses to History: A Compendium of Documents and Writings on the Return of Cultural Objects* (United Nations Educational, Scientific and Cultural Organization, 2009). 1; Alessandro Chechi, 'Multi-Level Cooperation to Safeguard the Human Dimension of Cultural Heritage and to Secure the Return of Wrongfully Removed Cultural Objects' in Silvia Borelli and Federico Lenzerini (eds), *Cultural Heritage, Cultural Rights, Cultural Diversity* (Martinus Nijhoff Publishers, 2012) 347, 367.

international laws, and more appropriate to both sides' interests.[3] Thus, an analysis of the practice of individuals, private museums, and auction houses is essential, and still a noteworthy issue when discussing the proposed customary rule in this book.

Chapter 7 focuses on the practice of individuals, private museums, and auction houses. This chapter aims to explore whether there is increasing public endorsement for states of origin's interests in their wrongfully removed heritage to be respected, which is the basic idea underpinning the proposed customary rule. Through the analysis of retuning cases, this chapter provides suggestions for individuals, private museums, and auction houses on how to avoid unnecessary negative headlines, reputational damage and becoming embroiled in recovery disputes, and more importantly, how to settle recovery disputes peacefully and quickly.

2. Stricter Policies at Acquisition and Acceptance

The 2006 high profile prosecution of former Getty Curator Marion True exposed how the Getty and other leading US museums had acquired scores of valuable art items from Italy and Greece with dubious provenance and added them to their collections.[4] This scandal ultimately led to stricter policies being drawn up by the museum groups, namely, not to accept any object when provenance is incomplete or uncertain.[5] In 2015, the Museums Association (MA) published a draft of its revised Code of Ethics, which requires all museums in the UK to exercise due diligence to verify the ownership of any item being considered. They must also: establish that the current holder is legitimately able to transfer title or lend the object; reject any item if there is suspicion that it was wrongfully taken during a time of conflict, stolen, illicitly exported or illicitly traded, unless explicitly allowed by treaties or other agreements; and contact appropriate authorities for any information regarding the legitimacy of items.[6] The museum guidelines are an important approach to respecting states of origin's interests in their wrongfully removed cultural heritage. As museums are some of the largest collectors of artefacts and other foreign cultural

3 Robert Peters, 'Remedying Historical Injustice: Ethical and Historical Considerations in Returning Cultural Materials' in Silvia Borelli and Federico Lenzerini (eds), *Cultural Heritage, Cultural Rights, Cultural Diversity* (Martinus Nijhoff Publishers, 2012) 141, 141.

4 Dan Glaister, 'Getty Museum Admits 350 More Treasures May Be Looted', *Guardian* 19 June 2006 <www.theguardian.com/world/2006/jun/19/arts.usa>; Elina Moustaira, *Art Collections, Private and Public: A Comparative Legal Study* (Springer, 2015), 116.

5 Neil Brodie, 'An Archaeologist's View of the Trade in Unprovenanced Antiquities' in Barbara T. Hoffman (ed), *Art and Cultural Heritage: Law, Policy and Practice* (Cambridge University Press, 2009) 52, 54; Neil Brodie et al, *Trade in Illicit Antiquities: The Destruction of the World's Archaeological Heritage* (McDonald Institute for Archaeological Research, 2001), 43.

6 Section 9 Combatting the Illicit Trade in Items and Section 2 Stewardship of Collections of MA's 2015 (Draft) Code of Ethics for Museums.

materials, the control of museum acquisition policies is extremely important in combatting illicit trade and suppressing the demand for cultural objects of dubious provenance.[7] If the codes of ethics are effectively implemented in practice, it will greatly help to prevent the acquisition or loan of foreign cultural objects of dubious provenance by museums, and reduce the incentives for looters engaging in illicit trafficking or conducting unauthorised excavations.[8] From this perspective, the ethical codes will help to preserve the integrity of cultural heritage.

In discussing the proposed customary rule, another important contribution to the ethical codes is that many museums typically no longer purchase or accept cultural objects that do not have a documented history stretching back past 1970. For example, the British Museum's acquisitions policy provides that it will normally only purchase and accept those heritage objects that have documentation to show a legal history back to November 14 1970.[9] This policy is influenced by the codes of ethics established by various museum groups, which align their guidelines with the 1970 UNESCO Convention, and strongly discourage museums from purchasing or accepting any object that cannot pass the 1970 test or lack an export permit from the state of origin. For example, the Museums Association directs museums in the UK not to accept any items that lack secure ownership history, unless there is reliable documentation to show that it was exported from the state of origin before 1970.[10] The Association of Art Museum Directors' (AAMD's) 2008 Guidelines, which have been adopted by most US museums and institutions, state that "member museums normally should not acquire a work unless provenance research substantiates that the work was outside its country of probable modern discovery before 1970 or was legally exported from its probable country of modern discovery after 1970".[11] While the date of 1970 has no legal significance, it creates a uniform set of expectations for museums as well as sellers and donors.[12] This is because when an object is documented as being outside of its state of origin before that date, it is less likely that any illegality is attached to the object as

7 Leila Amineddoleh, 'The Role of Museums in Sustaining the Illicit Trade in Culutral Property' 25 *Cardozo Arts & Entertainment Law Journal* 837, 838–839.

8 Janet Blake, *International Cultural Heritage Law* (Oxford University Press, 2015), 34.

9 'British Museum Policy on Acquisitions' <www.britishmuseum.org/pdf/Acquisitions.pdf>.

10 Section Illicit Trade of The UK Government, 'Memorandum Submitted by the Museums Association' <www.publications.parliament.uk/pa/cm199900/cmselect/cmcumeds/371/0032305.htm>.

11 Section E of 'Introduction to the Revisions to the 2008 Guidelines on the Acquisition of Archaeological Material and Ancient Art' <https://aamd.org/sites/default/files/document/AAMD%20Guidelines%202013.pdf>; Article 9.5 of MA's 2015 (Draft) Code of Ethics.

12 Manlio Frigo, 'Ethical Rules and Codes of Honor Related to Museum Activities: A Complementary Support to the Private International Law Approach Concerning the Circulation of Cultural Property' (2009) 16(1) *International Journal of Cultural Property* 49, 53; Neil Brodie and Colin Renfrew, 'Looting and the World's Archaeological Heritage: The Inadequate Response' (2005) 34 *Annual Review of Anthropology* 343, 352.

many national ownership laws postdate 1970. Thus, the 1970 cut-off date is sometimes viewed as a proxy for legality.[13] In this regard, it should be noted that the codes of ethics for museums are much higher than those required by law. For example, China and the US entered a bilateral agreement in 2009, which stipulated that the US would ban the import of antiquities dating from the Paleolithic period, starting in 75,000 BC, through to the end of the Tang dynasty, in 907 AD, and all monumental sculpture and wall art at least 250 years old.[14] The bilateral agreement took effect from January 16 2009. This means that US Customs will allow a Chinese object from the protected categories to enter the US if documents indicate that this item left China prior to January 16 2009, rather than the year of 1970. By adopting these higher standards, it can thus be argued that the codes of ethics show the commitment to acting professionally, fairly, ethically, honestly, and within the law.[15] However, questions arise regarding the practical implementation of the ethical codes, as they are not compulsory or enforceable in court. Despite not being legally binding, compliance with ethical and moral codes results in advantages when purchasing art works. For example, a buyer who acquires a cultural object from a dealer complying with the UNESCO International Code of Ethics for Dealers in Cultural Property, will most probably be considered a bona fide purchaser and be entitled to compensation for the return.[16]

As a result of the stricter policies, most museums and auction houses have tightened their policies and now follow up on what objects they can accept.[17] Suppressing the demand for cultural heritage objects with uncertain and cloudy provenance will greatly help to control the illegal excavation of culturally rich countries and subsequent movement of cultural objects. Museum guidelines reflect the commitment to combat the illicit trade of wrongfully removed heritage, which is essential for preserving the integrity of cultural heritage in states of origin. Thus, it can be concluded that the ethical and moral codes reflect a change in attitude among museum professionals, from viewing themselves as custodians of the objects in their collections to an acknowledgement that preserving the original site and context of cultural heritage is of equal importance.[18]

13 Patty Gerstenblith, 'The Meaning of 1970 for the Acquisition of Archaeological Objects' (2013) 38(4) *Journal of Field Archaeology* 364, 365.

14 Rhonda Schechter, 'Preventing Pillage and Promoting Politics: The Dual Goals of the 2009 US–China Bilateral Agreement to Restrict Imports of Chinese Cultural Property' (2009) 4 *Art Antiquity and Law* 317, 323.

15 Irini A. Stamatoudi, *Cultural Property Law and Restitution: A Commentary to International Conventions and European Union law* (Edward Elgar Publishing, 2011), 160.

16 Francesca Fiorentini, 'A Legal Pluralist Approach to International Trade in Cultural Objects' in James A.R. Nafziger and Robert Paterson (eds), *Handbook on the Law of Cultural Heritage and International Trade* (Edward Elgar Publishing, 2014) 589, 606.

17 Ralph Blumenthal and Tom Mashberg, 'The Curse of the Outcast Artifact', *The New York Times* July 12 2012 <www.nytimes.com/2012/07/15/arts/design/antiquity-market-grapples-with-stricter-guidelines-for-gifts.html?_r=0>.

18 Blake, *Cultural Heritage Law*, above n 8, 35.

3. Museums Codes of Ethics on the Returning Issue

In response to the increasing demands on foreign governments for the return of cultural items, both AAMD and MA addressed this issue in their updated codes of ethics for museums. First, museums are advised not to purchase or accept any item if it is suspected that the object may have been illegally removed in violation of that county of origin's laws or any international treaties, unless the museum is able to obtain permission from authorities in the state of origin.[19] By referring to the laws of states of origin, this requirement suggests that states of origin should be the ones to define when their cultural heritage has been illegally removed from their territories. Second, unlike the position adopted in the 2002 Universal Declaration, which is a way of refusing to engage in dialogue around the issue of repatriation, museums are now encouraged to deal sensitively and promptly with requests for return from states of origin.[20] Pursuant to the ICOM's code of ethics, museums should be prepared to "initiate dialogues for the return of cultural property to a country or people of origin".[21] Third, when a state of origin seeks the return of an object that can be proved to have been illegally exported or transferred, and shown to be part of that country's cultural or natural heritage, the museum should, if legally free to do so, take prompt and responsible steps to cooperate in its return.[22] As commented by Irini Stamatoudi, these provisions suggest that a return "may take place on a number of grounds expressly provided in the Code, without being limited only to situations of violations of national or international law".[23]

In discussing the proposed customary rule, these provisions provide for the return of cultural objects to their states of origin, and are in compliance with the principle of return embodied in the UNESCO and UNIDROIT Conventions. More importantly, they reflect the changing attitude regarding recovery claims, with museums less likely to avoid engaging in dialogue about the issue and more open to taking prompt and cooperative steps to resolve recovery claims.

4. Return Through Negotiation and Cooperation

As analysed above in Chapters 5 and 6, judicial cases show increasing recognition that cultural heritage wrongfully removed during both times of war and peace should be returned. In addition to the returns made through legal actions, there is a clear tendency for disputing parties to prefer more informal methods to resolve recovery disputes, without the need for litigation.[24]

19 Museums Assoication, 'Code of Ethics for Museums' <www.museumsassociation.org/download?id=1155827>.
20 Article 9.5 of MA's 2015 (Draft) Code of Ethics.
21 Article 6.2 of ICOM's 2006 Code of Ethics for Museums.
22 Article 6.3 of ICOM's 2006 Code of Ethics for Museums.
23 Stamatoudi, *Cultural Property Law and Restitution,* above n 15, 173.
24 For an overview of the variety of restitution solutions, see Cornu and Renold, *New Developments in Restitution,* above n 1, 18–22; James A.R. Nafziger and Robert Paterson,

The most welcomed approach is facilitating return through negotiation, accompanied with cultural cooperation measures.

In 2001, the Miho Museum, an antiquities museum near Kyoto, Japan, acknowledged for the first time that a rare Buddhist statue in its collection was stolen from Shandong Province, China, in 1994.[25] The museum said that the statue was bought from a London art dealer in 1995, but that it was not until four years later that scholars noticed the statue in the Miho catalogue and told the museum that it might have been stolen. The museum also stated that this stolen statue would be returned to the Chinese Government without payment. The return of a stolen Chinese statue by a Japanese museum is remarkable. Because Japan had not ratified international treaties that require countries to return stolen relics and the statue had not been reported stolen at the time of purchase, the Miho was under no legal obligation to give it back to China. However, Hiroo Inoue, the museum's director, explained that "the Miho Museum believes that art plays a significant role in creating greater tolerance and peace in the world". In response to this particular return, he elaborated that "in keeping with that philosophy, we have agreed to present the bodhisattva to the People's Republic of China in good faith".[26]

The return of this Chinese statue by the Miho Museum is a good illustration of how to resolve a recovery dispute peacefully and quickly through achieving mutual benefits for both sides. First, pursuant to the agreement signed with the Miho, China agreed to lend the statue to the Miho without charge until 2007, when an exhibition of Buddhist art and other works from Shandong was held at the museum to foster cultural collaboration between the two countries. In this regard, entering a bilateral agreement with requesting states can enrich holding museums' collections, as cooperation programmes usually contain art loan, information sharing, and collaboration in the areas of scholarship, conservation, and archaeological investigation. Second, the settlement releases museums from negative headlines, reputational damage, and impoverishment of their collections. For example, the agreement with the Miho Museum brought a conclusion to what was a major embarrassment for the Miho, which had prominently displayed the stolen statue in its catalogues and exhibits. As part of the agreement, the Chinese government stated publicly that it believed the Japanese museum had bought the statue in good faith on the open market and had not acted improperly. Third, for a requesting state

'Cultural Heritage Law' in James A.R. Nafziger and Robert Paterson (eds), *Handbook on the Law of Cultural Heritage and International Trade* (Edward Elgar Publishing, 2014) 1, 14–17; Sabrina Urbinati, 'Alternative Dispute Resolution Mechanisms in Cultural Property Related Disputes: UNESCO Mediation and Conciliation Procedures.' in Valentina Vadi and Hildegard Schneider (eds), *Art, Cultural Heritage and the Market* (Springer, 2014) 93, 113.

25 Calvin Sims, 'Japanese Agree A Stolen Statue Will Be Sent Back to China', *New York Times* April 18 2001 <www.nytimes.com/2001/04/18/arts/japanese-agree-a-stolen-statue-will-be-sent-back-to-china.html>.

26 Ibid.

of origin, settlements through cooperation and negotiation will avoid direct reliance on legal action. This is important because any legal action entails considerable economic and human expense, including the cost of litigation, investigating the circumstances of illegal removals, procuring evidence and witnesses, hiring attorneys, and learning the legal system of a foreign nation.

In practice, settlement through cooperation and negotiation has enabled not only China, but also other culturally rich states, in particular, Italy, Turkey, and Peru, to bring many wrongfully removed cultural objects home. What is noteworthy in these bilateral agreements is that the return of an item is more than a physical handover. Holding museums agreed to make restitution of objects of dubious provenance, but they did so in exchange for promises made by the foreign authorities entailing a commitment to the establishment of a continuing programme of cultural cooperation.[27] For example, in exchange for the return of all requested artefacts, Italy agreed to loan the Met a selection of archaeological objects or objects of equivalent beauty and artistic or historical significance, on a four-year rotating basis.[28] Furthermore, the Italy–Met agreement is a model of international collaboration because it establishes a 40-year long programme of cultural cooperation, including exchange of students and professors, and cooperation in the fields of restoration, research, and excavation.[29]

Although the return, embedded in cooperation and exchange in cultural heritage matters, may be only a token gesture in some cases, it is nevertheless an important approach to create incentives for both parties and to resolve recovery claims. The most obvious outcome is that an increasing number of wrongfully removed cultural heritage objects are returned home. As commented by Derek Fincham, "rather than simply encourage more prosecutions and a rigid law-and-order approach, perhaps a more productive short-term strategy would work in tandem with the law to encourage a collective shift in the behaviour of the dealer and collector community".[30] Cooperative approach has become a critical tool in negotiating mutually beneficial solutions out of court at a minimal cost and ensuring the proper allocation of cultural heritage objects on the basis of historic and cultural reasons, rather than the strict application of legal instruments. This approach may be alternatives that may overcome legal hurdles in resolving recovery disputes, create mutual benefits for the disputants, and enhance the preservation of cultural heritage. It should not be surprising that the UN General Assembly no longer demands outright

27 Cornu and Renold, *New Developments in Restitution,* above n 1, 12.

28 Article 4.1 of the Agreement between the Ministry for Cultural Heritage and Activities of the Italian Republic and the Metropolitan Museum of Art, New York, of February 21 2006 (Met–Italy Agreement).

29 Article 8.1 of the Met–Italy Agreement.

30 Derek Fincham, 'Social Norms and Illicit Cultural Heritage' in Francesco Francioni and James Gordley (eds), *Enforcing International Cultural Heritage Law* (Oxford University Press, 2013) 206, 209.

return in its resolution, but calls on states to negotiate mutual advantages besides the return of claimed objects taken during colonial occupation.[31]

However, it should be noted that this collaborative approach will encounter difficulties when cultural objects are possessed by an individual rather than a museum or research institute. For example, in a recent dispute over a Buddha statue, China claimed that the item was stolen from Fujian Province's Yangchun Village. The Buddha, which contains the remains of a mummified monk, was enshrined and worshipped by both Yangchun village and neighbouring Dongpu village for thousands of years, starting from the Song Dynasty (AD 960–1279). The Buddhist mummy is known as the statue of Zhanggong-zushi, which is the embodiment of God in the eyes of the locals. After the Buddha disappeared from its seat in 1995, it reappeared in public at an exhibition of "Mummies: Life beyond Death" by the Drents Museum in Hungary in 2015, and was later pulled out by its owner, Oscar Van Overeem, a Dutch private collector. Van Overeem purchased a Buddhist statue for US $20,500 in 1996 in Amsterdam from a collector who had acquired it in Hong Kong. Responding to pressure brought on by international attention, the Dutch collector first responded by agreeing to return the statue if it was proven to have belonged to a Buddhist community that still exists. However, although the Cultural Relics Bureau in Fujian has provided photos and historical records suggesting the statue was actually stolen from Yangchun village, the owner later changed his mind and attached three conditions to his return of the statue.[32] First, Van Overeem demanded the statue be enshrined at a grand temple such as Nanputuo Temple in Xiamen rather than at the small village temple at Yangchun. As a response, Nanputuo Temple stated that, since coming into being, its worship goes mainly to the Bodhisattva Guanyin and it has never worshiped any Buddhist mummy. Thus, it had no intention to enshrine and worship Zhanggong-zushi now. Second, Van Overeem requested the Chinese Government to provide him assistance in some scientific research in stone inscriptions, which is completely irrelevant to the statue. The Chinese Government agreed to make some arrangements, premised on the condition that an actual return is made. Third, he insisted the statue be included with other items of Chinese cultural heritage for sale. In that case, if someone were to buy all of the items for China, no one could determine the price paid for the

31 James A.R. Nafziger, 'Cultural Heritage Law:The International Regime' in James A.R. Nafziger and Tullio Scovazzi (eds), *The Cultural Heritage of Mankind* (Martinus Nijhoff/Brill, 2008) 145, 173.

32 Chloe Lyme, 'Battle for the Buddha: Angry Chinese Villagers sue Dutch Art Collector Who 'Refuses to Return Stolen Statue' Containing Mummified Remains of Meditating Monk', *Dailymail* November 20 2015 <www.dailymail.co.uk/news/peoplesdaily/article-3327398/Angry-Chinese-villagers-sue-Dutch-art-collector-refuses-return-stolen-statue-containing-mummified-remains-meditating-monk.html>; 'Chinese Mummy Buddha: Dutch Collector's Conditions for Repatriation Raise Questioning over His Sincerity', *Xinhua Net* December 10 2015 <http://news.xinhuanet.com/english/2015-12/10/c_134901207.htm>.

statue. This condition was rejected by the Chinese Government. The SACH stated that the Government never authorised anyone to deal with the Dutch collector for purchasing cultural relics and would never accept mixing up the return of Zhanggong-zushi with unrelated matters. Following the collapse of diplomatic efforts and private negotiation, the Yangchun villagers brought the case to a Dutch court for the return of the statue before their case is time-barred by a statute of limitation. The Dutch court will hold a first hearing for the dispute in July 2017.[33]

The dispute concerning the Buddhist mummy clearly reflects the limited application of the cooperative approach. Although cooperation and negotiation has come to play an important role in settling disputes, a solution can only be achieved if parties to a cultural heritage dispute recognise that mutual interests and values cannot be protected except by collaborative approach. In the absence of significant incentives, current possessors may be reluctant to resort to cooperation and negotiation to achieve an amicable settlement concerning cultural heritage. They would rely on their rights under the general law of possession and ownership, and turn a deaf ear to emotionally driven claims.[34] When discussing the proposed customary rule, cooperation and negotiation nevertheless helps to return cultural heritage objects to their states of origin. However, more often than not, it should be admitted that requested parties agree to return and cooperate because of their own significant interests, and there is no indication that such a cooperative approach can be applied widely to promote a large-scale return of wrongfully removed heritage.

5. Gradual Shaming of Illegal and Immoral Acquisition

After leading US museums were found in a close relationship with tomb robbers in Italy and Greece in 2006, the public's view regarding the idea of the "universal museum", which has been used to reject claims for return, has significantly changed.[35] The scandal revealed that the museums, who presented their role as preserving cultural diversity and providing a sense of a shared human cultural heritage, should be held responsible for the damage and looting of heritage sites.[36] The reason for this is simple: as long as there is a market for illicitly removed heritage, there will be supply. Those who purchase or accept these pieces are actually contributing to the destruction of the world's cultural heritage. In this regard, the scandal evoked increasing intolerance of illicit trafficking of cultural objects and, more importantly, a

33 'Dutch Court to Hold First Hearing for Buddha Statue Dispute in July', *People.cn* February 3 2017 <http://en.people.cn/n3/2017/0203/c90000-9173553.html>. At the time of writing, the Dutch court has not decided on this case.

34 Chechi, *Wrongfully Removed Cultural Objects,* above n 2, 368.

35 Glaister, *Getty Museum Admits 350 More Treasures May Be Looted,* above n 4.

36 Fincham, *Social Norms and Illicit Cultural Heritage,* above n 30, 217.

gradual shaming of museums' immoral acquisition and acceptance of questionable cultural objects. This changing attitude is clearly reflected in the case of *Ka Nefer Nefer*.[37] On July 28 2014, the Eighth Circuit Court of Appeals denied the request of the US Government to take further legal action regarding the St Louis Art Museum's (SLAM's) ownership of the 3,200-year-old Egyptian funerary mask of Ka Nefer Nefer. Despite the victory in the lawsuit, the museum received bitter criticism from the public.

In 1998, SLAM purchased the mask from Phoenix Ancient Art, a New York international art dealer. Years after the purchase, the mask became the centrepiece of a bitter ownership dispute between the museum, which claimed clear title, and Egypt, which alleged that the mask was stolen and illegally removed from Egypt.[38] After initial negotiations between SLAM and Egyptian authorities failed, the US Government judicially intervened on Egypt's behalf. The US Government filed a motion based on the NAPA, arguing that the mask was stolen before it was brought into the country, thereby violating the Tariff Act of 1930. However, instead of complying with the government's request, SLAM sued the US Government to assert its ownership. SLAM maintained that they purchased the mask in good faith[39] and that the statute of limitations had expired.[40] In April 2012, the US District Court dismissed the US Government's forfeiture complaint for failing to prove how the mask was stolen and smuggled, or how it was brought into the US contrary to law. Afterwards, the US Government filed a motion for the court to reconsider the dismissal of the case. However, in June 2014, the Court of Appeals affirmed the District Court's procedural ruling on the basis that the US Government's amended complaint was not submitted on time, nor did it show that the mask was ever stolen.

Although SLAM won the case, its continuing possession of the Egyptian mask received bitter criticism from the public. There are also multiple ongoing questions regarding this case. First, despite denying the government's forfeiture motion, the court did not question the authenticity of the Egyptian records that show the mask was excavated in 1952 and maintained in Egypt

37 *US v Mask of Ka-Nefer-Nefer*, No. 12–2578 (8th Cir June 12 2014), aff'ig 11-CV-504-HEA (ED Mo March 31 2012).

38 Malcolm Gay, 'For the St. Louis Art Museum, a Legal Victory Raises Ethical Questions', *Atlantic* May 30 2012 <www.theatlantic.com/national/archive/2012/05/for-the-st-louis-art-museum-a-legal-victory-raises-ethical-questions/257839/>.

39 SLAM maintains that they conducted due diligence and purchased the mask from reputable sources. Furthermore, SLAM claims that prior to the purchase, they inquired about its provenance with the Art Loss Register, the International Foundation for Art Research, INTERPOL, and consulted with the then director Mohammed Saleh, of the Cairo Museum. All of these institutions confirmed that this piece was licit and there were no reports of the mask missing at the time of the proposed purchase.

40 SLAM claimed that the US government received notice of the importation in 2005 but only filed the forfeiture complaint in 2011. Due to the fact that the statute of limitations in the US is five years, and more than this has passed, SLAM believes that they have rightful ownership of the mask.

as late as 1966, which conflicts with the museum's long-held claim suggesting that the mask was in Europe by 1952.[41] In other words, even though the museum claimed that it made the purchase with due diligence, it still accepted objects with dubious provenance. Second, there is a tendency for museums to hand over disputed objects when there are reasonable doubts indicating an object was stolen or illegally exported. However, SLAM went on the attack, filing its own pre-emptive lawsuit that claimed the statute of limitations had expired. "This is very unusual," Patty Gerstenblith commented on the museum's response to the forfeiture claim. "This is the first time I have seen a public institution like a museum deciding to expend its funds to pro-actively sue the government."[42] Especially when settlements through negotiation and cooperation have been recognised as a preferable solution to resolve recovery claims. "That is a shame", remarked Malcolm Gay, "To persevere in this litigious and outmoded view of antiquities collecting throws SLAM out of step with its fellow institutions, many of which have negotiated beneficial settlements for similar claims." Last, while American museums are largely self-regulated, many subscribe to the stricter guidelines adopted in 2008 by the AAMD governing the acquisition of archaeological material and SLAM is a member of the American Association of Museums. In this situation, the updated acquisition guidelines clearly direct members not to accept or purchase any art object when its provenance is incomplete or uncertain".[43] After the *Ka Nefer Nefer* case, Judge Diana Murphy agreed with the ruling in dismissing the government's forfeiture, but showed some sympathy with the other side:

> I concur in the court's opinion but write separately to express my concern about what the record in this case reveals about the illicit trade in antiquities . . . The substantive issues underlying this litigation are of great significance, and not only to museums which responsibly seek to build their collections. The theft of cultural patrimony and its trade on the black market for stolen antiquities present concerns of international import. These issues affect governments and the international art and antiquities markets, as well as those who seek to safeguard global cultural heritage.[44]

Although the gradual shaming of museums' immoral possession imposes no legal obligation for current possessors to relinquish wrongfully removed heritage in their collections, it nevertheless reflects the idea that the moral

41 Gay, *A Legal Victory Raises Ethical Questions,* above n 38.
42 Ibid.
43 Ibid.
44 Judith H. Dobrzynski, 'Maybe The Ka-Nefer-Nefer Dispute Isn't Over', *Blouin Artinfo* June 26 2014 <http://blogs.artinfo.com/realcleararts/2014/06/26/maybe-the-ka-nefer-nefer-dispute-isnt-over/>;
Center for Art Law, 'Case Review: US v Mask of Ka-Nefer-Nefer (8th Cir)' <https://itsartlaw.com/tag/ka-nefer-nefer/>.

duty to return highly valuable or significant cultural heritage items is strongly gaining ground. Additionally, the change in the public's attitude can serve as the catalyst to shift the public's perception about the right place to present foreign cultural heritage, especially historically removed heritage. Previously, many world-leading museums claimed to be "universal museums" as a way to refuse recovery claims; however, because of the gradual shaming of museums' immoral or illegal possession, new thinking has emerged. While millions of people visit the Parthenon Marbles in the British Museum each year, people also start to question: Is it proper to remove it from its original cultural setting, especially after learning that their removal damaged one of mankind's crowning achievements? Is the British Museum the best context for the Parthenon Marbles? Would it not be preferable for a cultural object to be placed in its original context? When the only difference between London and Athens having the Parthenon sculptures is emotion, should the sculpture not be returned to the side with the stronger emotional connection?[45]

6. Increasing Number of Objects Being Returned

In the last few decades, demands for the return of cultural heritage have increased, and there is greater recognition of the interest states of origin have in their wrongfully removed heritage. Many recovery claims for cultural objects that were largely unsuccessful in the late 20th century have now been negotiated and settled. These settlements are significant in discussing the proposed customary rule, as they constitute the acknowledgment that wrongfully removed cultural heritage should be returned to states of origin.

6.1. Reversing the Positions: Return of Khmer Statues From the US

In the 1970s, Cambodia went through a period of major political conflict and civil war. During this time of unrest, countless artefacts and statues were plundered from the country's historic sites and sold to museums and private collections in the West. The Cambodian Government has adopted different approaches to facilitate the return of artefacts, ranging from negotiating with the current possessors and offering to buy back certain items to asking for the US Government's involvement to apply civil forfeiture. These solutions have helped to bring a number of cultural heritage items back to Cambodia.

Among the cases, it is worth noting the return of the seven Khmer statues from the US, which came from the same Khmer temple, Prasat Chen, a site pillaged during the upheaval of Cambodia's civil war. "The dam has broken", said an expert on Khmer sculpture that helped Cambodia recover the statues. "One

45 Thomas Fitschen, 'The Resolution on the Return and Restitution of Cultural Property to the Countries of Origin Adopted by the General Assembly on December 13, 2001' (2002) 11(2) *International Journal of Cultural Property* 337, 358.

assumes they were looted at the same moment, then widely distributed."[46] The Met started the trend by voluntarily returning two of the statues in 2013. However, it should be noted that there has been a shift in the way the Met treats questionable antiquities. Previously, when Turkey claimed for the return of the Lydian Hoard collection from the Met in 1980s, the museum strongly fought repatriation through the courts. But this time, they voluntarily returned the two stolen statues to Cambodia without waiting for a lawsuit or court order. After evidence suggested they were illicitly taken, the Denver Art Museum, the Cleveland Museum of Art, and the Norton Simon Museum were all cooperative in returning the Khmer statues in their collections.

The remaining two statues were auctioned, one by Sotheby's and the other by Christie's. It is worth noting the changing reactions from these two auction houses in dealing with recovery claims. In March 2011, when Sotheby's first offered the Khmer statue at auction in New York, Cambodian officials claimed that it was illegally removed from the site Koh Ker during the 1970s and should be returned.[47] While the statue was removed from sale as a result of Cambodia's request for its restitution, Sotheby's neither consented to its return nor agreed to sell it to a private collector willing to donate it to Cambodia. Instead, it awaited a court decision on the matter of ownership. It was not until April 2012 that the US Government filed a forfeiture action against Sotheby's on the ground that the statue was illegally imported into the US. In December 2013, Sotheby's voluntarily decided to return the statue to Cambodia, after a lengthy court battle that ended in a settlement. Comparatively, in a recent auction case concerning another Cambodian sandstone figure, the response from Christie's was prompt, and more importantly, Christie's voluntarily paid to return the statue to its homeland. This case is remarkable because the returned object had already been sold at an auction in 2009, but after reviewing the sale and determining that the statue was stolen, Christie's contacted the buyer and bought it back. "Questions of repatriation are complex", said by Martin Wilson, chairman of Christie's Cultural Property Committee and General Counsel. "Christie's believes it can play a useful role in appropriate circumstances in helping to facilitate the resolution of certain cultural property issues between source countries and collectors where we actively engage with all affected parties to find fair solutions."[48] In particular,

46 Tom Mashberg and Ralph Blumenthal, 'Christie's to Return Cambodian Statue', *New York Times* May 6 2014 <www.nytimes.com/2014/05/07/arts/design/christies-to-return-cambodian-statue.html>; Art-Law Centre, University of Geneva, 'Khmer Statue—Cambodia and Sotheby's and the United States' <https://plone.unige.ch/art-adr/cases-affaires/khmer-statue-2013-cambodia-and-sotheby2019s-and-the-united-states>.

47 'Blood Antiquities: After Lengthy Fight, Sotheby's Agrees to Return Looted Khmer Statue', *Chasing Aphrodite* December 16 2013 <http://chasingaphrodite.com/2013/12/16/blood-antiquities-after-lengthy-fight-sothebys-agrees-to-return-looted-khmer-statue/>.

48 'Christie's Celebrates Return of 10th Century Statues to Cambodia at Official Ceremony in Phnom Penh' <www.christies.com/about-us/press-archive/details/?pressreleaseid=7298>.

Christie's recognised the meaning and value cultural heritage has for states of origin, stating in its press release: "as we can all see, this is a beautiful work of art. But beyond its artistic value there is also something just as important. It has a story to tell. It is the story of an amazing culture and the history of its people over many centuries."[49]

The return of the Khmer statues reflects an important shift in public attitude from museums and auction houses, not just in the US, but also worldwide. Instead of avoiding dialogue about the return of cultural heritage, museums and auction houses are now more alert to probing the provenance of cultural objects in their collections and inclined to resolve disputes through an amicable settlement. Museums have begun to carry out their own investigations into items with cloudy provenance. For example, after the New York art dealer Subhash Kapoor was arrested in 2011 for ordering the theft of 28 artefacts from two Indian temples, the National Gallery of Australia, which bought the Dancing Shiva statue from Kapoor for AUD 5.6 million in 2008, contacted the Indian Government to discuss the return of the statue.[50] In 2014, the Gallery relinquished the work, and the Australian Prime Minister returned it to India. The National Gallery of Australia stated in its press release that it "is continuing its cooperation with the department to fulfil Australia's international commitments and has voluntarily removed the statue from display".[51]

However, requested parties also agree to return items for selfish reasons, such as avoiding the impoverishment of their collections or reputational harm. Tess Davis, a heritage law expert who focuses on the illicit antiquities trade in South-East Asia commented: "I do believe that some—most, I hope—museums have changed because it's the right thing to do. But even the less moral institutions must realize that dealing with looted art—and especially war booty—is bad for business."[52] More than that, returning institutions agree to cooperate because they likely have already been advised by their lawyers of the slim chance of winning the case through litigation. In the US, available judicial practice has proved to be generally conducive to returning illegally removed cultural objects to states of origin and the courts are generally willing to condemn reckless professionals or art dealers. Hence, it is not finically worthwhile to fight the request in the courts. The same reason applies to the return of the Dancing Shiva statue. In reality, the National Gallery of Australia had very little option. The request stated that the statue was exported

49 Ibid.

50 Art Law Center, University of Geneva, 'Dancing Shiva Statue—India and National Gallery of Australia' <https://plone.unige.ch/art-adr/cases-affaires/dancing-shiva-statue-2013-india-and-national-gallery-of-australia>.

51 Australian Attorney-General's Department 'Request for Return of the Shiva Nataraja Idol' <https://nga.gov.au/COLLECTIONS/Asia/GALLERY.cfm?DISPLAYGAL=ASIAPROV_kapoor>.

52 Abby Seiff, 'How Countries Are Successfully Using the Law to Get Looted Cultural Treasures Back', *Art Journal* July 1 2014 <www.abajournal.com/magazine/article/how_countries_are_successfully_using_the_law_to_get_looted_cultural_treasur>.

from India in contravention of cultural heritage laws, namely India's Antiquity and Art Treasures Act 1972. According to Australia's Protection of Moveable Cultural Act of 1986, the act implementing the UNSECO Convention, Australia does not require a bilateral agreement with other signatories of the UNESCO Convention to return any illegally removed cultural heritage. Put simply, any object that was illegally exported from another UNESCO state and brought to Australia will be returned to that state. It is possible that without the evolving cultural heritage law as backup, voluntary returns and dispute avoidance settlements would not be successful in facilitating the return of illegally removed heritage to the states of origin.

6.2. *Return of the Machu Picchu Collection from Yale University*[53]

Between 1912 and 1916, Hiram Bingham, a history professor at Yale University, shipped to the US several artefacts that had been excavated at the Machu Picchu site. Peru sought the return of the artefacts exported by Bingham from the very beginning and formally requested the return in 1918 and 1920. In 2001, negotiations between Peru and Yale University resumed. While the National Geographic Society was in favour of returning the collection, Yale refused, saying it had fully complied with Peruvian legislation. During the period of 2003 to 2007, Peru reinforced its efforts to negotiate. While the two parties reached an agreement, it was not finalised. Following the failure of the 2007 agreement, Peru formally withdrew from negotiations and, in December 2008, Peru filed suit in the US against Yale University for the return of the collection, arguing that Yale violated Peruvian law by exporting the artefacts without the special permission of the Peruvian government, and by refusing to return them. However, in late 2010, Peru dropped the lawsuit and returned to the negotiating table, which was mostly due to the intervention of Christopher Dodd, a member of the Senate Foreign Relations Committee and chairman of its subcommittee on Latin America. His intervention led to the conclusion of the Memorandum of Understanding of 23 November 2010, in which Yale agreed to return the Machu Picchu collection to Peru, reversing a position that it held for nearly a century. Yale also recognised in the agreement that "the unique importance that Machu Picchu has come to play in the identity of the modern Peruvian nation".[54] After the return, Yale University

53 Randy Kennedy, 'Yale Officials Agree to Return Peruvian Artifacts', *New York Times* September 17 2009 <www.nytimes.com/2007/09/17/arts/design/17peru.html?_r=0>; Kianti Roman, 'Peru-Yale Center for the Study of Machu Picchu and Inca Culture opens', *Yale News* Octover 6 2011 <http://news.yale.edu/2011/10/06/peru-yale-center-study-machu-picchu-and-inca-culture-opens>; Art Law Center, University of Geneva, 'Machu Picchu Collection—Peru and Yale University' <https://plone.unige.ch/art-adr/cases-affaires/machu-picchu-collection-2013-peru-and-yale-university>.

54 'Statement from Yale University Regarding Machu Picchu Archaeological Materials', *Yale News* November 21 2011 <http://news.yale.edu/2010/11/21/statement-yale-university-regarding-machu-picchu-archaeological-materials>.

and the Universidad Nacional de San Antonio Abad del Cusco (UNSAAC) established the UNSAAC–Yale University International Centre for the Study of Machu Picchu and Inca Culture.

The controversy over the Machu Picchu collection is something of a test case, as it reflects the difficulty in recovering historically removed heritage, but provides a solution to resolve such disputes. From a strictly legal point of view, Yale was under no legal obligation to return the disputed artefacts. At the time of the Bingham expeditions, although the Peruvian law, namely the Civil Code of 1852 and the Supreme Decree of 27 April 1893, did vest ownership of any artefacts unearthed from Peruvian soil to the state,[55] the relevant statutes of limitation had elapsed. Despite the lack of legal obligations, the idea that there is a moral duty to return the Machu Picchu collection is strongly gaining ground. It is worth considering that Bingham and the National Geographic Society of the US did not support Yale University's approach, as they had affirmed that the contested objects belonged to Peru.[56] "Machu Picchu has tremendous symbolic value to Peru", said Johan Reinhard, an Inca specialist who is explorer in residence at the National Geographic Society. "By refusing to acknowledge Peruvian ownership, it may be losing the cultural battle."[57] Crucially, Senator Christopher Dodd said in a statement: "These artefacts do not belong to any government, to any institution or to any university—they belong to the people of Peru. I plan to work with both parties to resolve this dispute quickly, amicably, and return the artefacts to their rightful owners."[58] Thus, the strong ethical and moral considerations played a role in compelling Yale University to return Peru's cultural heritage. In discussing the proposed customary rule, the return of historically removed cultural heritage calls for the implementation of ethical and historical considerations into the legal regime of return. In many cases, claims for the return of wrongfully removed heritage objects are repeatedly based on the fact that the cultural rights of the claiming party have largely been ignored in the past. Thus, return is not merely a physical handover, but includes ethical, cultural, and historical considerations in an attempt to remedy past injustice and to recognise the special connection between states of origin and their cultural heritage.[59] This acknowledgment is an essential element in facilitating the return of historically removed heritage and creating the proposed customary rule.[60]

55 Article 522 of the Civil Code provided that all treasures and other buried objects that are found on vacant or public property belong to the finder. Article 1 of the Supreme Decree of 1893 prevented the mutilation, excavation and removal of artefacts from Peruvian sites.
56 Rosemary Listing, 'The Treasure Quest: Peru, Machu Picchu and the Yale Peruvian Expedition of 1911–1916 (Rosemary Listing)' (2011) 16(1) *Art Antiquity and Law* 67, 70.
57 Hugh Eakin, 'Inca Show Pits Yale Against Peru', *New York Times* February 1 2006 <www.nytimes.com/2006/02/01/arts/design/01mach.html>.
58 *Machu Picchu Collection,*above n 53.
59 Peters, *Remedying Historical Injustice,* above n 3, 155–156.
60 James D. Nason, 'Beyond Repatriation: Cultural Policy and Practice for the Twenty-First Century' in Professor Bruce Ziff (ed), *Borrowed Power: Essays on Cultural Appropriation* (Rutgers University Press, 1997) 290, 293.

Apart from the ethical and moral recognition, it should also be noted that the important reason for Peru to resolve the case is the mutual benefits from the cooperative partnership with Peru. In effect, the creation of the UNSAAC–Yale University International Centre is an ideal compromise for both parties. Instead of simply returning the questionable objects, Yale and Peru entered into a cooperative partnership to study and protect Peruvian cultural heritage. In this case, it can be argued that settlement concerning historically removed cultural heritage is not merely an outright return, but is always accompanied with cultural cooperation that generates mutual benefits for both parties. This requires different interests to be reconciled to reach a solution and it needs to be managed in a proper manner as reconciliation cannot be one-sided.

7. Conclusion

Although the practice of individuals, private museums and auction houses does not constitute state behaviour and cannot therefore create customary international law, they are important in reflecting the public attitudes and ethical considerations, and thus signalling the future development of the law. As analysed above, there is a clear tendency that states of origin's interests in their wrongfully removed heritage have been increasingly recognised and protected. Museums are called on not only to adopt stricter policies at acquisition and acceptance, but also to take prompt and responsible steps to deal with recovery claims. Additionally, recent cases have shown ethical and historical considerations have been taken into account rather than the mere application of legal instruments. Thus, while many recovery claims for cultural objects were largely unsuccessful in the late 20th century, they have now been successfully negotiated and settled. The gradual shaming of the continuing possession of wrongfully removed heritage further provides an opportunity for the recovery claims to be reconsidered. All these changes pave the way for the return of wrongfully removed cultural heritage and constitute the acknowledgment that wrongfully removed cultural heritage should be returned to their states of origin. They are important in developing the proposed customary rule.

The available practice reflects that the recognition of states of origin's connection with their heritage may play a role in facilitating outcomes that are more appropriate to states of origin' interests. However, it should be admitted that requested parties agreed to return wrongfully removed cultural heritage due to various reasons, for example, the willingness of courts to favour recovery claims and condemn reckless professionals, the developments in both international and national laws applicable to cultural heritage, the availability of a database of wrongfully removed cultural objects, and, particularly, the significant mutual benefits for the disputants. Although there is a supportive environment for states of origin to negotiate for their wrongfully removed heritage, current possessors often rely on their legal rights to ignore those recovery claims. All these brings uncertainty about whether the proposed customary rule can continue to develop, and eventually be recognised as a new customary rule.

Bibliography

'Blood Antiquities: After Lengthy Fight, Sotheby's Agrees to Return Looted Khmer Statue', *Chasing Aphrodite*, December 16 2013 <http://chasingaphrodite.com/2013/12/16/blood-antiquities-after-lengthy-fight-sothebys-agrees-to-return-looted-khmer-statue/>

'British Museum Policy on Acquisitions' (2007) <www.britishmuseum.org/pdf/Acquisitions.pdf>

'Case Review: US v Mask of Ka-Nefer-Nefer (8th Cir.)', Center for Art Law <https://itsartlaw.com/tag/ka-nefer-nefer/>

'Chinese Mummy Buddha: Dutch Collector's Conditions for Repatriation Raise Questioning over His Sincerity', *Xinhua Net* December 10 2015 <http://news.xinhuanet.com/english/2015-12/10/c_134901207.htm>

'Christie's Celebrates Return of 10th Century Statues to Cambodia at Official Ceremony in Phnom Penh' <www.christies.com/about-us/press-archive/details/?pressreleaseid=7298>

'Code of Ethics for Museums', Museums Association <www.museumsassociation.org/download?id=1155827>

'Dancing Shiva Statue—India and National Gallery of Australia', Art Law Center, University of Geneva <https://plone.unige.ch/art-adr/cases-affaires/dancing-shiva-statue-2013-india-and-national-gallery-of-australia>

'Dutch Court to Hold First Hearing for Buddha Statue Dispute in July', *People.cn* February 3 2017 <http://en.people.cn/n3/2017/0203/c90000-9173553.html>

'Introduction to the Revisions to the 2008 Guidelines on the Acquisition of Archaeological Material and Ancient Art' <https://aamd.org/sites/default/files/document/AAMD%20Guidelines%202013.pdf>

'Khmer Statue—Cambodia and Sotheby's and the United States', Art-Law Centre, University of Geneva <https://plone.unige.ch/art-adr/cases-affaires/khmer-statue-2013-cambodia-and-sotheby2019s-and-the-united-states>

'Machu Picchu Collection—Peru and Yale University', Art Law Center, University of Geneva <https://plone.unige.ch/art-adr/cases-affaires/machu-picchu-collection-2013-peru-and-yale-university>

'Memorandum Submitted by the Museums Association', UK Government <www.publications.parliament.uk/pa/cm199900/cmselect/cmcumeds/371/0032305.htm>

'Request for Return of the Shiva Nataraja Idol', Australian Attorney-General's Department March 26 2014 <https://nga.gov.au/COLLECTIONS/Asia/GALLERY.cfm?DISPLAYGAL=ASIAPROV_kapoor>

'Statement from Yale University Regarding Machu Picchu Archaeological Materials', *Yale News* November 21 2011 <http://news.yale.edu/2010/11/21/statement-yale-university-regarding-machu-picchu-archaeological-materials>

Amineddoleh, Leila, 'The Role of Museums in Sustaining the Illicit Trade in Culutral Property' 25 *Cardozo Arts & Entertainment Law Journal* 837

Blake, Janet, *International Cultural Heritage Law* (Oxford University Press, 2015)

Blumenthal, Ralph and Tom Mashberg, 'The Curse of the Outcast Artifact', *The New York Times* July 12 2012 <www.nytimes.com/2012/07/15/arts/design/antiquity-market-grapples-with-stricter-guidelines-for-gifts.html?_r=0>

Brodie, Neil, 'An Archaeologist's View of the Trade in Unprovenanced Antiquities' in Barbara T. Hoffman (ed), *Art and Cultural Heritage: Law, Policy and Practice* (Cambridge University Press, 2009) 52

Brodie, Neil et al, *Trade in Illicit Antiquities: The Destruction of the World's Archaeological Heritage* (McDonald Institute for Archaeological Research, 2001)

Brodie, Neil and Colin Renfrew, 'Looting and the World's Archaeological Heritage: The Inadequate Response' (2005) 34 *Annual Review of Anthropology* 343

Chechi, Alessandro, 'Multi-Level Cooperation to Safeguard the Human Dimension of Cultural Heritage and to Secure the Return of Wrongfully Removed Cultural Objects' in Silvia Borelli and Federico Lenzerini (eds), *Cultural Heritage, Cultural Rights, Cultural Diversity* (Martinus Nijhoff Publishers, 2012) 347

Cornu, Marie and Marc-André Renold, 'New Developments in the Restitution of Cultural Property: Alternative Means of Dispute Resolution' (2010) 17(1) *International Journal of Cultural Property* 1

Dobrzynski, Judith H., 'Maybe The Ka-Nefer-Nefer Dispute Isn't Over', *Blouin Artinfo* June 26 2014 <http://blogs.artinfo.com/realcleararts/2014/06/26/maybe-the-ka-nefer-nefer-dispute-isnt-over/>

Eakin, Hugh, 'Inca Show Pits Yale Against Peru', *New York Times* February 1 2006 <www.nytimes.com/2006/02/01/arts/design/01mach.html>

Fincham, Derek, 'Social Norms and Illicit Cultural Heritage' in Francesco Francioni and James Gordley (eds), *Enforcing International Cultural Heritage Law* (Oxford University Press, 2013) 206

Fiorentini, Francesca, 'A Legal Pluralist Approach to International Trade in Cultural Objects' in James A.R. Nafziger and Robert Paterson (eds), *Handbook on the Law of Cultural Heritage and International Trade* (Edward Elgar Publishing, 2014) 589

Fitschen, Thomas, 'The Resolution on the Return and Restitution of Cultural Property to the Countries of Origin Adopted by the General Assembly on December 13, 2001' (2002) 11(2) *International Journal of Cultural Property* 337

Frigo, Manlio, 'Ethical Rules and Codes of Honor Related to Museum Activities: A Complementary Support to the Private International Law Approach Concerning the Circulation of Cultural Property' (2009) 16(1) *International Journal of Cultural Property* 49

Gay, Malcolm, 'For the St. Louis Art Museum, a Legal Victory Raises Ethical Questions', *Atlantic* May 30 2012 <www.theatlantic.com/national/archive/2012/05/for-the-st-louis-art-museum-a-legal-victory-raises-ethical-questions/257839/>

Gerstenblith, Patty, 'The Meaning of 1970 for the Acquisition of Archaeological Objects' (2013) 38(4) *Journal of Field Archaeology* 364

Glaister, Dan, 'Getty Museum Admits 350 More Treasures May Be Looted', *Guardian* June 19 2006 <www.theguardian.com/world/2006/jun/19/arts.usa>

Kennedy, Randy, 'Yale Officials Agree to Return Peruvian Artifacts', *New York Times* September 17 2009 <www.nytimes.com/2007/09/17/arts/design/17peru.html?_r=0>

Listing, Rosemary, 'The Treasure Quest: Peru, Machu Picchu and the Yale Peruvian Expedition of 1911–1916 (Rosemary Listing)' (2011) 16(1) *Art Antiquity and Law* 67

Lyme, Chloe, 'Battle for the Buddha: Angry Chinese Villagers sue Dutch Art Collector Who 'Refuses to Return Stolen Statue' Containing Mummified Remains of Meditating Monk', *Daily Mail* November 20 2015 <www.dailymail.co.uk/

news/peoplesdaily/article-3327398/Angry-Chinese-villagers-sue-Dutch-art-collector-refuses-return-stolen-statue-containing-mummified-remains-meditating-monk.html>

Mashberg, Tom and Ralph Blumenthal, 'Christie's to Return Cambodian Statue', *New York Times* May 6 2014 <www.nytimes.com/2014/05/07/arts/design/christies-to-return-cambodian-statue.html>

Moustaira, Elina, *Art Collections, Private and Public: A Comparative Legal Study* (Springer, 2015)

Nafziger, James A.R., 'Cultural Heritage Law: The International Regime' in James A.R. Nafziger and Tullio Scovazzi (eds), *The Cultural Heritage of Mankind* (Martinus Nijhoff/Brill, 2008) 145

Nafziger, James A.R. and Robert Paterson, 'Cultural Heritage Law' in James A.R. Nafziger and Robert Paterson (eds), *Handbook on the Law of Cultural Heritage and International Trade* (Edward Elgar Publishing, 2014) 1

Nason, James D., 'Beyond Repatriation: Cultural Policy and Practice for the Twenty-First Century' in Professor Bruce Ziff (ed), *Borrowed Power: Essays on Cultural Appropriation* (Rutgers University Press, 1997) 290

Peters, Robert, 'Remedying Historical Injustice: Ethical and Historical Considerations in Returning Cultural Materials' in Silvia Borelli and Federico Lenzerini (eds), *Cultural Heritage, Cultural Rights, Cultural Diversity* (Martinus Nijhoff Publishers, 2012) 141

Prott, Lyndel, *Witnesses to History: A Compendium of Documents and Writings on the Return of Cultural Objects* (United Nations Educational, Scientific and Cultural Organization, 2009)

Roman, Kianti, 'Peru–Yale Center for the Study of Machu Picchu and Inca Culture opens', *Yale News* October 6 2011 <http://news.yale.edu/2011/10/06/peru-yale-center-study-machu-picchu-and-inca-culture-opens>

Schechter, Rhonda, 'Preventing Pillage and Promoting Politics: The Dual Goals of the 2009 US-China Bilateral Agreement to Restrict Imports of Chinese Cultural Property' (2009) 4 *Art Antiquity and Law* 317

Seiff, Abby, 'How Countries Are Successfully Using the Law to Get Looted Cultural Treasures Back', *Art Journal* July 1 2014 <www.abajournal.com/magazine/article/how_countries_are_successfully_using_the_law_to_get_looted_cultural_treasur>

Sims, Calvin, 'Japanese Agree A Stolen Statue Will Be Sent Back to China', *New York Times* April 18 2001 <www.nytimes.com/2001/04/18/arts/japanese-agree-a-stolen-statue-will-be-sent-back-to-china.html>

Stamatoudi, Irini A., *Cultural Property Law and Restitution: A Commentary to International Conventions and European Union law* (Edward Elgar Publishing, 2011)

Urbinati, Sabrina, 'Alternative Dispute Resolution Mechanisms in Cultural Property Related Disputes: UNESCO Mediation and Conciliation Procedures.' in Valentina Vadi and Hildegard Schneider (eds), *Art, Cultural Heritage and the Market* (Springer, 2014) 93

8 Return of Historically Removed Heritage

1. Introduction

Over the past two decades, many states of origin have begun to feel stronger and stronger about claims for their historically removed heritage. However, in the recovery of such heritage, legal claims are often complicated or simply impossible, for a number of reasons. As removals often occurred a long time prior, many claims are time barred, additionally many records and other evidence may have disappeared, international conventions are not retroactive and, most importantly, there is no law regulating the removal as being illegal. Despite these legal hurdles, there are indications that the time is coming where the future of historically removed cultural heritage is seriously considered.[1] Although many former colonisers and their heritage institutions are reluctant to investigate the past and largely stick to the existing global distribution of material cultural heritage of former colonies, new thinking has emerged and there are exceptions. Many claims for cultural objects that were unsuccessful in the late 20th century have now been successfully negotiated and settled.

This conclusion contains two parts. First is an examination of three return cases of historically removed heritage, which show that a dialogue about the future of historically removed objects is complicated and will not be a quick-fix. Second is a conclusion on the various rules, focussing on the idea that the states of origins' interests in their wrongfully removed heritage are being increasingly recognised. These rules can be drawn from the evolving law and return cases under three different categories: the return of looted heritage during wartime, the return of stolen and illegally exported heritage during peacetime, and the return of historically removed heritage. They all reflect a clear tendency that the states of origins' interests in their wrongfully removed heritage are being recognised more and more, which is significant in creating the proposed customary rule.

1 Jos van Beurden, 'How to Break the Deadlock in the Debate About Colonial Acquisitions?' in Valentina Vadi and Hildegard Schneider (eds), *Art, Cultural Heritage and the Market: Ethical and Legal Issues* (Springer, 2014) 165, 179.

2. Increasing Number of Objects, Taken in Early Times, Being Returned

In the late 1960s and 1970s, newly independent countries were anxious to recover their cultural heritage, as many were stored in the museums of former colonising states. In opposition to the claims raised by source and post-colonial countries, the directors of the main museums in Europe put forward the idea of the universal museum, arguing that claims for restitution were not justified unless the objects in question were removed as a result of a breach of law. However, this picture has changed, as the future of such heritage is seriously considered and an increasing number of objects taken in early times are being returned. The following section examines three cases of the return of historically removed heritage: the Shared Heritage Project between the Netherlands and Indonesia, the return of Hittite Sphinx from Germany to Turkey, and the return of Uigwe collection from France and Japan to South Korea.

2.1. Shared Heritage Project Between the Netherlands and Indonesia

At the time of decolonisation, the Netherlands and Indonesia had already begun the process of settling the problems arising from the long history of the Dutch presence in East Indies. However, the negotiations proceeded very slowly. In 1978, the Netherlands handed over some colonial art treasures of cultural and historical significance to Indonesia; however, an earlier request from Indonesia involved a list of 10,000 objects that it wished to have returned.[2] It was not until the end of the 20th century, that an important movement towards the settlement of cultural disputes occurred within a series of shared heritage initiatives and cultural cooperation.[3]

In 2000, Indonesia asked the Netherlands to exhibit collections that came from the former colonies of the East Indies on the grounds that "the Indonesian people had been unable to see parts of their cultural heritage stored in a foreign country".[4] This claim served as the first step towards a new round of difficult negotiations regarding the return of cultural heritage. In response, the National Museum of Ethnology in Leiden and the National Museum of Indonesia in Jakarta launched a joint project, the "Shared Cultural Heritage" in order to solve the issues related to the claims for the cultural heritage taken

2 Ibid, 167.

3 Andrzej Jakubowski, *State Succession in Cultural Property* (Oxford University Press, 2015), 300–302.

4 Cynthia Scott, 'Sharing the Divisions of the Colonial Past: An Assessment of the Netherlands—Indonesia Shared Cultural Heritage Project, 2003–2006' (2014) 20(2) *International Journal of Heritage Studies* 181, 183.

during colonisation. The joint project involves a wide range of cooperation, for example, the conservation of artefacts, and the study of the history of the collections preserved in both museums. As a result of the initiatives included in the framework of the Shared Cultural Heritage, a number of research projects were undertaken to exhibit newly reunified collections in both countries. For example, two large joint exhibitions of Indonesian artefacts took place at the National Museum in Jakarta (August 15–November 13 2005) and in the New Church in Amsterdam (December 15 2005–April 17 2006). Due to the Shared Cultural Heritage, the most significant pieces from both institutions were exhibited together to the Dutch and Indonesian public.

With regards to the proposed customary rule, the fundamental idea underpinned by the Shared Heritage Project is acknowledging the material objects as the heritage of both countries.[5] This cooperation allows parties to avoid the question as to "who owns the heritage", but focus more on the cultural exchange and cooperation that would allow a wider public to access their history and culture. It should be noted that the Netherlands–Indonesia approach cannot replace the rights of states of origin to claim permanent enjoyment and access to their historically removed heritage. But such an approach helps to constitute the acknowledgement that states of origin's interests in their wrongfully removed heritage should be respected.

2.2. Return of Hittite Sphinx from Germany to Turkey

In 2011, Germany eventually agreed to return a 3,500-year-old statue of Hittite sphinx to the Turkish Government, ending a war of words between Berlin and Ankara. The sphinx was brought to Berlin along with a second sphinx, which was later returned to Turkey, as an incomplete fragment between 1915 and 1917. It was restored in Berlin and then incorporated in the collection of the Pergamon Museum and included in its inventory between 1930 and 1934. Turkey has long demanded the second sphinx. In 1986, the Turkish Government sought the return of the statute by filing a request with the UNESCO Intergovernmental Committee for Promoting the Return of Cultural Property to its Countries of Origin or its Restitution in Case of Illicit Appropriation (ICPRCP), which offer a framework for bilateral negotiations between Germany and Turkey. According to the recommendation adopted in September 2010, the ICPRCP invited the parties "to hold comprehensive bilateral negotiations as soon as possible with a view to bringing this issue to a mutually acceptable solution".[6] In May 2011, the parties eventually

5 Jakubowski, *State Succession,* above n 3, 302.

6 Recommendation No. 2 of UNESCO, 'Intergovernmental Committee for Promoting the Return of Cultural Property to its Countries of Origin or its Restitution in Case of Illicit Appropriation, Sixteenth session' <http://unesdoc.unesco.org/images/0019/001925/192583e.pdf>.

reached a memorandum of understanding, according to which "the statue will be handed over to Turkey as a voluntary gesture of friendship".[7]

The return of sphinx statue clearly reflects the difficulty in recovery historically removed heritage and the limits of the existing framework for settlement. Although the origin of the statue was uncontested, one important reason for the case not being settled earlier is neither of the parties can prove its actual ownership. It was questionable whether the Sphinx was transferred to Germany only temporarily for restoration and research purposes, or whether it was part of a *partage* agreement that allowed Western museums and archaeologists to take a portion of objects found in the course of an excavation.[8] In other words, legal claims for Turkey are complicated or simply impossible.

As an alternative, the Turkish Government had sought the return by resorting to inter-governmental negotiation through the ICPRCP. The ICPRCP was created to assist UNESCO member states in dealing with cases that fall outside of the existing legal framework, including historical cases of cultural heritage being taken during remote colonial and imperial periods, and removals that occurred prior to the enforcement of the 1970 UNESCO Convention.[9] Since 1983, the ICPRCP has involved in several negotiations for the return to original states.[10] There is no denying that the efforts adopted by the UNESCO have played a significant role in bringing the issue of returns to the public's attention, engendering an atmosphere favourable to returns, encouraging states to address claims for return, and exerting influence on domestic policies and cultural heritage law. However, the scarce return reflects the fact that the authority of the ICPRCP or even UNESCO for adopting practical and implementable solutions in resolving the disputes surrounding historically removed cultural heritage is rather limited.[11] The ICPRCP has no jurisdictional power to rule in disputes between states. Rather, it may act in an advisory capacity only, thereby offering a framework for discussion and bilateral negotiations.[12] Thus, states are not compelled to bring a case before it or to abide by its recommendations on the return of a disputed cultural object.

7 Press and Information Office of the Federal Government, 'Turkey to Receive Hittite Sphinx' <www.bundesregierung.de/ContentArchiv/EN/Archiv17/_Anlagen/2011-05-13-pm-sphinx-translation.pdf?__blob=publicationFile&v=1>.

8 University of Geneva, 'Bogazköy Sphinx—Turkey and Germany' <https://plone.unige.ch/art-adr/cases-affaires/bogazkoy-sphinx-2013-turkey-and-germany>, 3.

9 Article 3(2) a state can bring a case before the ICPRCP only if bilateral negotiations with the state in which the requested object is located have failed or been suspended.

10 UNESCO, 'Recent Examples of Successful Operations of Cultural Property Restitutions in the World' <www.unesco.org/new/en/culture/themes/restitution-of-cultural-property/successful-restitutions-in-the-world/>.

11 Francesco Francioni and Federico Lenzerini, 'The Destruction of the Buddhas of Bamiyan and International Law' (2003) 14(4) *European Journal of International Law* 619, 639.

12 The Committee should be responsible for, first, seeking ways and means of facilitating bilateral negotiations for the restitution or return of cultural property to its original states;

When Turkey's requests for return went unanswered for years, the Turkish Government stepped up its restitution campaign against Germany. Culture Minister Ertugrul Gunay announced that the Government would not renew the excavation licence of German archaeologists, if the sphinx was not returned. This led to the termination of the excavation licence of the German Archaeological Institute in the ancient Roman town of Aizanoi in western Turkey, where it had worked since 1926.[13] Therefore, it can be argued that the aggressive strategy adopted by Turkey and the needs for archaeologic cooperation are the main reasons that convinced Germany to return the sphinx.

In discussing the proposed customary rule, the return of the Hittite sphinx symbolises an important victory in Turkey's efforts with regard to its historically removed heritage. However, it may have limited influence in the creation of the proposed customary rule and also Turkey's future claims for recovery. The press release issued by the German Government simply stated that transfer of the sphinx to Turkey is "a voluntary gesture of friendship". It further clarifies that "the two sides agreed that the case of the sphinx is unique and cannot be compared with other cases".[14] In other words, Germany is careful in using the terms to avoid future requests that other states of origin may refer to the case of sphinx statue as a legal precedent.

2.3. Return of Uigwe to South Korea

The Uigwe is a collection of Royal Protocols from the over 500-year-long Joseon Dynasty (1392–1910) in Korea. The value of the Uigwe lies within its rarity, in that it provides a detailed account of many aspects of the life of the Korean royal family, including the records of all the procedures, protocols, formalities, and requirements needed to conduct important ceremonies, as well as the details on the construction of royal buildings and tombs and other various cultural activities of the royal family.[15] However, these priceless ancient books were taken from Korea by the French during its 19th century invasion, and the Japanese seized copies during its colonial rule of the Korean Peninsula, from 1910 to 1945.

2.3.1. Return from France

Starting from the early 1990s, the South Korean Government, civil groups, scholars, and historians have been demanding the return of Uigwe. In 1992,

---

second, promoting multilateral and bilateral cooperation with a view to the restitution and return of cultural property to its original states (Article 4 of the ICPRCP Statutes).

13 Susanne Gusten, 'Turkey Presses Harder for Return of Antiquities', *New York Times* May 25 2011 <www.nytimes.com/2011/05/26/world/europe/26iht-M26C-TURKEY-RETURN.html?pagewanted=all&_r=0>.

14 *Turkey to Receive Hittite Sphinx*, above n 7.

15 UNESCO, 'Uigwe: The Royal Protocols of the Joseon Dynasty' <www.unesco.org/fileadmin/MULTIMEDIA/HQ/CI/CI/pdf/mow/nomination_forms/republic_of_korea_uigwe.pdf>.

the embassy of South Korea in France formally requested their return. When the then-French President, Francois Mitterrand, visited Seoul in 1993, he returned one of the stolen royal books and promised to return the rest of the collection. However, in France, this return saw resistance from the country's museums and cultural institutions. One of the most crucial issues involved in this situation is whether the President violated the law by handing over what is considered to be French property. France has upheld the principle of the "inalienability" of public heritage, meaning that if works that are now in French museums and collections are listed as "national treasures", they are not allowed to be transferred abroad. But in the past two decades, France's former colonised countries are demanding their treasure and history back.[16] Thus, French museums and cultural institutions are concerned as to whether this return would set a precedent that will result in an increasing number of recovery claims in the future, leading to the depletion of their collections. "Demands for restitutions of all kinds will now be presented by many countries, and there will be no justification for refusing them", said a letter to the French Cultural Minister, Jacques Toubon, with signature from 700 members of the National Library's staff.[17] However, President Mitterrand conceded that the world's museums were full of seized art objects. "That is the past", he added. "We cannot change it, but today we act differently."[18] Jack Lang, a former French Culture Minister, was even more direct in addressing the substance of the dispute. "These documents were seized by illegal means, by force, during colonial times", he said. The return was "a gesture of friendship, a gesture of reparation, a gesture of justice".[19] However, the resistance from France's museums and cultural institutions nevertheless impeded further negotiation and, while President Mitterrand promised to return the rest of the Uigwe collection, there was no follow up regarding the recovery.

In 2007, a Seoul-based civic group called Cultural Action filed a lawsuit with the Paris administrative court asking for an official return of the royal books from the National Library of France. The group's demand was refused by the French court in December of 2009. In its statement, the court acknowledged, for the first time in history, that the cultural heritage was illegally stolen by French troops back in 1866. However, the court still rejected the recovery claim on the basis that the disputed documents were kept in the National Library of France and since the items in the National Library are national property, the circumstances and conditions of the texts' acquisition cannot preclude the books from being considered French

16 Laurent Carpentier, 'French Museums Face A Cultural Change over Restitution of Colonial Objects', *Guardian* November 3 2014 <www.theguardian.com/world/2014/nov/03/france-museums-restitution-colonial-objects>.

17 Alan Riding, 'Return Of Booty Protested In France', *New York Times* September 29 1993 <www.nytimes.com/1993/09/29/books/return-of-booty-protested-in-france.html>.

18 Ibid.

19 Ibid.

national assets.[20] After failing the lawsuit, in March of the same year, the Korean Government requested the return of 297 copies of Uigwe on a permanent lease. On November 12 2010, French President Nicholas Sarkozy and President Lee Myung-bak finally agreed on the return of the Uigwe to South Korea on a five-year renewable loan at APEC and the G20 Seoul Summit. Under the agreement, France retains formal ownership of the documents, which allows France to bypass the ban on the transfer of property of French cultural heritage.[21] In the agreement, France also recognised that the manuscripts were part of the identity of the Korean people and form a fundamental element of Korean history.[22] In 2011, 297 copies of ancient royal documents, comprising 191 Uigwe, were returned to Korea, a gap of nearly 150 years from when they were first removed by French troops. The return marks the end of years of negotiations between governments and relentless efforts by activists to have the priceless artefacts repatriated.[23]

2.3.2. Japan Returned Uigwe to South Korea

In addition to France's possession of Uigwe, the Imperial Household Agency of Japan houses 145 Uigwes of 70 kinds, taken from the Odaesan archive in 1922 under Japanese colonial rule.[24] The main obstacle for the return of the Korean objects was the failure of the post-war restitution programme in East Asia, which was firmly opposed by Japan.[25] It was not until June 22 1965 that South Korea and Japan signed a separate agreement on the repatriation of cultural objects removed in the early 20th century, which allowed certain cultural objects to be returned. However, after the 1965 return, contradictory opinions on the return of the remaining Korean arts from both sides closed any further negotiations.[26] For South Korea, the set of returned cultural objects constituted only the first step in a broader restoration of lost cultural heritage. Inversely, although agreeing to partial repatriation, Japan considered all the appropriations and removals made after 1910 as lawful on the grounds that the 1910–1945 annexation of Korea was lawful under the rules of the

20 Claire Lee, 'The Long Journey: Repatriating "Uigwe" ', *Korea Herald* December 7 2010 <www.koreaherald.com/view.php?ud=20101207000942>.

21 Beurden, *How to Break the Deadlock,* above n 3, 167.

22 Ibid, 167.

23 Lee, *Repatriating 'Uigwe',* above n 20.

24 Danielle Demetriou, 'Japan Returns Looted South Korean Documents to Homeland', *Telegraph* December 6 2011 <www.telegraph.co.uk/news/worldnews/asia/japan/8937503/Japan-returns-looted-South-Korean-documents-to-homeland.html>.

25 Jakubowski, *State Succession,* above n 3, 291–292.

26 Several returns were made to Korea through friendly donations from Japan from individuals. For example, in 1987, a Japanese businessman returned the tomes of the Goryo Dynasty to Seoul National University. Melissa (YoungJae) Koo, 'Notes: Repatriation of Korean Cultural Property Looted by Japan—Can a Sincere Apology Resolve the Centuries-old Korea/Japan Disputes?' (2015) 16 *Cardozo Journal of Conflict Resolution* 625, 635–636.

international law in force at the time. Thus, Japan was rightfully entitled to take the cultural heritage objects, by virtue of its sovereign capacity.[27] Consequently, the contradictory opinions with regards to issues of repatriation remained a hurdle, preventing any further negotiations in the following years.

However, the situation has changed since the late 1980s, particularly through the engagement of Japan in UNESCO activities.[28] In 1989, Japan created the Japanese Funds in Trust Program for the Preservation of the World Cultural Heritage under the UNESCO regime.[29] This programme was created to support efforts made by national authorities in the field of the preservation of cultural heritage, especially through the provision of technical assistance. In 2000, in collaboration with South Korea, Japan provided financial assistance to the government of North Korea for preserving the Complex of Koguryo Tombs situated near Pyongynang, which was successfully added to the World Heritage List in 2004.[30] The restoration of cultural heritage also creates a supportive environment for the discussion of cultural heritage issues, which eventually led to the Pyongynang Declaration signed by Japan and North Korea in 2002. The Declaration reads that:

> Establishing a fruitful political, economic and cultural relationship . . . through the settlement of unfortunate past between them and the outstanding issues of concern would be consistent with the fundamental interests of both sides, and would greatly contribute to the peace and stability of the region.[31]

Pursuant to the Pyongynang Declaration, both parties agreed that "they would sincerely discuss . . . the issue of cultural property", which eventually opened the possibilities for cultural disputes to be resolved.[32] In the same year, Japan ratified the 1970 UNESCO Convention and in 2007 ratified the 1954 Hague Convention. Meanwhile, South Korea accelerated negotiations for the restitution of certain treasures removed by Japan from the present North Korean territory, including the Bukgwandaecheopbi monument. The disputed monument was taken by the Japanese army at the time of the Russo-Japan War of 1904–1905 as war booty, but was rediscovered at the Yasukuni Shrine in Tokyo. In 2005, the Yasukuni Shrine announced that it would return the monument to South Korea by the end of that year, the 60th anniversary

27 Jakubowski, *State Succession,* above n 3, 295.

28 Geoffrey R. Scott, 'Spoliation, Cultural property, and Japan' (2008) 29(4) *University of Pennsylvania Journal of International Law* 803, 850–860.

29 UNESCO, 'Japanese Funds-in-Trust for the Preservation of the World Cultural Heritage' <http://whc.unesco.org/en/partners/277>.

30 UNESCO 'Preservation of the Koguryo Kingdom Tombs' <http://whc.unesco.org/en/list/1091>.

31 Ministry of Foreign Affairs of Japan, 'Japan-DPRK Pyongyang Declaration' <www.mofa.go.jp/region/asia-paci/n_korea/pmv0209/pyongyang.html>.

32 Ibid.

of the end of the Second World War.[33] The monument was to be on display at the newly constructed National Museum in Seoul for up to one year and eventually handed over to North Korea, from where the monument was originally taken. The return enjoyed a warm welcome from both sides, as the head of South Korea's Cultural Properties Administration stated that "the return means efforts to heal our painful injuries from the shared past of Korea and Japan", signifying the start of repatriation of stolen Korean cultural heritage from Japan.[34]

Furthermore, this friendly donation has significantly promoted a cultural collaboration between Japan and North and South Korea. In 2005, Japanese experts and North Korean officials agreed to carry out a joint research project into ancient tombs on the outskirts of Pyongyang, even though Japan and North Korea did not have any diplomatic relations. Additionally, in May 2006, 90 historical treasures from North Korea, including an 11th century bronze statue, were loaned to South Korea for a six-month exhibition in Seoul.[35] The continuous cooperation without being affected by diplomatic issues paves the way for further negotiations for return. On August 10 2010, Japanese Prime Minister, Naoto Kan, offered a renewed apology to South Korea for Japan's brutal colonial rule, as part of a statement marking the 100th anniversary of his nation's annexation of the Korean Peninsula in 1910: "For the enormous damage and suffering caused during this colonial rule, I would like to express once again our deep remorse and heartfelt apology."[36] In the statement, Mr Kan offered to return historical documents and other cultural objects taken from the Korean Peninsula during the Japanese Occupation. In October 2011, the Japanese Foreign Ministry announced that Japan had agreed to transfer a total of 1,205 looted archives of Korean books, including 167 volumes of Uigwe.[37]

The settlement between Japan and South Korea is a remarkable precedent for China and other states of origin, not only because the returned Korean arts were removed pursuant to Japan's devastating plunder rule in the early 20th century, but also because it is a good illustration that repatriation can be made through cooperation without affecting any diplomatic or legal positions. It should be noted that when the Uigwa was returned to South Korea, neither party changed their positions towards the legality of Korean arts taken during the 1910–1945 annexation of Korea, but rather focused on the issues

33 The Yasukuni Shrine in Tokyo is a memorial dedicated to soldiers and other persons who died fighting on behalf of the Emperor of Japan, including the officers convicted for the commission of war crimes during the Second World War. 'Japan Returns Historic Victory Monument to Korea', *Chosun* October 20 2005 <http://english.chosun.com/site/data/html_dir/2005/10/20/2005102061026.html>.

34 Koo, *Repatriation of Korean Cultural Property Looted by Japan,* above n 26, 635–636.

35 Scott, *Spoliation, Cultural property, and Japan,* above n 28, 887.

36 Martin Fackler, 'Japan Apologizes to South Korea on Colonization', *New York Times* August 10 2010 <www.nytimes.com/2010/08/11/world/asia/11japan.html?_r=1>.

37 Lee, *Repatriating 'Uigwe',* above n 20.

of repatriation and cultural cooperation. At this point, it can be observed that national and international organisations, for example, UNESCO, can play a significant role in removing the biggest obstacle to better bilateral ties and creating supportive and cooperative environments for negotiation.

2.4. The Return of Chinese Cultural Heritage from Japan

With regards to the return of the looted Chinese heritage from Japan, the crux of the issue is whether Chinese individuals have a basis to take legal action against the current Japanese possessors or the Japanese Government. Japan has insisted that the matter of war reparations from the Second World War was settled pursuant to the 1972 Joint Communique and no individual claim may now be brought. According to the Chinese side, however, Japan cannot rely on treaties with the Chinese Government to absolve its liability to remedy individual claims for unlawful acts during the Second World War. In addition to individual claims, it is necessary to explore whether China can recover its heritage removed by the Japanese by following in Korea's footsteps.

At this point, it can be observed that a similar approach has already been adopted by China and Japan. After the 1972 Joint Communique, a separate Treaty of Peace and Friendship was concluded on August 12 1978, which stated that "in the spirit of good neighbourliness and friendship and in accordance with the principles of mutual benefit and non-interference in each other's internal affairs, the Contracting parties shall foster contacts and endeavours . . . to furthering economic and cultural relations between the two countries".[38] In 1979, Japan and China signed the Japan–China Cultural Exchange Agreement, through which the two countries have conducted various cultural exchanges, both at the government and private levels.[39] For example, in 1999, the Chinese Cultural Ministry co-organised large-scale cultural exhibitions with Japan, named Touring Japan 1999.[40] The Japanese Embassy in China organised activities to mark the Year of Sino-Japanese Friendship and Culture, which played an active role in enhancing the mutual understanding and friendship of the two peoples. However, the relationship between China and Japan has always been affected by Japan's continued efforts to revise the view of its history of military aggression and China has sought redress for many unlawful Japanese acts during wartime.[41]

38 'Treaty of Peace and Friendship between Japan and People's Republic of China' <www.mofa.go.jp/region/asia-paci/china/treaty78.html>.

39 Ministry of Foreign Affairs of Japan, 'Japan–China Relations (Basic Data)' <www.mofa.go.jp/region/asia-paci/china/data.html>.

40 Ministry of Foreign Affairs of the People's Republic of China, 'Cultural Exchange' <www.fmprc.gov.cn/mfa_eng/wjb_663304/zzjg_663340/yzs_663350/gjlb_663354/2721_663446/2722_663448/t15970.shtml>.

41 China also has accused Japan of failing to fully come to terms with its wartime aggressions and has questioned the sincerity of its apology for its acts of atrocity during the war, particularly the visits by its Prime Minister Abe to the Yasukuuni Shrine in Tokyo.

In September 2014, the fourth International Conference of Experts on the Return of Cultural Property was held in China by the Gansu Administration of Cultural Heritage and Dunhuang Research Academy. This conference reopened possibilities for China and Japan to work collaboratively in the protection of cultural heritage.[42] Its significant achievement was the "Declaration of Dunhuang", according to which Chinese, South Korean, and Japanese authorities proclaimed their joint desire to "construct, in East Asia, a common area based on non-violence, symbiosis and search for harmony".[43] The Declaration was created to call on feasible measure to ensure that information related to archaeological heritage can be published in a timely manner and registered in the record of national cultural heritage.[44] Despite its purpose being not to amend past wrongs, the Declaration was significant in the creation of a cooperative and friendly environment between Japan and China, which may pave the way for the future return of Chinese cultural heritage from Japan.

As analysed above, while legal actions are often complicated or simply impossible, states of origins' interests in their historically removed heritage are being recognised more and more. Returns have evolved so that they are not only based on a strict legal analysis or limited to situations where there has been a violation of national or international laws, but also on the basis of a wide range of non-legal factors, including an awareness that cultural heritage is particularly important to the original states. The idea that there is a moral duty to return highly valuable or significant cultural heritage items is steadily gaining ground.[45] As a result, an increasing number of cultural objects taken in early times are being returned. The evolving law and returning cases have shown a tendency that a state of origin should be treated as the owner of representative cultural objects and that other states should collaborate in securing the return of wrongfully removed core heritage object.[46] However, it should also be admitted that a dialogue about the future of historically removed objects is complicated and requires more than a quick fix.

Martin Fackler, 'In Textbook Fight, Japan Leaders Seek to Recast History', *New York Times* December 28 2013 <www.nytimes.com/2013/12/29/world/asia/japan-fights-a-political-battle-using-history-texts.html?_r=0>.

42 Song Han, 'The 4th International Conference of Experts on the Return of Cultural Property Opens', *China Culture* September 12 2014 <www.chinaculture.org/info/2014-09/12/content_563202.htm>.

43 Guy Faure and Scientific World, *New Dynamics Between China and Japan in Asia: How to Build the Future from the Past?* (World Scientific Pub. Co, 2010), 83.

44 Xueling He, 'Dunhuang Declaration Adopted', *China Culture* September 16 2014 <www.chinaculture.org/info/2014-09/16/content_563722.htm>.

45 Marie Cornu and Marc-André Renold, 'New Developments in the Restitution of Cultural Property: Alternative Means of Dispute Resolution' (2010) 17(1) *International Journal of Cultural Property* 1, 3.

46 Alessandro Chechi, *The Settlement of International Cultural Heritage Disputes* (Oxford University Press, 2014) 52, 285; Norman Palmer, 'Itinerant Art and the Architecture of Immunity from Legal Process: Questions of Policy and Drafting' (2011) 16(1) *Art, Antiquity & Law* 1, 7.

3. Increasing Recognition That States of Origins' Interests in Their Wrongfully Removed Heritage Should Be Respected

Various conclusions can be drawn from the previous return cases and the evolving law applicable to the return of cultural heritage discussed in the previous chapters. These conclusions can be considered trends in the sense that the interests of the states of origin in their wrongfully removed heritage have been increasingly respected and such heritage should be returned. These trends are significant evidence in constituting the proposed customary rule and, more importantly, in facilitating the claims for the return of historically removed heritage.

3.1. Respect for the Integrity of Cultural Heritage of States of Origin

As a collection of objects with historical, artistic or scientific significance, cultural heritage is considered material evidence of a nation's civilisation and an ideal means to enhance the identity and memory of its people. The return of wrongfully removed heritage is not only a redress for wrongful acts, but also a reunion for the integrity of the country's origins. The increasing respect for the integrity of countries' cultural heritage is evident in the following aspects. First, there is a strong recognition that cultural heritage is of great significance to the states of origin. For example, when the £3 million Iraqi Emergency Heritage Management Project was announced, Tobias Ellwood, the UK's Minister for the Middle East and North Africa, commented that "the new funding for the British Museum to train Iraqi experts in rescue archaeology will build on the progress we are already making to preserve art and archaeological sites for future generations and promote a sense of Iraqi national identity".[47] Second, cultural heritage of states of origin should be protected from destruction and illegal removal during times of both war and peace. The prosecutions of the major Nazi war criminals firmly established the confiscation, destruction and damage to cultural heritage as a war crime subject to prosecution and punishment, and provided the first truly international enforcement of the international law protecting cultural heritage.[48] Additionally, many source states have enacted ownership law and export controls to protect their heritage from destruction and illegal removal during peacetime. Third, it is increasingly recognised that return is a prerequisite for the

47 UK Government, 'New Scheme to Protect Cultural Sites from Destruction' <www.gov.uk/government/news/new-scheme-to-protect-cultural-sites-from-destruction>.

48 M. Cherif Bassiouni, 'Reflections on Criminal Jurisdiction In International Protection of Cultural Property' (1983) 10(2) *Syracuse Journal of International Law and Commerce* 281, 293.

preservation of the integrity of the cultural heritage of the states of origin.[49] Artworks stolen or clandestinely excavated from their context and then traded for commercial gain provide little information about the history and culture of the (often unknown) places from where they were taken and the civilizations to which they belonged. However, this loss can be remedied when a looted and smuggled object is returned to its state of origin.[50] Cultural heritage is a source of pride and identity for the nation's inhabitants, a material evidence of the nation's civilization, and serves as a link between the past and the present. Every state should be able to recover and retain those cultural objects that are significant to its history, identity, and memory, and also to the integrity of its cultural heritage.

3.2. *Return with Due Regard for the Laws of the States of Origin*

The evolving laws and practices have shown a clear tendency for states to accept that the states of origin should be the ones to define when their cultural objects have been illegally exported from their territories, or stolen and otherwise illegally removed.[51] Evidence can be found in the following aspects: first, the enactment of domestic legislation implementing international and regional conventions, such as the 1970 UNESCO Convention and 1995 UNIROIT Convention; second, the adoption or revision of conflict of laws legislation favouring the laws of states of origin; and third, the development of national laws in the market states taking heed of the cultural heritage laws of the states of origin.[52]As Lyndel Prott mentions, "a further way of dealing with state claims of ownership over items not in their possession but alienated or exported contrary to the rights of the state was for a court to recognise the rights of the state of origin".[53] It is increasingly recognised that states of origin are the only competent bodies to define the content and scope of their cultural treasures, and also to define when their cultural objects have been illegally removed from their territories.[54]

49 Irini A. Stamatoudi, *Cultural Property Law and Restitution: A Commentary to International Conventions and European Union law* (Edward Elgar Publishing, 2011), 227.
50 Simon Mackenzie and Penny Green, 'Introduction: A Context for the Engagement of Criminology and Archaeology' in Simon Mackenzie and Penny Green (eds), *Criminology and Archaeology: Studies in Looted Antiquities* (Hart Publishing, 2009) 1, 2.
51 Stamatoudi, *Cultural Property Law and Restitution,* above n 49, 217.
52 Chechi, *Settlement of Cultural Disputes,* above n 46, 286.
53 Lyndel Prott, 'The Ethics and Law of Returns' (2009) 61(1–2) *Museum International* 101, 102.
54 Stamatoudi, *Cultural Property Law and Restitution,* above n 49, 218.

3.3. Return of Illegally Removed Heritage

The relevant laws and returning practices reflect a clear trend towards the view that the states of origin should be able to recover any cultural heritage illegally that was taken during a time of conflict, stolen or illicitly exported, unless explicitly allowed by treaties or other agreements.[55] This has been consistently recognised in all international, regional and national legal instruments. For cultural heritage looted during armed conflicts, an occupying power must prevent the illicit export of cultural heritage from the occupied territory and return the illicitly exported property to the competent authorities of the occupied territory. With regards to stolen and illegally exported objects, laws in the specially affected states have been introduced to recognise that foreign states have sufficient interests to argue for repatriation, a factor that provides strong evidence for the creation of the proposed customary rule. This increasing recognition of the return of illicitly removed heritage is further reflected in the sense of international cooperation. At this point, the 1970 UNESCO Convention serves as a starting point for creating a framework for the regulation of trade in cultural heritage by calling on states to protect cultural heritage from theft and illegal export and to assist each other in recovering illegally exported cultural heritage.[56] Over the last few decades, a growing number of cultural heritage objects have been returned worldwide under the mechanism provided by international conventions and the spirit of international cooperation.[57]

3.4. International Endorsement for the Return of Historically Removed Heritage

In 1973, the United Nations General Assembly (UNGA) passed the first of a series of resolutions on this subject. The Restitution of Works of Art to Countries Victims of Expropriation stated that "the restitution of such works would make good the serious damage suffered by countries as a result of such removal".[58] The Resolution addressed the importance attached by some countries to the return of their cultural heritage as being "of fundamental spiritual, historical and cultural value to them, so that they may constitute

55 Patrick J Boylan, 'Illicit Trafficking in Antiquities and Museum Ethics' in Kathryn Walker Tubb (ed), *Antiquities: Trade or Betrayed: Legal, Ethical, and Conservation Issues* (Archetype Publications Ltd, 1995) 94, 105.

56 Patty. Gerstenblith, 'The Meaning of 1970 for the Acquisition of Archaeological Objects' (2013) 38(4) *Journal of Field Archaeology* 364, 364.

57 Gao Sheng, "Recovering Illegally Removed Cultural Property and Improving Cultural Property Protection: A Chinese Perspective' (2009) (1) *Art Antiquity and Law* 1, 12.

58 Norman Palmer, 'Alternative Procedures, Litigation: The Best Remedy?' in Lyndel Prott (ed), *Witnesses to History: A Compendium of Documents 2009 and Writings on the Return of Cultural Objects* (United Nations Educational, Scientific and Cultural Organization, 2009) 358, 13–14.

collections representative of their heritage".[59] In the last 40 years, the UNGA has issued a number of resolutions encouraging the return of cultural heritage to original states, which is consistent with the fundamental ideal running through the proposed customary rule.[60]

In December 2015, the UNGA published the most recent Resolution on the "Return or Restitution of Cultural Property to the Countries of Origin", reaffirming the key idea running through a number of international resolutions: cultural heritage that has a fundamentally spiritual, historical and cultural value should be returned to the countries of origin.[61] Special attention was paid to the "Ancient Olympia Recommendation", which calls on member states to mobilise for the return of stolen cultural treasures, with express reference to the return of the Parthenon Marbles.[62] This clearly shows that there is an overwhelming norm calling on art collecting states to consider the return of cultural heritage to states of origin, regardless of when they were taken.[63] Furthermore, the Resolution enjoyed wide acceptance, as it was co-sponsored by a total of 74 states, which included many original states as well as many member states of the European Union and the US.[64] It is thus undeniable that the position of the cultural nationalist continues to gain increasing worldwide support, favouring the return of historically removed heritage and the creation of the proposed customary rule.[65]

As analysed above, the evolving law and returning cases have shown a tendency that a state of origin should be treated as the owner of representative cultural objects and that other states should collaborate in securing the return

59 Alessandro Chechi, 'Multi-Level Cooperation to Safeguard the Human Dimension of Cultural Heritage and to Secure the Return of Wrongfully Removed Cultural Objects' in Silvia Borelli and Federico Lenzerini (eds), *Cultural Heritage, Cultural Rights, Cultural Diversity* (Martinus Nijhoff Publishers, 2012) 347, 353.

60 For details of the UN resolutions, see UNESCO, 'Resolutions adopted by the United Nations General Assembly about Return and Restitution of Cultural Property' <www.unesco.org/new/en/culture/themes/restitution-of-cultural-property/resolutions-adopted-by-the-united-nations-general-assembly-about-return-and-restitution-of-cultural-property/>.

61 United Nations General Assembly, Resolution A.67/L.34 of 5 December 2012 about Return and Restitution of Cultural Property <www.un.org/ga/search/view_doc.asp?symbol=A/67/L.34>, 3.

62 UNESCO, 'Ancient Olympia Recommendation' <www.unesco.org/fileadmin/MULTIMEDIA/HQ/CLT/pdf/Ancient_Olympia_Recommendation.pdf>.

63 Michael Reppas, 'Deflowering of the Parthenon: A Legal and Moral Analysis on Why the Elgin Marbles Must be Returned to Greece' (1999) 9 *Fordham Intellectual Property,Media and Entertainment aw Journal* 911, 962.

64 *Ancient Olympia Recommendation,* above n 62.

65 Michael J. Reppas, II, 'Empty "International" Museums' Trophy Cases of Their Looted Treasures and Return Stolen Property to the Countries of Origin and the Rightful Heirs of those Wrongfully Dispossessed' (2007) 36(1) *Denver Journal of International Law and Policy* 93, 120–121.

of wrongfully removed cultural heritage.[66] States of origins' interests in both their illegally and historically removed heritage are being recognised more and more. This recognition is significant in developing the proposed customary rule and indicating that the future of historically removed heritage is seriously considered.

4. Conclusion

This book examines state practices to argue for a new customary rule, which would provide an answer for the lack of legal basis when claiming for the return of historically removed heritage. The developing state practices reflect that there is an increasing recognition of the interests of the states of origin in their wrongfully removed heritage: first, with regard to illegally removed heritage during war or occupation, available state practice has recognised that an occupying power not only needs to prevent looting and illegal export of cultural relics taken from occupied territory, but also needs to return such artefacts at the end of war. Second, regarding illegal removal as a result of theft, illegal excavation and illegal export, state practice has shown a growing recognition of returning such heritage to their states of origin, particularly through the enforcement of foreign ownership and export laws. This growing recognition is significant in suggesting that the proposed customary rule is emerging, which will eventually pave the way for the return of historically removed heritage. As a result, there are indications that a time approaches when the interests of the states of origin in their historically removed heritage are increasingly respected and the future of such heritage is seriously considered. At the UNESCO International Conference on the Return of Cultural Objects to their Countries of Origin in Athens in 2008, one conclusion was: "In recent years a clear tendency towards the return of cultural objects to their countries of origin has been developed on legal, social and ethical grounds."[67]

However, this research also admits that, at this stage, the proposed customary rule has not reached the stage of being recognised as a new customary rule due to a lack of universal agreement in terms of state practices. For example, the evolving state practice has clearly reflected an increasing recognition that cultural heritage looted during armed conflicts should be returned to the countries from which they were taken. However, the unresolved issues of war repatriations during the First and Second World Wars have constituted a powerful deterrent to the creation of the proposed customary rule. Also, although there is an increasing recognition that foreign states should have sufficient

66 Chechi, *Settlement of Cultural Disputes,* above n 52, 285; Palmer, *Questions of Policy and Drafting,* above n 46, 7.

67 UNESCO, 'Conclusions of the Athens International Conference on the Return of Cultural Objects to their Countries of Origin' <www.unesco.org/culture/laws/pdf/Conclusions>.

interests to argue for the return of their stolen and illegally exported removed heritage, the uniformity among specially affected states is still lacking. In summary, while the proposed customary rule is emerging, it is still in the very early stages of development. More evidence of state practices are required so that the proposed customary rule can continue to develop, and eventually be recognised as a new customary rule.

Bibliography

'Ancient Olympia Recommendation', UNESCO, 2013 <www.unesco.org/fileadmin/MULTIMEDIA/HQ/CLT/pdf/Ancient_Olympia_Recommendation.pdf>

'Conclusions of the Athens International Conference on the Return of Cultural Objects to their Countries of Origin', UNESCO, 2008 <www.unesco.org/culture/laws/pdf/Conclusions>

'Cultural Exchange', Ministry of Foreign Affairs of the People's Republic of China, November 15 2000 <www.fmprc.gov.cn/mfa_eng/wjb_663304/zzjg_663340/yzs_663350/gjlb_663354/2721_663446/2722_663448/t15970.shtml>

'Intergovernmental Committee for Promoting the Return of Cultural Property to its Countries of Origin or its Restitution in Case of Illicit Appropriation, Sixteenth session', UNESCO, September 21–23 2010 <http://unesdoc.unesco.org/images/0019/001925/192583e.pdf>

'Japan–China Relations (Basic Data)', Ministry of Foreign Affairs of Japan, 2012 <www.mofa.go.jp/region/asia-paci/china/data.html>

'Japan-DPRK Pyongyang Declaration', Ministry of Foreign Affairs of Japan, September 17 2002 <www.mofa.go.jp/region/asia-paci/n_korea/pmv0209/pyongyang.html>

'Japan Returns Historic Victory Monument to Korea', *Chosun* October 20 2005 <http://english.chosun.com/site/data/html_dir/2005/10/20/2005102061026.html>

'Japanese Funds-in-Trust for the Preservation of the World Cultural Heritage', UNESCO <http://whc.unesco.org/en/partners/277>

'New Scheme to Protect Cultural Sites from Destruction', UK Government, October 28 2015 <www.gov.uk/government/news/new-scheme-to-protect-cultural-sites-from-destruction>

'Preservation of the Koguryo Kingdom Tombs', UNESCO <http://whc.unesco.org/en/list/1091>

'Recent Examples of Successful Operations of Cultural Property Restitutions in the World', UNESCO <www.unesco.org/new/en/culture/themes/restitution-of-cultural-property/successful-restitutions-in-the-world/>

'Resolution A.67/L.34 of 5 December 2012 about Return and Restitution of Cultural Property', United Nations General Assembly <www.un.org/ga/search/view_doc.asp?symbol=A/67/L.34>

'Resolutions adopted by the United Nations General Assembly about Return and Restitution of Cultural Property', UNESCO <www.unesco.org/new/en/culture/themes/restitution-of-cultural-property/resolutions-adopted-by-the-united-nations-general-assembly-about-return-and-restitution-of-cultural-property/>

'Treaty of Peace and Friendship between Japan and People's Republic of China', 1978 <www.mofa.go.jp/region/asia-paci/china/treaty78.html>

'Turkey to Receive Hittite Sphinx', Press and Information Office of the Federal Government, May 13 2011 <www.bundesregierung.de/ContentArchiv/EN/Archiv17/_Anlagen/2011-05-13-pm-sphinx-translation.pdf?__blob=publicationFile&v=1>

'Uigwe: The Royal Protocols of the Joseon Dynasty', UNESCO <www.unesco.org/fileadmin/MULTIMEDIA/HQ/CI/CI/pdf/mow/nomination_forms/republic_of_korea_uigwe.pdf>

Art Law Centre, University of Geneva, 'Bogazköy Sphinx—Turkey and Germany', University of Geneva, 2013 <https://plone.unige.ch/art-adr/cases-affaires/bogazkoy-sphinx-2013-turkey-and-germany>

Bassiouni, M. Cherif, 'Reflections on Criminal Jurisdiction in International Protection of Cultural Property' (1983) 10(2) *Syracuse Journal of International Law and Commerce* 281

Beurden, Jos van, 'How to Break the Deadlock in the Debate About Colonial Acquisitions?' in Valentina Vadi and Hildegard Schneider (eds), *Art, Cultural Heritage and the Market: Ethical and Legal Issues* (Springer, 2014) 165

Boylan, Patrick J, 'Illicit Trafficking in Antiquities and Museum Ethics' in Kathryn Walker Tubb (ed), *Antiquities: Trade or Betrayed: Legal, Ethical, and Conservation Issues* (Archetype Publications Ltd, 1995) 94

Carpentier, Laurent, 'French Museums Face a Cultural Change over Restitution of Colonial Objects', *Guardian* November 3 2014 <www.theguardian.com/world/2014/nov/03/france-museums-restitution-colonial-objects>

Chechi, Alessandro, 'Multi-Level Cooperation to Safeguard the Human Dimension of Cultural Heritage and to Secure the Return of Wrongfully Removed Cultural Objects' in Silvia Borelli and Federico Lenzerini (eds), *Cultural Heritage, Cultural Rights, Cultural Diversity* (Martinus Nijhoff Publishers, 2012) 347

Chechi, Alessandro, *The Settlement of International Cultural Heritage Disputes* (Oxford University Press, 2014)

Cornu, Marie and Marc-André Renold, 'New Developments in the Restitution of Cultural Property: Alternative Means of Dispute Resolution' (2010) 17(1) *International Journal of Cultural Property* 1

Demetriou, Danielle, 'Japan Returns Looted South Korean Documents to Homeland', *Telegraph* December 6 2011 <www.telegraph.co.uk/news/worldnews/asia/japan/8937503/Japan-returns-looted-South-Korean-documents-to-homeland.html>

Fackler, Martin, 'In Textbook Fight, Japan Leaders Seek to Recast History', *New York Times* December 28 2013 <www.nytimes.com/2013/12/29/world/asia/japan-fights-a-political-battle-using-history-texts.html?_r=0>

Fackler, Martin, 'Japan Apologizes to South Korea on Colonization', *New York Times* August 10 2010 <www.nytimes.com/2010/08/11/world/asia/11japan.html?_r=1>

Faure, Guy and Scientific World, *New Dynamics Between China and Japan in Asia: How to Build the Future from the Past?* (World Scientific Pub. Co, 2010)

Francioni, Francesco and Federico Lenzerini, 'The Destruction of the Buddhas of Bamiyan and International Law' (2003) 14(4) *European Journal of International Law* 619

Gerstenblith, Patty., ‘The Meaning of 1970 for the Acquisition of Archaeological Objects’ (2013) 38(4) *Journal of Field Archaeology* 364

Green, Simon Mackenzie and Penny, ‘Introduction: A Context for the Engagement of Criminology and Archaeology’ in Simon Mackenzie and Penny Green (eds), *Criminology and Archaeology: Studies in Looted Antiquities* (Hart Publishing, 2009) 1

Gusten, Susanne, ‘Turkey Presses Harder for Return of Antiquities’, *New York Times* May 25 2011 <www.nytimes.com/2011/05/26/world/europe/26iht-M26C-TURKEY-RETURN.html?pagewanted=all&_r=0>

Han, Song, ‘The 4th International Conference of Experts on the Return of Cultural Property Opens’, *China Culture* September 12 2014 <www.chinaculture.org/info/2014-09/12/content_563202.htm>

He, Xueling, ‘Dunhuang Declaration Adopted’, *China Culture* September 16 2014 <www.chinaculture.org/info/2014-09/16/content_563722.htm>

Jakubowski, Andrzej, *State Succession in Cultural Property* (Oxford University Press, 2015)

Koo, Melissa (YoungJae), ‘Notes: Repatriation of Korean Cultural Property Looted by Japan-Can a Sincere Apology Resolve the Centuries-old Korea/Japan Disputes?’ (2015) 16 *Cardozo Journal of Conflict Resolution* 625

Lee, Claire, ‘The Long Journey: Repatriating “Uigwe” ’, *Korea Herald* December 7 2010 <www.koreaherald.com/view.php?ud=20101207000942>

Palmer, Norman, ‘Alternative Procedures, Litigation: The Best Remedy?’ in Lyndel Prott (ed), *Witnesses to History: A Compendium of Documents 2009 and Writings on the Return of Cultural Objects* (United Nations Educational, Scientific and Cultural Organization, 2009) 358

Palmer, Norman, ‘Itinerant Art and the Architecture of Immunity from Legal Process: Questions of Policy and Drafting’ (2011) 16(1) *Art, Antiquity & Law* 1

Prott, Lyndel, ‘The Ethics and Law of Returns’ (2009) 61(1–2) *Museum International* 101

Reppas, Michael, ‘Deflowering of the Parthenon: A Legal and Moral Analysis on Why the Elgin Marbles Must be Returned to Greece’ (1999) 9 *Fordham Intellectual Property, Media and Entertainment aw Journal* 911

Reppas, Michael J., II, ‘Empty “International” Museums’ Trophy Cases of Their Looted Treasures and Return Stolen Property to the Countries of Origin and the Rightful Heirs of those Wrongfully Dispossessed’ (2007) 36(1) *Denver Journal of International Law and Policy* 93

Riding, Alan, ‘Return of Booty Protested In France’, *New York Times* September 29 1993 <www.nytimes.com/1993/09/29/books/return-of-booty-protested-in-france.html>

Scott, Cynthia, ‘Sharing the Divisions of the Colonial Past: An Assessment of the Netherlands–Indonesia Shared Cultural Heritage Project, 2003–2006’ (2014) 20(2) *International Journal of Heritage Studies* 181

Scott, Geoffrey R., ‘Spoliation, Cultural property, and Japan’ (2008) 29(4) *University of Pennsylvania Journal of International Law* 803

Sheng, Gao, ‘‘Recovering Illegally Removed Cultural Property and Improving Cultural Property Protection: A Chinese Perspective’ (2009) (1) *Art Antiquity and Law* 1

Stamatoudi, Irini A., *Cultural Property Law and Restitution: A Commentary to International Conventions and European Union law* (Edward Elgar Publishing, 2011)

Index

For Product Safety Concerns and Information please contact our EU
representative GPSR@taylorandfrancis.com
Taylor & Francis Verlag GmbH, Kaufingerstraße 24, 80331 München, Germany

www.ingramcontent.com/pod-product-compliance
Ingram Content Group UK Ltd.
Pitfield, Milton Keynes, MK11 3LW, UK
UKHW022119190926
475702UK00013B/1524
* 9 7 8 0 3 6 7 8 9 0 4 5 2 *